DATE DUE

Developments in Geotectonics 5

GLOBAL TECTONICS AND EARTHQUAKE RISK

Further Titles in this Series

Developments in Geotectonics 5

GLOBAL TECTONICS
AND EARTHQUAKE RISK

BY

CINNA LOMNITZ

Institute of Geophysics, National University of Mexico, Mexico

ELSEVIER SCIENTIFIC PUBLISHING COMPANY
Amsterdam — London — New York 1974

ELSEVIER SCIENTIFIC PUBLISHING COMPANY
335 JAN VAN GALENSTRAAT
P.O. BOX 211, AMSTERDAM, THE NETHERLANDS

AMERICAN ELSEVIER PUBLISHING COMPANY, INC.
52 VANDERBILT AVENUE
NEW YORK, NEW YORK 10017

LIBRARY OF CONGRESS CARD NUMBER: 72-87960

ISBN 0-444-41076-7

WITH 72 ILLUSTRATIONS, 26 COLORED MAPS AND 50 TABLES

PRINTED IN THE NETHERLANDS

To the memory of my father
Dr. Kurt Richard Lomnitz
(1894-1961)

Preface

The mobilistic theories which, under the name of "sea-floor spreading", have overtaken and largely redirected the mainstream of geological thought during the last decade, yield a reasonably coherent explanation of the occurrence and geographical distribution of earthquakes. The seismic evidence for sea-floor spreading, while undoubtedly impressive, is still bedeviled by contradictions and uncertainties: mostly these have to do with our imperfect knowledge about the nature of the interaction between oceanic plates and continental borders. On the whole, though, the evidence in favor of sea-floor spreading is now overwhelming enough for normal attitudes of scientific skepticism safely to be set aside. What we have is essentially a new global view about the origin and nature of the forces which shape the surface of the earth; the study of this worldwide system of forces and displacements constitutes a new branch of the earth sciences, known as *global tectonics.*

A basic insight of global tectonics is the recognition that thermal instability must produce convective motion in a large part of the earth's mantle. Because of an extremely low heat conductivity, the radioactive heat generated in the mantle cannot be dissipated by conduction alone. Computed velocities of convective overturn are in substantial agreement with the known properties of mantle materials, and with the observed magnitudes of surface displacements during geologic time.

The connection between global tectonics and earthquake risk can easily be grasped, once it is realized that large earthquakes are rare occurrences in terms of the human lifespan. Predicting the earthquake risk for a given locality or region involves the extrapolation of a time series of widely spaced events, from which only an exceedingly small and inhomogeneous sample is available. Hence it has become necessary to understand the earthquake process on a global tectonic basis, in order to optimize the information in terms of the scanty available data. Two major cases occur in the practice of earthquake risk estimation. In places such as California (and more generally, in what we have termed "transduction zones"), the earthquake faults may be mapped quite readily on the ground or from the air. The risk is tied in with well-known, or at least technically locatable, active structures. The motion on such structures can be monitored and their behavior in time can be studied.

On the other hand, no such detailed study of fault mechanics is possible in the case of subduction zones, e.g., the coast of southern Mexico, Central America, or South America. Here geologic faults break the ground surface very rarely: most seismic activity occurs at depth and cannot be correlated with surface structures. As a first approximation, the entire continental margin tends to be active. Lacking well-defined local structures, a stochastic approach to earthquake risk seems inevitable.

One of the earliest examples of statistical treatment of earthquake risk may be found in the work of Sir Alfred Schuster, who applied significance testing to periodicity studies of earthquake recurrence. A century later, the problem of periodicities in earthquake time series remains essentially unsolved — a sobering thought to earthquake statisticians. On the other hand, many outstanding seismologists have been actively interested in theoretical problems of earthquake risk. The names of Omori, Turner, Byerly, Gutenberg, Richter, Rothé, Tsuboi, Knopoff, Aki, Karnik, Vere-Jones, and many others are associated with advances in earthquake statistics. Perhaps the most significant achievements are connected with the name of Sir Harold Jeffreys, who applied statistical methods to many areas of seismology. He showed in 1932 that the aftershock sequence from the Tango earthquake could be modelled after a nonstationary Poisson process — an outstanding result in the stochastic theory of earthquake processes. The consequences of this discovery are extremely far-reaching.

One event which had an important effect on the whole of seismology was the introduction of the magnitude scale by C.F. Richter in 1935. The magnitude parameter remains the most viable measure of earthquake size, though it may well become supplanted by the seismic moment at some future time. The statistical distribution of earthquake magnitudes in space and time has been studied since the early 1940's; the approach to these so-called "seismicity studies" has been predominantly empirical. The lack of a well-defined probabilistic model of the earthquake process has been a serious drawback in these studies, whose inconclusive and frequently tautological results were once ironized by Perry Byerly: "The longer it's been since the last one, the closer we are to the next one".

The present work is mainly an attempt to contribute toward a viable approach of geostatistical treatment of earthquake risk. It is not intended as a summary of the state of the art: thus, no effort was made to survey the numerous methods of site evaluation based on tectonics, geology, and soils engineering. It was felt that these methods were still rudimentary and self-contradictory to an extent which defied systematization. It seemed preferable to try putting together some of the research materials which I had found useful in my own work, and which I had trouble looking up elsewhere. Such data may be needed for quite specific purposes: a new town is perhaps being planned, a nuclear reactor needs to be built near a fault, or a village razed by an earthquake is to be relocated. There is only one way to perform such tasks in a satisfactory manner, and that is through the closest kind of cooperation between seismologists, geologists, land-use specialists, sociologists, economists, civil engineers, and politicians. Beyond the lip service generally paid to "interdisciplinary efforts", it is essential that each team member gain a vivid and coherent understanding of global tectonics and of the statistics of earthquake recurrence. Is it possible, even for a non-specialist, to achieve this in a reasonable time and still do justice to the complexity and the intellectual challenge of the subject? I sincerely believe so.

It is a pleasure to thank my friends, colleagues, and students at the National University of Mexico for the intellectual and material environment which made the completion of this work possible. Professor David Vere-Jones of Victoria University (New Zealand) carefully read and annotated the manuscript for Part II. Mr. José Lauro Ramírez ably designed and drafted the illustrations. The maps were drafted from computer output by

Mrs. Stephanie Killian (Lamont-Doherty Geological Laboratory of Columbia University) and Mr. Manuel Araneda (University of Chile).

Many colleagues around the world have kindly supplied information about the historical seismicity of their respective regions. I realize the provisional nature of this information and I hope to receive many corrections. Since anything worth correcting is worth printing, I should be pleased to stand corrected in a future edition.

Finally, I should like to thank Dr. Larissa Lomnitz for the constant challenge and stimulation which she has contributed to this research since its inception, for her companionship and help during the decade of its gestation, and for making its completion seem like just another reward for the many experiences that we have found worth sharing.

Contents

Part III. World Seismicity

PART I

GLOBAL TECTONICS

But now perceive the secret urging
of nature's innermost design,
as, from the darkest depths emerging
the earth brings forth a living sign!

Faust II, Act. 1.

CHAPTER 1

Continuity and Change

SYNOPSIS

Geologic history is the history of the dynamic interaction between lithospheric plates. Since the breakup of Pangaea geologic change has occurred largely at the edges of plates, that is, along active continental margins and island arcs, and along the seams of mid-oceanic ridges.

We may distinguish four principal modes of interaction between plates (Fig.1.1). One of these, *subduction*, has been explored theoretically and observationally to a significant extent. Subduction is known to occur along island arcs, such as the Tonga–Kermadec region, where two plates of approximately equal thickness converge. Its opposite case is *extrusion*, where two thin plates grow apart and away from each other. Apparently, this can only occur on mid-oceanic ridges.

Transcursion may occur either between two oceanic plates or between an ocean and a continent, e.g., in North America between the Pacific plate and the American continent.

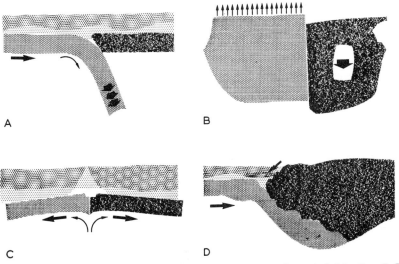

Fig.1.1. The four modes of interaction between lithospheric plates. A. Subduction. B. Transcursion. C. Extrusion. D. Accretion.

Finally, *accretion* is the result of a slow collision between an ocean and a continent, the latter growing at the expense of the former.

EVIDENCE OF CHANGE

In western South America it is clear that these modes of interaction have alternated at different times, so that the continental margin has undergone successively subduction, transcursion, and accretion. Tanya Atwater (1970) has proposed a historical sequence involving subduction followed by transcursion in western North America (Fig.1.2). New evidence for such reversals or changes in the direction of tectonic forces is now being found in other parts of the world.

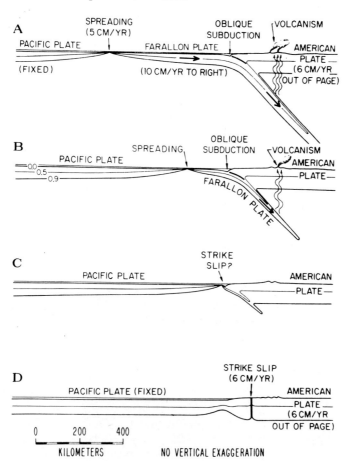

Fig.1.2. Evolution of plate interactions at the coast of California from Early Tertiary (A) to present (D), according to Atwater (1970). The numbered lines are isotherms, normalized with reference to temperature at top of upper mantle. As the spreading center reaches the continental border, subduction is replaced by transcursion.

It has become difficult to conceive of geologic history without accepting the existence of large-scale horizontal motions in the earth's lithosphere. The importance and complexity of tectonic changes rule out any static theory of geologic evolution. So far, geologic evidence has been of little use in support of global tectonics, but potentially it should provide a decisive and valuable clue in this regard.

Geological problems still awaiting a satisfactory dynamical explanation are impressive for their scope and importance to the earth sciences. To list but a few of the major problems:

(1) *Mountain building.* The large modern mountain chains of the world are complex structures which were built up in stages during the past 200 million years. The Himalayas, for instance, contain miles of former ocean-floor sediments which have been squeezed together and elevated; the adjacent continental areas are much older. The subcontinent of India itself is geologically foreign to the rest of Asia and appears to have been originally a part of East Africa.

The South American Andes are lower than the Himalayas, but they contain the steepest large-scale relief in the world. There is a drop of 14,700 m from the top of Mt. Llullaillaco to the bottom of Bartholomew Deep, off the coast of Chile. Such large differences in surface elevation cause stresses of a magnitude that no known material could resist statically for many millions of years.

Some mountain chains (including the Chilean Andes) have roots reaching 70 km into the earth's mantle. Their mass is held up partly by buoyancy in the mantle. Other areas, viz. the high Bolivian plateau, seem to lack adequate roots and their equilibrium remains a major mystery.

(2) *Volcanism.* The heat flow from the interior through the earth's crust is approximately the same everywhere — about 1.5 μ cal. cm^{-2} sec^{-1} on the average. Higher heat flows are found locally on mid-ocean rises, along active continental borders, and in volcanic areas.

Volcanism is a major causative agent in the formation of the earth's crust. The current rate of solid material, steam, and gases expelled by the earth's volcanoes could account, not only for the mass of the continents but of the oceans and the atmosphere as well, if projected backward to the origin of the earth's crust. Yet volcanism appears to be a fairly shallowseated, secondary phenomenon. What is its relationship to the large-scale motions of the continents? How do magmas originate, how do they circulate or move in the earth's crust, and how do they interact with other crustal materials?

(3) *Earthquakes.* The hypothesis of sea-floor spreading has provided a plausible explanation of why earthquakes occur along the borders of the Pacific Ocean and not of the Atlantic Ocean. The latter is not the edge of a plate. Earthquakes occur along the boundaries between two lithospheric plates which move relatively to one another.

However, many details of this picture are still unclear or contradictory. Studies of focal mechanisms show that the fault planes of earthquakes under the edges of continents are not parallel to the dipping lithospheric plates, and do not mark the upper or lower boundaries of the plates. In many cases, earthquake activity extends throughout the whole continental border, while the dipping plate is active at some depths and inactive at others. Deep earthquakes tend to concentrate in relatively small regions or "nests", rather than along the leading edges of the dipping plates.

Hence, while the general relationship between earthquakes and deformations of the earth's lithosphere appears firmly established, the mechanism of the process remains obscure. There can be no question of systematic earthquake prediction until the major regularities of the seismic process have been determined on a quantitative basis.

(4) *Ocean trenches.* A trench is a linear offshore deep occurring along plate boundaries which are zones of convergence. Some trenches are steep, rocky canyons, others are gentle, flat valleys filled with sediments. Benioff (1951) assumed that the trenches marked the outcrops of the dipping zones of weakness now called "Benioff zones". In the early days of sea-floor spreading it seemed natural to assume that they delineated the front of subduction where the oceanic plate dips under the continent.

However, the expected evidence of crumpling and thrusting of the ocean floor in the trenches has not materialized. Instead, the data show that most trenches are graben-like structures and that their subsiding floors are bound by normal range faults. Normal faulting also appears to be common on the continental slopes. The sediments in the trenches are mostly flat and show little evidence of intense folding, as might be expected if the ocean floor were being consumed by underthrusting in those areas. Further observations are required to determine the actual mechanism of sea-floor subduction near continental margins.

(5) *Magnetic lineations.* The presence of elongated magnetic anomalies over the sea floor represents the primary geophysical evidence of sea-floor spreading. These magnetic lineations are assumed to be caused by the emplacement of lavas at the center of the active oceanic rises during periods of alternating polarities of the earth's magnetic field. Symmetrical patterns of magnetic anomalies centered about oceanic rises have been found in all major oceans.

However, in some areas the oceanic rise intersects a continental margin, such as the west coast of Mexico. Tentative interpretations assume that the North American continent has been "overriding" the rise; but the justification for this assumption is weak on theoretical grounds. In other areas, such as the North Pacific Ocean adjoining the Aleutian Trench, the age sequence of magnetic lineations is reversed so that the youngest sea floor is closest to the trench. If subduction took place at the trench this would seem to imply a reversal in direction of sea-floor spreading occurring after the particular portion of the Pacific Ocean had been generated.

Actually the pattern is consistent with sea-floor spreading, as the trend of the anomalies changes sharply in the northeast Pacific. However, a satisfactory correlation with observations in other regions will require a considerable research effort, in order to reconstruct the detailed history of the Pacific Ocean Basin, and other major oceans.

GEOLOGIC CONTINUITY

The geologic time scale can be divided into three stages (which correspond roughly to Prehistory, Ancient History, and Modern History). The earliest stage is the *Precambrian*, i.e. the period extending from the formation of the earth's crust to the appearance of the first fossil life forms on earth.

Since fossils play the same role in geologic history as writing in human history, the absence of fossils in Precambrian rocks means that their age and history has been poorly known until recently, when more sophisticated methods (radioactive dating) became available. Precambrian rocks are very widespread: they comprise the central platforms, or shields, of the major continental masses. Precambrian shields underly most of northern

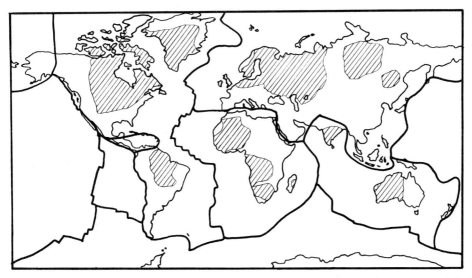

Fig.1.3. Major shield areas of the world, with outlines of lithospheric plates. (After Bostrom and Vali, 1971.)

Canada, Brazil, Siberia, Australia, Africa, India, and probably Antarctica (Fig.1.3). Minor Precambrian blocks occur elsewhere, e.g., in southern Mexico and Central America; but their original connection with the shields is still unknown.

The appearance of life on the earth's surface initiates the *second stage* in geologic history. During this stage the land masses were essentially grouped together in a single large island-continent called Pangaea. Present continents are seen as fragments of Pangaea which have drifted apart during the past 200 million years. Apparently, the breakup of Pangaea greatly accelerated the development and diversification of species, particularly of land animals and plants.

The *third stage* of geologic history begins with the opening of the North Atlantic Ocean and continues into the present. This stage includes the Cenozoic and the Late

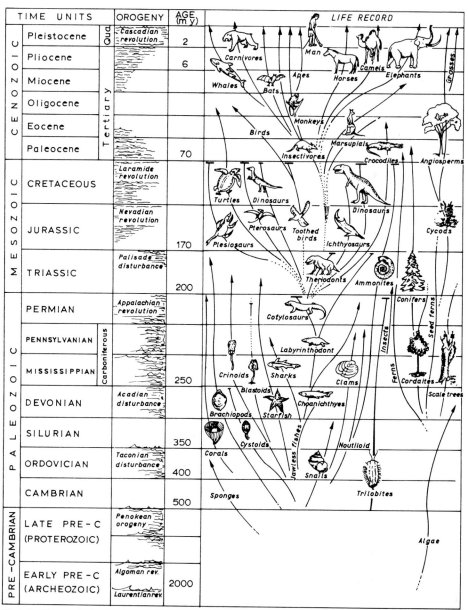

| TIME UNITS | | OROGENY | AGE (m y) | LIFE RECORD |

Fig.1.4. The geologic time scale, modified after Dunbar (1960). Approximate ages for the onset of some time units is given in millions of years before present.

Mesozoic, particularly the Cretaceous. Fig.1.4 shows the principal geologic periods. *Geologic maps* describe the present distribution of rocks belonging to these several periods on the surface of the earth.

The continuity of geologic history reveals that the forces which are now shaping the surface features of the earth have been active for many millions of years, perhaps since the earth's crust was formed some 3,500 million years ago. Volcanism has existed since the Precambrian, and it seems safe to assume that earthquakes were associated with large-scale deformations involved in mountain building throughout geologic history. Traditionally, geologists have tended to view these deformations as the result of vertical movements of the earth's crust. Thus, the transgressions and regressions of the sea over large areas of present-day continents were explained by coastal subsidence or emergence, with horizontal motions representing but a secondary consequence of such vertical displacements.

The consistency of a static theory depends largely on assuming the absence of large horizontal motions in the earth's interior. We know that the earth's outer core is fluid. Convective motion in the core represents the most likely explanation for the origin of the earth's magnetic field. But it has never been demonstrated that the solid mantle of the earth can be free from such convective motion, even though its viscosity may be as high as that of silicate glasses at room temperature.

Hydrodynamical calculations by Tozer (1965) and others indicate that convective instability in the earth's mantle is reached when the temperature gradient exceeds a certain amount, which depends on the viscosity, the diffusivity, the coefficient of thermal expansion, and the acceleration of gravity. The figures which have been proposed for these parameters by various authors seem to indicate that the critical temperature gradient *is exceeded*, not only in the earth but in the planets and in the moon as well. The radioactive content of terrestrial rocks and of extraterrestrial materials (lunar rocks, chondrites) is sufficiently high to sustain a regime of stationary convection for periods of time which exceed the age of the solar system.

Thus, the difficulty confronting a static view of the earth's evolution is to prove that the mantle can be hydrostatically stable under any reasonable set of geophysical assumptions. If convection is taking place in the earth's mantle it follows that large-scale horizontal motions must occur beneath the crust; such motions are likely to attain important surface expressions. The computed velocities of convection in the mantle are of the order of centimeters per year, in agreement with the proposed velocities of sea-floor spreading. Such velocities are also consistent with the known creep properties of silicate materials. In conclusion, the existence of large-scale horizontal motions in the earth's lithosphere follows from the likelihood that the earth's mantle is convecting; and this likelihood seems extremely difficult to disprove on the basis of present-day knowledge of the physical conditions which prevail in the interior of the earth.

Once a regime of stationary convection is established in a planet it can be shown that such a regime can be stable. Small perturbations increase the heat turnover very rapidly, independently of the melting point. Shallow inhomogeneities influence the convection pattern at depth, and vice versa. Thus, the evolution of oceans and continents must be viewed as the result of the interaction of convection currents with the free surface; in fact, the lithosphere itself must participate in the convection. Continental masses may represent an aggregation of mantle differentiates adrift on the convection currents, according to this view.

The process is thermodynamically irreversible. Thus, the evolution of the earth can occur only in the direction of increasing differentiation. Volcanism is a process of local distillation of the lithosphere. Continental growth is due to the asymmetry of convection currents, as the flow lines are more concentrated in the downgoing limbs than in the zones of upwelling (De la Cruz, 1970). In conclusion, continuity and change in the earth as known from geologic history must be understood as a consequence of the dynamic stability of the earth's interior. The earth is an irreversible thermodynamical system which includes many complex interacting processes: gravitational differentiation, convective mixing, circulation of internal heat sources (radioactive materials) and heat sinks (subsiding fragments of lithosphere). The earth's crust is drifting on the convecting mantle: it sinks or regenerates much like the crust of basalt which floats on the molten lava pool in the crater of a volcano.

CHAPTER 2

Geologic History

HISTORY OF PANGAEA

The initial period of formation of Pangaea is conjectural. We know only that a great island-continent existed as a geographical unit during the Paleozoic and the Early Mesozoic, and that it embraced the present continental cores of Europe, Asia, Africa, Australia, Antarctica, and the Americas.

Life evolved initially in shallow seas along the coasts of Pangaea. The first land animals included insects and spiders, turtles, and lizards; plants included ferns and pine trees. Reptiles and cycads became dominant during the Mesozoic; they developed a great variety of species adapted to a wide range of environmental conditions. The reptiles produced efficient marine swimmers such as the ichthyosaurs, various species of river crocodiles, great land predators such as the tyrannosaurs, many varieties of swamp-dwelling dinosaurs, and the earliest flying vertebrates, the pterosaurs. Most of these species became extinct after the breakup of Pangaea into separate continents.

Any historical reconstruction of Pangaea must take into account the large systematic geologic changes which occurred in certain epochs. Thus, extensive glaciation of southern Pangaea (South America, Australia, South Africa, and India) took place during the Permian. About the same time there was extensive compression and folding in northern Pangaea, as well as volcanism along the coasts. The interior of the island-continent was raised, and shallow inland seas disappeared in many areas. Similar periods of tectonic activity had occurred during the Ordovician and Silurian, the Mississippian, and the Pennsylvanian. Such major changes indicate that Pangaea has been subjected to episodes of continental drift and sea-floor spreading throughout its whole history.

GEOCHRONOLOGY

The existence of land connections between parts of Pangaea made it possible for land animals and plants to spread fairly uniformly over continental areas prior to Cenozoic times. Until quite recently this circumstance was explained by assuming the existence of narrow land bridges (similar to the Isthmus of Panama) between the major continents. These land bridges were supposed to have somehow broken down during the Cretaceous, in order to account for the separate evolution of species after the breakup of Pangaea.

The worldwide distribution of fossils makes it possible to use certain "index fossils" as markers for geologic dating. Table 2.1 shows the paleontological time scale and its equivalents in million of years. Fossil dating after the breakup is mostly based on marine life, as the terrestrial life forms became increasingly distinctive and specialized in each of the new continents. Even earlier, the best worldwide correlations were provided by shallow-water marine species, because of their fairly rapid geographical diffusion.

TABLE 2.1

Paleontological time scale

Age (million years)	Period	Typical fossils
Paleozoic		
500	Cambrian	trilobites, brachiopods
400	Ordovician	trilobites, brachiopods, cephalopods, corals, fishes
350	Silurian	trilobites, brachiopods, crinoids, scorpions
300	Devonian	trilobites, brachiopods, sharks, amphibians
250	Carboniferous	trilobites, brachiopods, insects, reptiles
Mesozoic		
200	Triassic	no trilobites; amphibians, dinosaurs
170	Jurassic	amphibians, large dinosaurs, ichthyosaurs, birds
120	Cretaceous	idem, turtles, pterodactyls
Cenozoic		
70	Tertiary	mammals, birds
1	Quaternary	primates

Absolute dates of geologic strata are assigned on the basis of the isotope ratios in certain minerals. The following isotopes have the right range of half-lives to be used for this purpose: ^{238}U, ^{235}U, ^{232}Th, ^{87}Rb, and ^{40}K. Some relatively short-lived isotopes, such as ^{14}C, are used in dating more recent quaternary deposits. Uranium-238 has a half-life of 4,500 million years, while the half-life of carbon-14 is only 5,568 years.

The basic assumption in radioactive dating is that the rock contained no decay products at the time of its formation. For example, the original rock is assumed to contain ^{238}U but no ^{206}Pb, the stable end product of disintegration of ^{238}U. Similarly, the rock is assumed to contain initially ^{40}K but no ^{40}A: a plausible assumption in the case of igneous rocks, since argon-40 is volatile gas.

The analytical determination of decay products is carried out in the laboratory by chemical and mass-spectrographic separation. The isotope ratios between different members of a decay series can thus be used to estimate the age of the rock:

$$\frac{\text{amount of parent isotope}}{\text{amount of daughter isotope}} = \exp\ (\text{age} \times \text{decay constant} - 1) \qquad [2.1]$$

Age estimates using different isotopes tend to differ by fairly wide margins. Differences of 50% are not uncommon. However, the discrepancies are sufficiently systematic and well-studied to afford confident statements about the accuracy of a given estimate, particularly when results from several methods are available.

On the basis of the oldest known radioactive ages of continental rocks, the formation of Pangaea may be put at 3,000–3,500 million years ago. The total age of the earth is probably more than twice that timespan. Ages of various geologic periods are given in Table 2.1, though the boundaries between the periods are anything but sharp.

DATING OF ROCKS IN THE FIELD

Many non-geologists assume that surface rocks and sediments are all modern, and that older strata are only accessible through deep excavation or drilling. Actually, there is no need to dig in order to find rocks many millions of years old. The exposed heartland of Pangaea, Precambrian in age, is now accessible throughout vast areas forming the cores of the major continents: eastern Canada, Scandinavia, Siberia, southeast Africa, India, Brazil, and western Australia. These so-called "shield" areas have suffered comparatively little geologic change for the past billion years, except for intrusion, metamorphism, and erosion. Precambrian outcrops represent nearly one-fifth of the surface of all continents.

The rest of the land surface is represented by younger rocks. Modern sedimentary fill is mostly confined to river valleys, flood plains, deserts, and beaches. Elsewhere, rocks of intermediate age crop out in mountain slopes, along the walls of canyons or across broad eroded areas of the land. Geologic maps show the location and age classification of these outcrops for any particular region.

In order to *specify an outcrop* in the field it is initially sufficient to give its lithology (sandstone, limestone, granite, etc.) and its approximate age or stratigraphic relationship to surrounding rocks. The basic lithological classification is as follows:

Sedimentary rocks (arrow indicates increasing metamorphism)	sandstone limestone→marble shale→schist→gneiss
Volcanic rocks or extrusives (% quartz)	rhyolite (65%+) andesite, trachyte (55–65%) basalt (45–55%)
Intrusive rocks (% quartz)	granite (65%+) granodiorite, diorite, syenite (55–65%) gabbro (45–55%)

Volcanic rocks occur as lava flows or ash flows (tuffs, breccias). They can be more or less consolidated (welded tuffs, ignimbrites) or metamorphosed (metavolcanics). An intrusive rock is a rock which has not reached the surface (eruption) but has cooled at depth. Jointly, extrusives and intrusives are called *igneous rocks*. Sedimentary rocks are derived from older rocks through erosion and redeposition, though limestones are largely derived from skeletons of plankton which settled on the floors of shallow seas.

Once the basic lithology of an outcrop has been decided it is often useful to relate it to the *stratigraphy* of the region. A stratigraphic unit which can be identified and traced over a broad area is called a *formation*, and carries the name of its type locality. Example: the Pierre Shale is a formation of Upper Cretaceous age which was deposited in a sea which once covered the Great Plains of North America (Montana, Nebraska, the Dakotas). It is underlain by the Niobrara Chalk and capped by the Fox Hill Sandstone, all of Cretaceous age.

TABLE 2.2

Classification of fossils

Phylum	Class	Examples
Protozoa	—	foraminifera, radiolaria
Porifera	—	sponges
Coelenterata	Hydrozoa	graptolites
	Anthozoa	corals
Brachiopoda	—	brachiopods
Bryozoa	—	moss animals
Echinodermata	Asteroidea	starfish
	Echinoidea	sea-urchins
	Crinoidea	sea-lilies
	Blastoidea	blastoids
	Cystoidea	cystoids
Mollusca	Pelecypoda	clams, oysters
	Gastropoda	snails
	Cephalopoda	squids, ammonites
Annelida	—	segmented worms
Arthropoda	Crustacea	crabs
	Myriapoda	centipedes
	Arachnoidea	spiders, trilobites
	Insecta	insects
Vertebrata	Pisces	fishes
	Amphibia	frogs, salamanders
	Reptilia	turtles, dinosaurs
	Aves	birds
	Mammalia	mammals

A formation may often be identified by its characteristic fossils. For example, the Niobrara Chalk is known to contain fossils of flying reptiles (pterosaurs) and large marine dinosaurs. Fossil leaves are somewhat less useful for purposes of identification, since many plant forms tend to embrace whole geologic eras and are less characteristic of a specific period. A general classification of animal fossils (Table 2.2) is given for the orientation of the non-specialist.

Proper identification of igneous rocks is obviously impossible in this fashion, since they contain no fossils. Occasionally a lava flow may be dated by inference from adjacent sediments. Otherwise, radioactive dating may be necessary. Formerly amounts of rock weighing a hundred pounds or so were required for age determinations, but currently a good-sized hand specimen is adequate for most purposes.

TECTONIC REVOLUTIONS

Sea-floor spreading originated as a result of convection currents, simultaneously with the incipient differentiation of the earth's crust into oceans and continental masses. This process has not been smooth and gradual. There is ample evidence that periods of relative quiet in geologic history have been interrupted by periods of great geologic activity. The latter periods are called "orogenies", "disturbances", or "revolutions".

Precambrian geologic history is still rather little known. Yet several major revolutions are known to have occurred in the Precambrian. For example, in the Canadian Shield two major revolutions (the Laurentian and the Algoman) are traditionally recognized during the *earliest* Precambrian. The Algoman Revolution produced a major regional uplift which was eventually followed by peneplanation of the entire shield, much as it is today. Later, the Penokean Revolution caused folding and intrusion toward the end of the Precambrian era in Canada.

The Cambrian period was relatively calm and stable; but during the Ordovician there was a cycle of tectonism, volcanism, and vertical movements (submergence and emergence). After a further period of quiet, which embraced most of the Silurian, there began the Caledonian Revolution, with mountain building across Scotland, northern France, southern Germany and Austria, Algeria, and southern Siberia.

The Acadian Revolution, which folded and intruded the Appalachians, occupied much of the Devonian and was accompanied by intense volcanism. This revolution also affected northwestern Europe (the North Atlantic Ocean did not exist at the time), and continued fitfully throughout the Carboniferous culminating in the Appalachian Revolution of the Upper Permian.

Major mountain building during Permian time included the Appalachians, the Urals, the Variscan chains, and perhaps the earliest folding in Tibet and in the Andes. At this time the drift of Pangaea reached its southernmost position, as shown by the extensive glaciation of the southern continents. This drift was reversed and followed by a period of emergence of Pangaea during the Triassic. Tectonic forces also suffered a reversal at that time: in the Appalachian area, compression was succeeded by tension. The resulting block faulting is known as the Palisade disturbance.

The Jurassic was a time of growing tectonic unrest, particularly in North America, due to the beginning of the creation of the Atlantic Ocean. The Nevadian Revolution indicates a period of intense activity (emplacement of large batholiths) along the west coast of North America. As the breakup of Pangaea proceeded one finds extensive submergence during much of the Cretaceous, followed by regional compression along an east—west axis. This caused the episode known as the Laramide Revolution, with large-scale thrusting in the Rocky Mountains, the Andes, and other Circum-Pacific mountain systems.

THE BREAKUP OF PANGAEA

About 200 million years ago, toward the end of the Permian, the northern orogenic seam of Pangaea developed a crack; mantle material was extruded along the new ridge, and North America began to drift away from Europe.

Fig. 2.1 shows the reconstructions of the sequence of events which eventually led to the breakup of Pangaea. The separation of North and South America from Europe and Africa became established chiefly during Cretaceous time. India split off from Africa and ultimately became welded to Asia at the Himalayas.

The breakup of Pangaea coincides with the most radical period of change in geologic

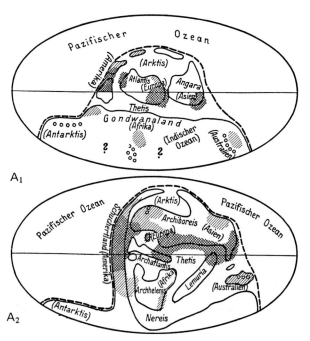

Fig.2.1. Sequence of the breakup of Pangaea: A. According to Gutenberg (1927). B. According to Le Pichon (1968). C.According to Dietz and Holden (1970).

17

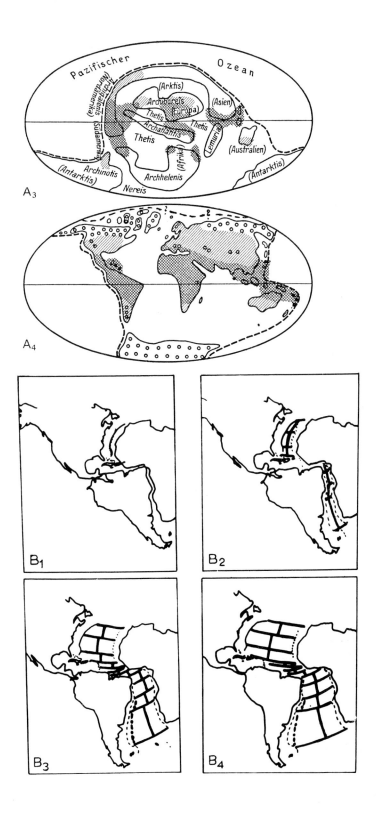

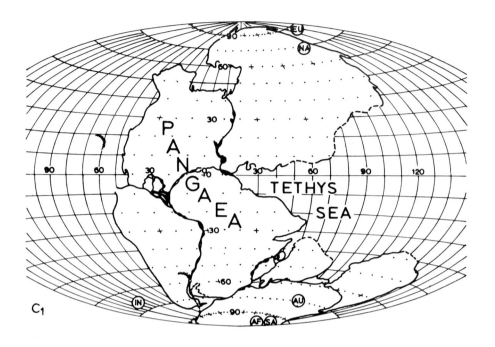

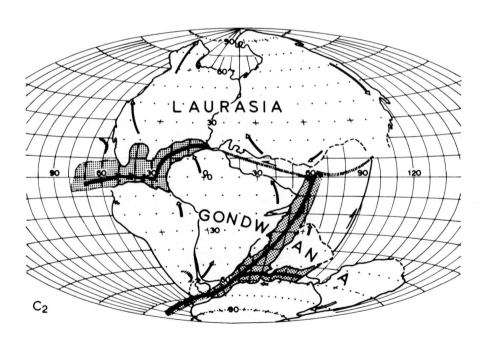

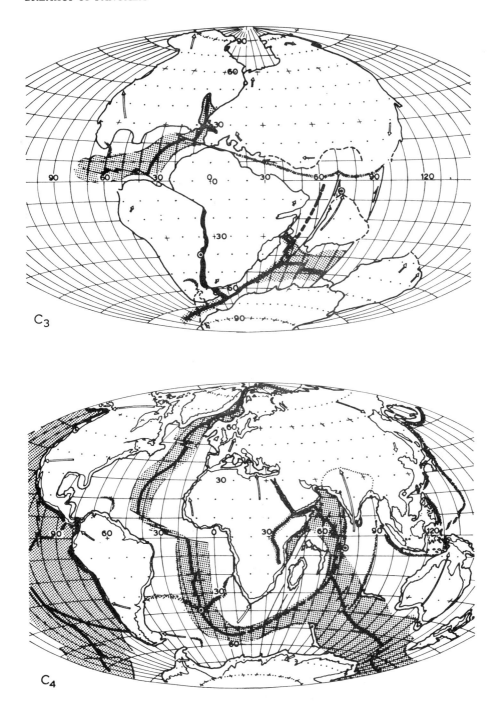

Fig.2.1C (for legend see p.16).

history: the end of the Mesozoic Era. The dinosaurs, which had become the dominant life form on land, now became extinct. Only the marine turtles were able to survive on a worldwide scale. However, many sea animals (ammonites and belemnites) which had become specialized in shallow-sea environments, also became extinct.

Continental drift and tectonism caused important climatic changes, which required new adaptive responses. A new class of vertebrates, the Mammalia, originated and spread rapidly over all continents. These mammals had evolved an internal, metabolic temperature control, including evaporation through the skin. This, in addition to their unique reproductive system which enhances the survival rate of the young, proved superior to the less adaptive saurians.

About the same time, or perhaps as early as in Lower Cretaceous, the first Angiosperma appeared. These represented as great an advance to the vegetal world as the mammals represented among the animals. Flowering plants were superior to the cycads and gymnosperms of the Mesozoic for quite the similar reasons: because of their improved temperature control, which allowed them to hibernate during the cold seasons and to sprout new leaves as the warm weather returned. Also, the sexual reproduction through flowers and fruits greatly improved the survival rate for the seed. Deciduous trees and grasses displaced most of the older plants and soon became the dominant vegetation during the Cenozoic. Today the few characteristic survivors of Mesozoic land forms (e.g. iguanas, crocodiles, cycads, tree ferns) are mostly found in tropical and subtropical environments, where they manage to hold on to a relatively undemanding ecological niche.

In conclusion, the new climatic conditions of the post-breakup environment stimulated the ascendancy of new types of animals and plants, endowed with metabolic and reproductive systems which could effectively adapt to rapid environmental changes. Of course, these new genera came to dominate chiefly on land, as the conditions in the oceans were less severely changed. Nevertheless, the steepening of the active coasts due to continental divergence must have had some effect on the extinction of shallow-sea invertebrates such as the ammonites, which had become the most common mollusks during the Mesozoic.

The Cenozoic Era (which extends into the present) is usually assumed to begin towards the end of the Laramide Revolution, about 70 million years ago. At this time the present continents were all separated and had acquired nearly their present shape and configuration. The increasing rate of geologic change (mountain building, volcanism) due to continental drift became reflected in a great diversification of land species. Thus, the main divisions of the Cenozoic period (Paleocene, Eocene, Oligocene, Miocene, Pliocene, Pleistocene) were established by Lyell on the basis of the survival ratios of species from each of these periods.

In summary, the fossil record reflects the changing geophysical conditions which have affected the earth's crust as a result of continental drift. The breakup of Pangaea is the major event which determined the course of geologic evolution from the beginning of the Cenozoic and into the present time, a time of rapid change in geologic history.

CHAPTER 3

Earthquakes

INTRODUCTION

From earliest antiquity the cause of earthquakes has been associated with the idea of internal stresses in the earth. The alleged origin of such stresses may seem as fanciful to us today as our present ideas could appear to scientists two thousand years hence. Aristotle's theory on the cause of earthquakes has been aptly paraphrased by Shakespeare[1]:

Diseased nature oftentimes breaks forth
in strange eruptions; oft the teeming earth
is with a kind of colic pinch'd and vex'd
by the imprisoning of unruly wind
within her womb; which, for enlargement striving,
shakes the old beldame earth, and topples down
steeples and moss-grown towers.

Theological preoccupations during the Middle Ages put a temporary end to speculations about the origin of earthquakes. The Wrath-of-God theory of earthquakes had its origin in Old Testament interpretations of natural disasters, such as the destruction of Sodom and Gomorrah, and the fall of Jericho, which may have been early instances of seismic activity in the Jordan Trough. Naturalistic explanations of earthquakes were formally banned as heresy by a Father of the Church in the 5th Century[2].

Meanwhile, the Chinese had developed an elaborate system of earthquake reporting throughout all provinces of the Empire. Official concern with earthquakes was motivated by the belief that these phenomena meant impending changes in government. The famous Han court astronomer, Chang Heng (78–139) designed the first serviceable seismograph, which was probably based on the principle of the pendulum (Fig.3.1). Old Chinese records stored in provincial capitals for centuries, were recently unearthed to compile a 2000-year seismic history of China. Similar records in Japan go back to A.D. 599 and were found to be sufficiently detailed for estimating the magnitudes of major earthquakes since that date.

---

[1] Henry IV, Part I, Act III, Scene I.
[2] "Alia est heresis quae terrae motum non Dei iussione et indignatione fieri, sed de nature ipsa elementorum opinatur, cum ignorat quid dicat Scriptura: Qui conspicit, etc." St. Philastrius of Brescia *Diversarum Hereseon Liber*, Corpus Script. Eccl. Lat., 38, Ch. 102 (Tempsky, Vienna, 1898).

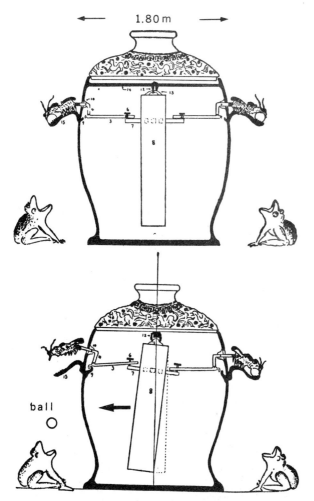

Fig.3.1. A proposed reconstruction of the Chang seismograph. Two of the eight ejection mechanisms are shown, with a suggestion of how the central mass *8* might cause a ball to be ejected (the true mechanism was probably different). No examples of this seismograph survive. (After C.T. Wang, reproduced in Needham, 1959.)

Elsewhere, earthquake observations have been considerably less reliable or complete. As late as 1625, Francis Bacon claimed that the American continent was noted for its low seismicity, "for Earth-quakes are seldome in those Parts". It took European scientists another two centuries to realize that Europe and Asia Minor were not the most seismic regions on earth.

By the early 19th Century doubts about the divine causation of earthquakes had appeared throughout Christianity.

The Rev. Camilo Henriquez commented on the 1822 Valparaiso earthquake that God should not be thought so unreasonable as to vent His wrath against His own temples.

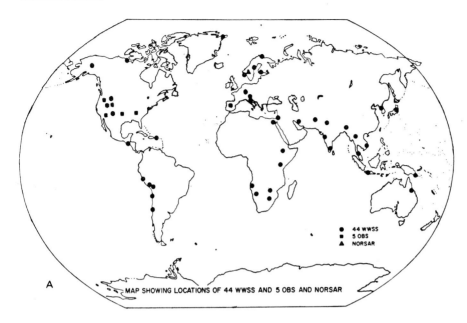

A MAP SHOWING LOCATIONS OF 44 WWSS AND 5 OBS AND NORSAR

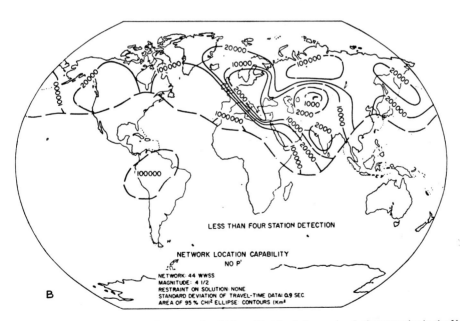

LESS THAN FOUR STATION DETECTION

NETWORK LOCATION CAPABILITY
NO P'

NETWORK: 44 WWSS
MAGNITUDE: 4 1/2
RESTRAINT ON SOLUTION: NONE
STANDARD DEVIATION OF TRAVEL-TIME DATA: 0.9 SEC
AREA OF 95 % CHI² ELLIPSE CONTOURS (Km²

B

Fig.3.2. Location capability of a network of 44 worldwide stations, plus 5 observatories in the United States (A). The area of the 95% confidence ellipse is contoured in B. (After Evernden, 1971.)

Elsewhere, a revival of interest in the earth sciences led to the discovery of fossil life much older than man; this gave rise to misgivings about the Biblical chronology of Genesis.

In 1835 Charles Darwin was visiting the coast of Chile as a member of the Beagle expedition, when he experienced the great Concepción earthquake. His description contains the first detailed measurements and discussions of tectonic uplift due to an earthquake. Darwin suggested that earthquakes might be among the major causes of mountain building throughout the earth.

The theory of the earth's interior began to attract the attention of some of the best scientists of the time, including Laplace, Poisson, Lamé, Lord Rayleigh, and others. Yet observational seismology remained backward until the turn of the present century, when crude but reliable seismographs became available. Today there are over 1000 operational seismographic stations in the world and earthquakes of magnitude 4.5 or over can be located and catalogued most anywhere on earth (Fig.3.2).

EARTHQUAKE PARAMETERS

Seismic events are defined by their location (latitude, longitude, depth), their time of occurrence, and their energy. The latter is difficult and cumbersome to determine. Instead, several measures of *earthquake size* have been used, none of which is entirely satisfactory.

The most common measure of earthquake size is Richter's magnitude M. The magnitude of an earthquake is computed from the logarithm of the amplitude of seismic waves. Several definitions are possible, depending on which kind of waves are measured. The Richter scale uses the maximum waves in the seismogram (surface waves), and is roughly logarithmic in energy E. Two approximate relationships which have been proposed are:

$$\log_{10} E = 1.5\,M + 11.4 \tag{3.1}$$

and

$$\log_{10} E = 1.7\,M + 10 \tag{3.2}$$

where E is in ergs. The largest recorded earthquakes have reached Richter magnitudes of up to 8.9 (which yields an energy of order 10^{25} ergs). Magnitude has dimensions of log (erg) and may adopt negative values.

Some agencies in charge of epicenter determination, such as the National Oceanic and Atmospheric Administration of the United States, use a magnitude scale based on the amplitudes of body waves, particularly the P signal. This is the *body-wave magnitude m*. There is no direct one-to-one correspondence between m and M; an approximate relationship is:

$$M = 1.59\,m - 3.97 \tag{3.3}$$

The amplitudes of seismic waves vary from station to station, depending on the azimuth and on the radiation pattern at the source. Hence the magnitude varies in different directions from the epicenter, and even the average magnitude from many stations may depend on the geographical distribution of seismographic stations.

The *seismic moment* M_0, largely known through the work of Brune (1968), is a measure of earthquake size which attempts to overcome the disadvantages of the various magnitude scales. It depends only on the physical mechanism at the source, and is computed by means of the Fourier spectrum of seismograms. For shallow earthquakes there is a fairly good correspondence between seismic moment and Richter magnitude. A useful relationship for large earthquakes is:

$$\log_{10} M_0 = 19.9 + M \qquad [3.4]$$

where M_0 is in dyne-cm.

The strength of shaking on the earth's surface is usually reported on a non-instrumental scale, called an intensity scale. One of the most widely accepted intensity scales is the Modified Mercalli Scale (Table 3.1), which has 12 degrees. The rating of an earthquake by intensity can supposedly be done by anybody; actually it requires an

TABLE 3.1

Modified Mercalli Scale (abridged)

I.	Not felt
II.	Felt by persons at rest or on upper floor.
III.	Hanging objects swing. Light vibration.
IV.	Vibration like heavy truck. Windows and dishes rattle. Standing cars rock.
V.	Felt outdoors. Sleepers wakened. Small objects fall. Pictures move.
VI.	Felt by everybody. Furniture displaced. *Damage:* broken glassware, merchandise falls off shelves. Cracks in plaster.
VII.	Felt in moving cars. Loss of balance while standing. Church bells ring. *Damage:* broken chimneys and architectural ornaments, fall of plaster, broken furniture, widespread cracks in plaster and masonry, some collapse in adobe.
VIII.	Steering trouble in moving cars. Tree branches broken off. Cracks in saturated soils. *Destruction:* elevated water tanks, monuments, adobe houses. *Severe to mild damage:* brick construction, frame houses (when unsecured to foundation), irrigation works, embankments.
IX.	"Sand craters" in saturated silty sands. Landslides. Cracking of ground. *Destruction:* unreinforced brick masonry. *Severe to mild damage:* inadequate reinforced concrete structures, underground pipes.
X.	Widespread landslides and soil damage. *Destruction:* bridges, tunnels, some reinforced concrete structures. *Severe to mild damage:* most buildings, dams, railway tracks.
XI.	Permanent ground distortion.
XII.	Nearly total destruction.

experienced observer, and there are several schools of thought. Some agencies rate a locality by the highest-ranking earthquake effect observed anywhere within the locality, while other institutions prefer to make a mental average of all observed effects. Such procedural variations may entail systematic differences in intensity rating of the order of a full degree or more.

Relationships between the magnitude M, the intensity I, and the focal distance R (in km) have been proposed for a number of regions. For example, the formula by Esteva and Rosenblueth (1964):

$$I = 8.16 + 1.45\,M - 2.46\log_{10} R \qquad\qquad [3.5]$$

has been tested with good results in North America, including California and Mexico.

For small focal distances (less than 100 km) the focal depth h becomes an important parameter. Kazim Ergin (1969) proposes:

$$I_0 - I = n\log_{10}(R/h) \qquad\qquad [3.6]$$

where I_0 is the intensity at the epicenter and n is either 3 or 5. Sometimes n may be 3 in one direction and 5 in another, for one and the same earthquake. Formula [3.6] may be used for distances beyond 100 km, by adding an exponential attenuation term to the right-hand side.

Instead of the intensity I, the peak ground motion Y may directly be measured. Depending on the type of instrument, Y may be given in terms of displacement, velocity, or acceleration. A general formula to be used is:

$$Y = b_1\,e^{b_2 M} R^{-b_3} \qquad\qquad [3.7]$$

where R is in km, Y is in c.g.s. units, and the values of b_1, b_2, b_3 are given in Table 3.2.

In practice few instrumental measurements of ground motion are likely to be available

TABLE 3.2

Peak ground motion

	$Y =$ acceleration[1]	$Y =$ velocity	$Y =$ displacement
b_1	2,000	16	7
b_2	0.8	1.0	1.2
b_3	2	1.7	1.6

[1] Formula by Esteva and Rosenblueth (1964) for hard ground.

in an epicentral region, and engineers must often rely on intensity reports in the Mercalli scale. A convenient rule-of-thumb relationship for converting Mercalli intensity reports to ground acceleration is:

$$\log_{10} a = \frac{I}{3} - \frac{1}{2}$$ [3.8]

where a is the approximate acceleration in cm/sec^2. The shallower the earthquake, the more peaked is the intensity distribution at the surface. This is easy to understand on first principles. Using a light source as an analogy, one finds that the intensity decreases as the square of the distance to the reflector; the same is true in the case of earthquake ground accelerations (Fig.3.3). This analogy suggests that the maximum acceleration in epicentral areas is proportional to the radiated seismic power per unit area of ground surface.

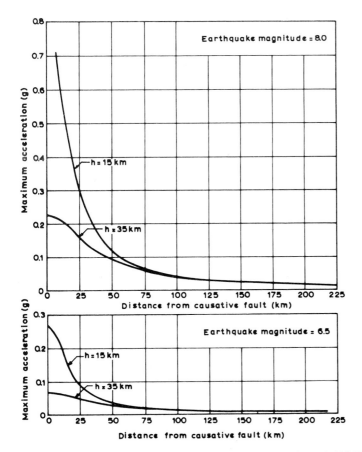

Fig.3.3. Accelerations in basement rock inferred by Seed et al. (1968) from data by Esteva and Rosenblueth (1964). Above, magnitude 8.0; below, magnitude 6.5. These values are two to ten times lower than those observed by Esteva and Rosenblueth on "hard ground".

Since the pattern of energy radiation is strongly non-uniform, the distribution of intensities in an epicentral region is quite uneven.

SEISMIC WAVES

In any elastic solid the deformation ϵ which results from a small stress σ is given by Hooke's Law:

$$\epsilon = \sigma/G \qquad\qquad\qquad [3.9]$$

where G is a characteristic stress called the *modulus* of the material. Depending on whether the deformation is measured normally or tangentially to the applied stress one gets two different moduli.

This behavior, which is common to all solids, has the important consequence that elastic waves propagate in a solid with two different velocities. The faster wave propagates in the compressional mode and is called the P-wave; the other wave is called the S-wave and propagates in the shear mode.

The elastic moduli G of a material for any arbitrary mode of deformation may all be expressed in terms of the constants λ and μ, called Lamé's constants. Thus, the velocities of P and S are given by:

$$v_P = \sqrt{(\lambda + 2\mu)/\rho} \qquad\qquad\qquad [3.10]$$

$$v_S = \sqrt{\mu/\rho} \qquad\qquad\qquad [3.11]$$

where ρ is the density of the material. Poisson's ratio $\lambda/2(\lambda+\mu)$ measures the relative lateral constriction of a bar which is axially stretched.

The wave propagation in an elastic, infinite, homogeneous solid is governed by the wave equation:

$$\frac{1}{v^2} \ddot{\epsilon} = \Delta^2 \epsilon \qquad\qquad\qquad [3.12]$$

In the case of the P-wave ϵ is a cubical dilatation and $v = v_P$; for the S-wave ϵ is a shear strain and $v = v_S$. Eq.3.12 implies that any local disturbance gives rise to sinusoidal waves travelling outwards with characteristic velocities v_P and v_S.

If the solid has a free surface the disturbance also excites certain characteristic oscillations which propagate along the surface and are called *surface waves*, in distinction to P and S which are called *body waves*. A somewhat similar distinction also occurs in fluids, viz. water waves on the surface, and sound waves in the body of the liquid. Surface waves in solids are of two kinds: Rayleigh waves, which tend to distort the surface into a wavy shape, and Love waves, which produce a shearing deformation in the plane of the free

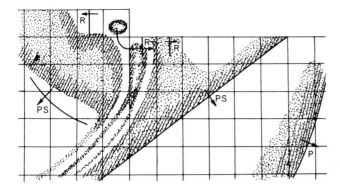

Fig.3.4. Photoelastic fringe pattern produced by the passage of a Rayleigh wave from left to right, around a step. Part of the Rayleigh wave energy is reflected at the step, part is transmitted around the corner, and part is transformed into body waves (P, S, and conical PS waves). (After Dally and Lewis, 1968.)

surface (Fig.3.4.). Earthquake damage to structures on the surface of the earth is mostly due to surface waves.

The velocity of a surface wave depends on the frequency of the wave: this property gives rise to *dispersion*. The velocity also depends strongly on the near-surface structure, particularly in respect to layering. If the solid is homogeneous or has no layers near the surface there will be Rayleigh waves but no Love waves. The velocity of Rayleigh waves reaches up to 0.92 v_S in earth materials: the velocity of Love waves is intermediate between v_S near the surface and v_S in the basement layer.

Surface sediments may lose most of their cohesion under strong shaking and sometimes behave almost like a liquid. When the rigidity μ is smaller than $\rho g l$ (where ρ is the density and l is the wavelength) the surface waves become shorter and higher, resembling choppy gravity waves on the surface of a liquid. The theory of such gravitationally perturbed surface waves has been discussed by Freeman Gilbert (1967), and their actual occurrence in sedimentary basins during large earthquakes is very probable (Lomnitz, 1970a). Because of their short wavelengths and large associated strains these waves may be responsible for torsional effects which cause spectacular engineering failures, particularly in elongated buildings on soft ground.

MECHANISM AT THE SOURCE

A seismic event may be defined in at least three different ways: (a) as a mechanical rupture localized in the earth's lithosphere or upper mantle; (b) as part of a stochastic process of energy transfer from the earth's interior toward the surface; (c) as a radiation of elastic waves which propagate through the interior of the earth and along its surface.

The science of seismology has been traditionally concerned with the study of earthquakes as elastic waves, and of the medium which they sample when they travel from the focus to the station. As a result, much more is known about the internal structure of the earth than about the mechanism of earthquakes at the focus, or about the process of earthquake generation. The actual process may be summarized as follows:

(1) A non-hydrostatic stress field is generated in a finite region about the fault. The deviatoric stress in the focal region is likely to reach values of the order of 100 bars.

(2) A rupture occurs along the fault, and the stored elastic energy in the stress field is reduced by the amount of energy radiated as seismic waves or transformed into heat or potential energy.

(3) The medium is gradually restored to a state of equilibrium, through the release of residual strains by means of aftershocks and fault creep.

Approximately, the radiation pattern from a fault has a fourfold symmetry about the focus. Space is divided by four right solid angles into two quadrants of initial compression and two quadrants of initial dilatation (Fig.3.5).

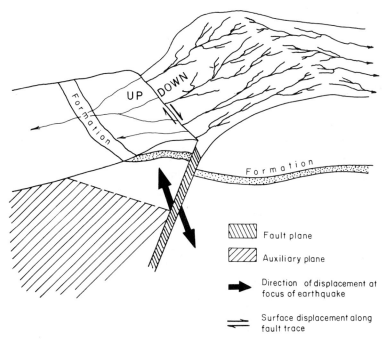

Fig.3.5. A right-hand strike-slip fault (or transcurrent fault), showing the fault plane and the auxiliary plane. There is also a minor component of reverse faulting (left side up).

One of the two nodal planes is the fault plane. Any method of projective geometry which utilizes the first motions on seismograms to find the fault plane at the source is called a *fault-plane solution*.

The most commonly used method of fault-plane solution is the Wulff stereo net. It is a polar projection of a sphere on its own equatorial plane. If the earthquake focus occupies the center of the sphere, the quadrants of compression and dilatation are bounded by two mutually orthogonal great circles on the lower hemisphere (Fig.3.6). The advantage of the Wulff net is that orthogonality is preserved in the projection. The exact plotting position of each station on the lower hemisphere depends on the earth structure along the seismic ray from the focus to the station. Tables and graphs based on average models of the earth's interior are available for computing the angle of the ray at the origin as a function of distance.

Every fault-plane solution consists of *two* orthogonal planes. One of these is the fault plane; the other is the nodal plane of motion with respect to the fault plane. In other

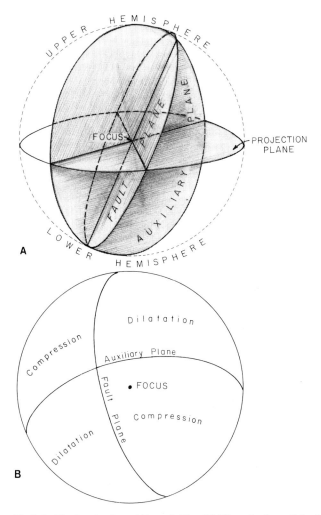

Fig.3.6. The focal sphere (A), and (B) a Wulff projection of the lower hemisphere on the equatorial plane, for the mechanism of Fig.3.5.

words, the normal to the second plane yields the vector of motion. Hence, if we can tell which of the two planes is the fault plane (and this is frequently possible on geological or seismological evidence), we may obtain the direction of motion as well. Characteristic patterns corresponding to normal faulting, reverse faulting, and transcurrent faulting are easy to recognize (Fig.3.7).

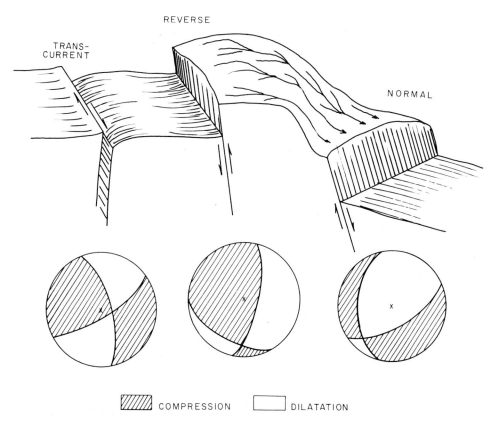

Fig.3.7. Major types of faulting, and their expression on the focal sphere projection. Reverse faulting yields compressions at most distant stations, while normal faulting yields dilatations at the same stations.

The actual radiation patterns are influenced by the regional strain, the source dimensions, and the direction of propagation. The radiation pattern also depends on the frequency of the seismic wave. At low frequencies the source dimension becomes small as compared to the wavelength and therefore the asymmetry of the radiation pattern is negligible; for this reason it is standard practice to use low-frequency P-waves in fault-plane solutions.

The most important parameter in problems of focal mechanism is the seismic moment M_0:

$$M_0 = \mu\, A\, \bar{u} \qquad\qquad\qquad [3.13]$$

where μ is the rigidity, A is the fault plane area and $\bar{u}$ is the mean relative displacement between both sides of the fault. The amplitude of long-period waves is proportional to the seismic moment. Since the magnitude is calculated by measuring the amplitude of 20-second Rayleigh waves, there exists a close relationship between the seismic moment and the Richter magnitude M (eq.3.4).

The slip along a fault zone for a given time interval is obtained by adding the seismic moments together (Brune, 1968; Davies and Brune, 1971):

$$\sum \bar{u} = \frac{1}{\mu A_0} \sum M_0 \qquad [3.14]$$

where A_0 is the total area of the fault zone. This simple calculation affords a check on the relative displacement predicted at plate boundaries by the theory of sea-floor spreading.

The average shear stress on the fault is related to the energy divided by the seismic moment M_0:

$$\bar{\sigma} = \mu E/M_0 \qquad [3.15]$$

where E is the elastic energy and μ is the rigidity. Since the total elastic energy is not accessible to measurement we define the *apparent* stress at the source as:

$$\bar{\sigma}_{app} = \eta E_s/M_0 \qquad [3.16]$$

where E_s is the energy radiated as long-period seismic waves (frequencies up to 1 Hz). E_s can be estimated by using the Gutenberg-Richter formula:

$$\log_{10} E_s = 5.8 + 2.4 m \qquad [3.17]$$

where m is the body-wave magnitude. A more reliable computation uses the amplitude spectral density of seismic waves. The apparent stress is proportional to the ratio between the spectral amplitudes at high frequency and at low frequency.

The results of such calculations show that apparent stresses of up to 10,000 bars occur in earthquakes. If we call "seismic efficiency" the ratio $E_s/E = \eta$ of energy conversion into seismic waves, the true stresses $\bar{\sigma} = \eta \bar{\sigma}_{app}$ may be estimated on the basis of several considerations. It turns out that the efficiency η varies between 0.1% and 1%, so that the true deviatoric stresses in the focal region reach values of up to 100 bars. The stress drop in earthquakes may be inferred from field observations.

ELASTICITY AND ANELASTICITY

Hooke's Law *Ut tensio sic vis* represents a general statement of linear stress–strain behavior in solids. It is a constitutive equation for small strains:

$$\epsilon = \frac{\sigma}{M} [1 + \varphi(t)] \qquad [3.18]$$

implying that the strain in the material is proportional to the applied stress at all times. The constitutive equation of the theory of elasticity is obtained from [3.18] by neglecting the creep function $\varphi(t)$. In principle, this is contrary to the Second Law of Thermodynamics, since it means that work can be done against internal forces without producing entropy.

All solids obey eq.3.18 within a certain strain range close to the origin. This is called the "linear range"; it is dependent on temperature and pressure. For purposes of stress-wave propagation one can assume that the entire solid earth is in the linear range. Some criticism has been intermittently voiced, to the effect that the generalized Hooke's Law is not applicable to brittle materials nearing fracture, to plastic flow, to convection in the earth, and so on. This criticism is unfounded. Experimental proof of linear creep behavior in igneous rocks at stresses up to 0.0005μ was provided by Lomnitz (1956). These experimental results are confirmed by every known evidence on the stress–strain behavior of polycrystalline materials; they have never been disproved. Linearity does not negate nonlinearity. It seems unreasonable to insist on applying a linear constitutive equation to solids subjected to deviatoric stresses in the kilobar range, at which actual microfracture in crystals can be recorded, or to slow-rate unidirectional flow which proceeds for such long time spans that the memory function $\varphi(t)$ cannot possibly preserve any physical meaning in terms of the original position of particles or crystals.

Let the internal structure of the material be represented by a random network of elementary springs and dashpots (Fig.3.8). Each spring-dashpot couple or equivalent elementary network may be assigned an eigenfrequency ω, such that the strain rate of the material may be represented by:

$$\dot{\epsilon}(t) = \text{constant} \cdot \int_0^\infty f(\omega) e^{-\omega t} d\omega \qquad [3.19]$$

If the elementary eigenfrequencies are uniformly distributed up to some maximum value $\omega_{max} = \omega_0$ we may integrate [3.19] as follows:

$$\dot{\epsilon}(t) = \text{constant} \cdot (1 + \omega_0 t)^{-1} \qquad [3.20]$$

which gives a constitutive equation of the form (cf. eq.3.18):

$$\epsilon(t) = \frac{\sigma}{M} [1 + q \log(1 + \omega_0 t)] \qquad [3.21]$$

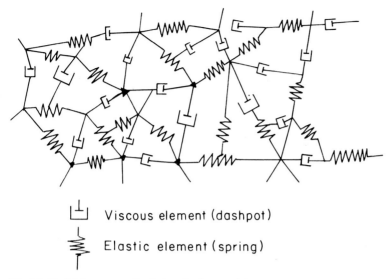

⊔ Viscous element (dashpot)

≩ Elastic element (spring)

Fig.3.8. Model for a generalized viscoelastic material.

In 1955 eq.3.21 was tested experimentally in igneous rocks (Lommitz, 1956, 1957). It has since proved to fit the stress–strain behavior of other polycrystalline materials in the linear range. Mott and Nabarro (1948) have proposed that ω_0 represents the vibration frequency of a vacancy in a crystal lattice; in metals ω_0 may be as high as 10^{10} Hz. The value of ω_0 in rocks has not been determined except for its lower bound, which is of the order of 10^4 Hz at room temperature and atmospheric pressure.

Jeffreys (1965, 1972) later generalized [3.21] by introducing an additional parameter α:

$$\varphi(t) = q\,(1 + \omega_0 t)^{-\alpha} \tag{3.22}$$

which reduces to [3.21] as $\alpha \to 0$. The introduction of this generalization becomes necessary if one wishes to fit data from the damping of the free nutation (14 months) and even longer periods. For purposes of stress-wave attenuation and free vibrations of the earth (periods up to one hour) the logarithmic form [3.21] appears to be adequate. A complete description of the stress–strain behavior of a linear solid requires the determination of two elastic moduli (λ and μ) and two creep moduli (q_p and q_s). In general it is found that $q_s > q_p$.

We may generalize the constitutive equation [3.18] for an arbitrary stress input $\sigma(t)$; this was done by Boltzmann and later by Volterra. The solution is obtained by superposition of the elementary responses due to small stress increments $d\sigma$. In the limit we obtain:

$$\epsilon(t) = \frac{1}{M}\left[\sigma(t) + \int_0^t \dot{\sigma}(\tau)\,\varphi(t-\tau)\,d\tau\right] \qquad [3.23]$$

which represents the most general statement of Hooke's Law. By the known properties of convolution transforms we may write [3.23] in the form:

$$\epsilon(t) = \frac{1}{M}\left[\sigma(t) + \int_0^{\infty} \sigma(\tau)\,\dot{\varphi}(t-\tau)\,d\tau\right] \qquad [3.24]$$

In the case of the logarithmic creep function we obtain:

$$\epsilon(t) = \frac{1}{M}\left[\sigma(t) + \omega_0\,q\,\sigma * (1 + \omega_0 t)^{-1}\right] \qquad [3.25]$$

where the symbol $*$ stands for the convolution transform. Obviously, this equation reduces to the elastic case when $q = 0$.

Consider now a stress wave $\sigma(t) = M \exp(i\omega t)$ propagating in the earth. From [3.25] we find:

$$\epsilon(t) = e^{i\omega t}\left[1 - q\,\omega_0\,e^{\omega/\omega_0}\,Ei\,(-\omega/\omega_0)\right] \qquad [3.26]$$

The factor inside square brackets describes the amplitude of the strain wave as a function of normalized frequency $\Omega = \omega/\omega_0$. The amplitude damping increases with the frequency. The wave is also dispersive, but the amount of dispersion is negligible in body waves.

An important parameter for the study of attenuation in the earth is the dimensionless specific loss factor $1/Q$. In close analogy with the theory of electric networks $1/Q$ represents the proportion of energy dissipated during a strain cycle, as referred to the peak strain energy stored during the cycle. A general expression for the loss factor in linear materials is:

$$1/Q = \int_0^{\infty} \sin \omega t\,\dot{\varphi}(t)dt / \left[1 + \int_0^{\infty} \cos \omega t\,\dot{\varphi}(t)dt\right] \qquad [3.27]$$

Introducing the logarithmic creep function we obtain:

$$\frac{1}{Q} = \frac{q[(\frac{\pi}{2} - Si\,\Omega)\cos\Omega + Ci\,\Omega\,\sin\Omega]}{1 + q[(\frac{\pi}{2} - Si\,\Omega)\sin\Omega - Ci\,\Omega\,\cos\Omega]} \qquad [3.28]$$

where $\Omega = \omega/\omega_0$ is the normalized frequency. The symbols Si and Ci stand for the sine and cosine integral functions. They may be computed by means of the rapidly converging algorithms:

$$Si\,x = \sum_{n=0}^{\infty} (-1)^n x^{2n+1}/(2n+1)(2n+1)! \qquad [3.29]$$

$$\text{Ci } x = 0.5772157 + \log x + \sum_{n=1}^{\infty} (-1)^n x^{2n}/2n (2n)! \qquad [3.30]$$

In agreement with theory, the specific loss factor $1/Q$ varies between zero at $\omega = 0$ and zero at $\omega = \infty$. It has at least one maximum in the middle frequency ranges. For the logarithmic creep function $1/Q$ exhibits an extremely wide, horizontal plateau over a broad frequency range; within this range, experimental determinations of $1/Q$ yield a quasi-constant value. For small values of q, such as occur in the solid earth, the value of $1/Q$ along this plateau is approximately $\pi q/2$.

Hence, if we assume $Q^{-1} = \pi q/2$ within the earth's lithosphere and upper mantle it becomes possible to discuss the attenuation data from surface waves and free oscillations of the earth (Fig.3.9). The data are suggestive of discontinuities around 100 km (low-velocity zone), 270–350 km, and 1,000 km. They can be inverted to obtain the distribution of the creep modulus q with depth.

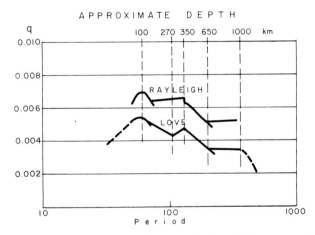

Fig.3.9. Attenuation of seismic waves in the earth's upper mantle, showing inferred discontinuities at 100, 270–350, 650, and 1000 km.

In conclusion, linear theory permits a unified description of stress–strain behavior, including low-strain creep and stress-wave propagation, in the solid earth. Creep rates can be predicted from measurements of $1/Q$ and vice versa, in good agreement with laboratory measurements. No detailed knowledge of the attenuation mechanisms at the molecular or crystal level is required within the linear range.

At large strains the behavior of rocks depends on many factors, including pore water content, pressure, temperature, chemical and mineralogical impurities, in addition to the strain rate. Confining pressure is not the most critical factor. Failure is commonly preceded by a loosening of the grain structure, accompanied by microfracturing. The behavior of a polycrystalline material prior to fracture may be classified as "brittle" or "ductile"; but this distinction is irrelevant within the linear range.

There has been much discussion about the possible use of creep and attenuation data to determine whether convection in the earth's mantle occurs or not. Unfortunately, the relevance of internal energy dissipation to the problem of convection seems limited. Convection is a process of mass transfer, which is driven by density gradients. Essentially, no internal strains are involved if the flow lines are circular and concentric. The motion is braked (rather than driven) by shear in the boundary layers. Hence the occurrence of convection must be decided on the basis of whether the heat conductivity of the mantle is sufficiently high to prevent density instability. The energy dissipation associated with mass transfer cannot by itself prevent flow from occurring, unless one postulates a material which becomes stiffer under increasing temperature and stress. Such a hypothetical material would seem to be physically unrealizable.

The shear boundary layers which confine a convection cell from top to bottom may be subjected to strains beyond the linear range. Considerable heat dissipation may also be occurring in those parts of a convection cell where flow lines are constrained to change their curvature. Thus convection provides a mechanism which accounts for the low-velocity layer and other inhomogeneous regions of the mantle. However, the anelastic behavior of materials in these anomalous zones is not necessarily reflected in the bulk properties of the mantle, as derived from the attenuation of mantle waves and free oscillations.

EQUIVALENT VISCOSITY OF THE MANTLE

A material described by the logarithmic creep law will flow like a viscous liquid under long-term shear stress. The effective viscosity η may be obtained from:

$$\dot{\varphi}(t) = M/\eta = \omega_0 \, q \, (1 + \omega_0 \, t)^{-1} \tag{3.31}$$

which indicates that the viscosity increases with time. In a convecting mass this has the effect of slowing the rate of convection, which in turn raises the temperature gradient and increases the driving force. As a result the system is self-regulating and seeks a stationary state with minimum dissipation.

Thus, the effective viscosity in a convecting mantle depends on the rate of heat transfer of the system. The mantle materials will flow neither faster nor slower than is necessary in order to dispose of the excess heat which is causing convective instability. Short-term parameters such as $1/Q$ and q lose significance under long-term stationary flow.

What amount of time can be considered "long-term"? Using the approximation:

$$\eta \approx Mt/q \tag{3.32}$$

which may be readily derived from [3.31], we obtain for $\eta = 10^{21}$, $M = 10^{11}$ and $q = 0.01$ a "relaxation time" of the order of 3 years. Any convective regime in the mantle which can maintain itself for a period of at least three years becomes self-regulating, i.e., the effective viscosity is independent of the short-term material constant q. This conclusion is in substantial agreement with Tozer's (1970) approach to the thermal history of the convecting mantle.

AFTERSHOCKS

As we have seen, the elastic energy stored in the deviatoric stress field about the fault is reduced after an earthquake by an amount which depends on the stress drop. For a stress drop of 50% the energy drop will be 75% (because the energy is proportional to the square of the stress). This represents a negative energy perturbation in the earth. If the earth is a steady-state thermodynamic system there will be some influx of energy into the depleted region, in order to restore stationary conditions.

This energy transient towards the epicentral area takes various aspects: mass transfer, heat flow, electrical and chemical potentials, and so on. Every one of these flows is governed by an Onsager equation of the form:

$$J_k = \text{grad } \Delta\sigma \sum_i L_{ik} v_k \qquad\qquad [3.33]$$

where J_k is the flow of a phase k, v_k is the corresponding specific volume, and the L_{ik} are Onsager's coefficients. The flow at every point in the system is proportional to the gradient of the stress perturbation $\Delta\sigma$, i.e. the gradient of the stress drop. Equations similar to [3.33] may be written for heat flow, electromagnetic effects, and so on (Lomnitz, 1961).

Now, the state of strain in the focal region after an earthquake is far from a state of equilibrium. All the strain release was effected through displacement along a finite crack within the medium. Model experiments by Gzovsky (1954) have shown that such displacements generate residual strain concentrations, particularly near both extremes of the fault (the so-called "butterfly strains"), but also elsewhere around any inhomogeneities within the region. As the regional stress level builds up again these residual strains reach critical levels and trigger many small earthquakes called *aftershocks*.

The occurrence of aftershocks appears to be governed by the rate of energy influx. According to Prigogine (1947) the entropy production s in a stationary system after a perturbation at time $t=0$ is of the general form:

$$s(t) = s_0 + \frac{\alpha_1}{t + \beta} + \frac{\alpha_2}{(t + \beta)^2} + \ldots \qquad\qquad [3.34]$$

where α_1, $\alpha_2 \ldots$, β are constants of the process. Since the rate of energy influx is propor tional to $s(t)-s_0$, the process agrees with Omori's (1894) Law for aftershocks:

$$n(t) = p/(t + q)$$ [3.35]

where n (t) is the number of aftershocks per unit time, and p, q are constants. The magnitude of the aftershocks being stationary, the quantity $n(t)$ is proportional to the rate of seismic energy release in the region.

The spatial distribution of aftershocks may be predicted from the residual strain pattern. In many transcurrent faults the aftershock strain distribution shows a characteristic concentration near the ends of the fault break, in the shape of a butterfly (Fig.3.10). In the case of reverse or normal faulting the aftershock pattern is elliptical on a horizontal projection. In low-magnitude earthquakes the aftershock activity is often localized along the original fault break, or on its closest branch-faults.

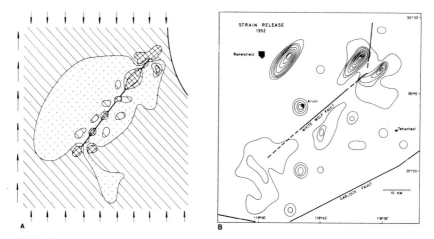

Fig.3.10. A comparison of aftershock strains. A. Observed photoelastic fringes in a fault model in gelatin (after Gzovsky, 1954). B. Strains calculated from the energy release of the 1952 Kern County aftershock sequence.

If aftershocks were due to creep recovery, as has been proposed in the past, their mechanisms should be reversed: an earthquake due to normal faulting should be followed by reverse-faulting aftershocks, and vice versa. The observations show, on the contrary, that the focal mechanisms of aftershocks are consistent with the tectonic stresses which generated the main shock. Therefore, aftershocks cannot be caused by a process of stress relaxation.

The thermodynamical model of aftershock sequences as stress recovery processes is still relatively unknown. It has important potential implications for global tectonics, such as the quantitative description of certain features including magmatism and metamorphism in seismic regions. The theory also predicts thermal and electromagnetic transients which have not yet been observed, but which may be verifiable in the field. In short, aftershock research represents today one of the more promising experimental approaches toward an understanding of the cause of earthquakes.

EARTHQUAKES AND EXPLOSIONS

An explosion is a relatively simple type of seismic source. Compared with an earthquake it can be described as a point source; the initial wave front is spherical and compressional. If the explosion is confined underground the seismic signal at distant stations is a fairly simple P-wave pulse. The amount of energy converted into S-waves and surface waves near the explosion is relatively minor, so that the general aspect of the seismogram is rather distinctive (Fig.3.11).

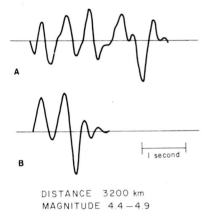

DISTANCE   3200 km
MAGNITUDE 4.4 — 4.9

Fig.3.11. Seismograms of two events of similar location and magnitude recorded on a short-period instrument. A. Earthquake. B. Nuclear explosion. (After Davies and Smith, 1968.)

The yield of an explosion is expressed in terms of equivalent tons of TNT. A yield of one ton corresponds approximately to $4 \cdot 10^{16}$ ergs. Thus, a nuclear explosion of 20 kilotons (called a "nominal bomb", or Hiroshima-type bomb) has a yield of $8 \cdot 10^{20}$ ergs. The seismic signal from such an explosion depends on whether it is detonated in the atmosphere, in the ocean, or in an underground cavity. For underground tests the equivalent body-wave magnitude may be estimated approximately by:

$$m = 0.67 \log_{10} Y + K \pm 0.3 \qquad\qquad [3.36]$$

where Y is the yield in kilotons, and the constant K is 4.25 for close coupling in granite and 3.25 for close coupling in dry alluvium. Thus, a nominal bomb detonated in granite could produce a seismic event of body-wave magnitude m up to 5.4. This would be equivalent to a Richter magnitude (cf.eq.3.3) of $M = 5.2$.

TABLE 3.3

Magnitude—energy—yield[1]

m	M	$E(\times 10^{21}$ ergs)	Y(Mton)
5.6	5	0.008	0.1
6.3	6	0.205	1.2
6.5	6.4	1.0	2.5
6.6	6.5	1.4	3.1
6.6	6.6	2.0	4.0
6.7	6.7	2.8	5.0
6.8	6.8	4.0	5.6
6.8	6.9	5.6	6.5
6.9	7.0	8.0	10.0
7.0	7.1	11.2	12
7.0	7.2	15.8	14
7.1	7.3	22.4	16
7.1	7.4	31.6	20
7.2	7.5	44.7	25
7.3	7.6	63.1	32
7.3	7.7	89	40
7.4	7.8	126	50
7.5	7.9	178	63
7.5	8.0	251	80
7.6	8.1	355	94
7.6	8.2	501	110
7.7	8.3	708	145
7.8	8.4	1.000	180
7.8	8.5	1.400	220
7.9	8.6	2.000	280
8.0	8.7	2.800	360
8.0	8.8	4.000	420
8.1	8.9	5.600	630

[1]For nuclear explosions in granite.

The "Cannikin" explosion of November 6, 1971 had a yield of 5 megatons and produced a seismic event of Richter magnitude 7.0, in close agreement with predictions. Table 3.3 gives an equivalence of seismic magnitudes in terms of nuclear yield for underground explosions.

The widespread public anxiety on the subject of underground testing seems to imply that the effects of nuclear explosions should be much different from those of natural earthquakes. Millions of dollars were spent between 1960 and 1967 in the hope of finding a way to tell an earthquake from an explosion. Differences do exist, but they are rather subtle and require numerical processing of the seismograms. Immediate effects such as the triggering of large earthquakes at a distance are within the realm of possibility but have never been substantiated.

Of course, no one can predict what long-term effects nuclear tests may produce. At present, the number of underground tests has been over 500 in the Nevada Testing Site alone. Nevada tests have triggered small aftershocks within about 20 km of the explosion, but correlation with more distant events has not been significant. This is perhaps unfortunate, since some kind of cumulative effect on the environment is entirely possible and even likely. At present we do not know what form this effect might take or when it might appear.

CHAPTER 4

Plate Tectonics

INTRODUCTION

In 1922 the American press reproduced a declaration by Professor Andrew C. Lawson, of the University of California, taking issue with the problem of earthquake prediction. The declaration was couched in fairly optimistic terms, and said in part[1]:

"If the amount of strain which the earth's crust will endure has been ascertained, and the rate at which the earth's crust is creeping toward the breaking point has been learned, when and where the break will occur is a mere matter of calculation".

It has taken more than 40 years for this hypothetical vision to become close to reality. Today we know that large blocks of the earth's lithosphere are endowed with mobility in response to convective processes at depth, and we know that the differential motion between these blocks is the cause of earthquake activity. Once the rate of displacement is known we may directly infer the mean annual rate of seismic energy release.

The details of the process are a great deal more complex than Lawson anticipated. A significant proportion of earthquakes occurs on fault structures which had previously been believed to be inactive. Some earthquake faults cut across scarps of Pleistocene age: this indicates that tectonic patterns are changing in time spans as short as 100,000 years.

In some regions, such as Turkey or Chile, historic earthquakes tend to occur in an orderly spatial succession. In these cases the larger structures (Anatolian Fault, Chile Trench) seem to dominate the tectonic process to such an extent that sequential patterns begin to emerge within a relatively short period of observation. Elsewhere it may take a geologic era to discern these regional patterns.

Thus, even in those regions where *"the rate at which the earth's crust is creeping toward the breaking point has been learned"*, there remain many other things to be learned as well. But the advances made during the decade of 1960–1970 have indeed been dramatic, and they would surely have made Professor Lawson feel that his optimism of 1922 was beginning to be justified at last.

THE PLATE CONCEPT

Large-scale dynamic motions of the earth's outer shell, or *lithosphere*, are impeded by the rigidity of the silicate materials which predominantly make up its composition. The

---
[1] *Christian Science Monitor*, February 14, 1922.

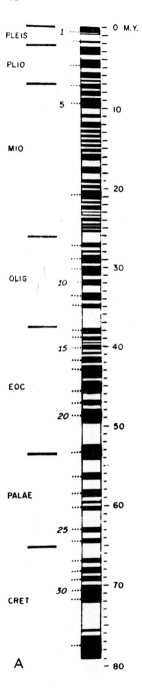

Fig.4.1. A. Scale of magnetic inversions during the last 80 million years (after Heirzler et al., 1968). B. Diagram of sea-floor spreading.

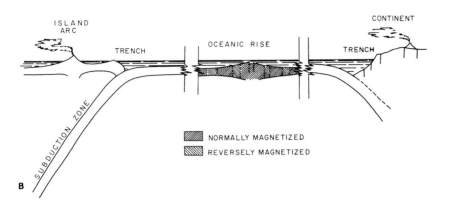

theory of plate tectonics assumes that the lithosphere can be divided into a small number of rigid plates, which move as units. Obviously, this assumption cannot be taken too literally: the rigidity of a basaltic layer 5,000 km wide by 100 km thick can hardly be compared to that of a paving block. Yet the concept proves useful in dealing with the mechanics of sea-floor spreading and particularly with the geometry of interaction between oceans and continents.

Where two plates move away from each other the intervening space between the plates is filled by hot material ascending from the upper mantle. As the hot lava solidifies its iron ore particles are frozen in the prevailing orientation of the earth's magnetic field. This process continues as more material is extruded and the two plates grow apart. Finally, the oceanic crust on both sides of the seam will be imprinted with a continuous record of the fluctuations of the earth's magnetic field (Fig.4.1). These lineations form parallel stripes on the magnetic survey charts of the oceans, which can be traced, correlated, and dated by radioactive methods.

Foremost among the lineations are the records of the *inversions* of the earth's magnetic field. These changes in polarity have occurred quite frequently and they provide excellent markers for world-wide time correlations. The more recent inversions serve to define the four youngest magnetic epochs, named after Brunhes (normal polarity, 0–700,000 years before present), Matuyama (reversed, 700,000 years–2.5 million years). Gauss (normal, 2.5–3.36 m.y.), and Gilbert (reversed, 3.36–5 m.y.). Within these broad periods there are also several shorter reversals called "events" (Jaramillo, normal, 0.87–0.93 m.y.; Olduvai, normal, 1.85–2.00 m.y.; and so on), which can be identified by the magnetic lineations and also by the magnetic stratigraphy of sea-floor sediments. A great many older inversions of the earth's magnetic field have been detected into the period of formation of the Atlantic Ocean, thus affording a complete chronology of the sea-floor spreading process.

Velocities of sea-floor spreading calculated in this fashion are fairly consistent over the major ocean basins. They range from 1 to 6 cm/year. A spreading ridge is not a continu-

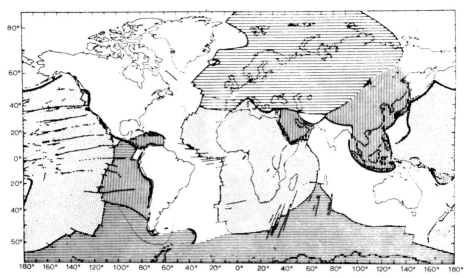

Fig.4.2. Major lithospheric plates of the world, after Morgan (1968). This was the earliest published version of plate geometry; many plate boundaries have since been modified or questioned.

ous structure: it shows frequent axial offsets. The faults which connect two spreading ridge segments are called "transform faults". They have the notable property of being arcs of concentric circles; their center is the pole of relative rotation between the adjoining plates. Fig.4.2. shows the plates originally proposed by Morgan (1968).

GEOMETRY OF SEA-FLOOR SPREADING

The basic ideas of sea-floor spreading were developed about 1960 by Hess, Dietz, Wilson, Vine, Matthews, and many others. The idea of plate tectonics was originated around 1968 by Morgan, Le Pichon, McKenzie, and others. These ideas have revolutionized tectonics in a very short time; but some of them have their roots in observations going back several decades.

Some 50 years ago Wegener argued forcefully that the similarity of the Atlantic coasts of Africa and South America was an indication of continental drift. In those days it was not known that a continuous rift zone, the Mid-Atlantic Ridge, is the original seam along which these continents were formerly joined. It is now possible to reconstruct their initial fit with excellent accuracy (Fig.2.1).

This means that the South Atlantic Ocean was generated from a crack between South America and Africa. There is no indication of active borders between the South Atlantic Ocean and its adjoining land masses. Thus, the African plate and the South American plate each include one half of the South Atlantic Ocean. By extending this method of reasoning it is possible to divide the earth's surface into six major plates (Fig.4.2). These plates are: the Pacific plate, the Americas plate, the African plate, the Eurasian plate, the Nasca plate, and the Antarctic plate. Several smaller plates have also been proposed, such as the Cocos plate (between Central America and the Galápagos rise), the Caribbean plate, the Indian Ocean plate, and so on.

The boundaries of lithospheric plates are defined on the basis of current tectonic activity, particularly earthquakes. The pattern of earthquake epicenters can be used to outline the plate boundaries in considerable detail. Other indications of tectonic activity are deep-sea trenches, oceanic rises, active volcanoes, modern mountain ranges, gravity anomalies, and ongoing movements of the surface of the earth.

TECTONICS OF SEA-FLOOR SPREADING

There are four basic modes of interaction between plates: extrusion, subduction, accretion, and transcursion (cf. Chapter 1, p.3). Each of these modes of interaction is associated with characteristic types of tectonism.

Extrusion is associated with rifting of the ocean floor; subduction with thrust faulting; accretion with block faulting, and transcursion with transcurrent faulting. In general, extrusion and accretion are related to tension, subduction to compression, and transcursion to horizontal shear.

Pure subduction of active margins by oceanic plates is probably less frequent than was originally supposed. The dipping lithospheric plates under the continents are called "Benioff zones", after the seismologist who first described the pattern of earthquakes under certain active areas. However, Benioff zones which reach their full development down to 600 km in the mantle are rare.

Shallow earthquakes form a continuous belt along plate boundaries, but deep-focus earthquakes tend to cluster in a few regions (Japan Sea, Fiji Basin, western Argentina, Banda Sea). Intermediate earthquakes, with focal depths of order 100–300 km, also have a tendency to form clusters or "nests" in many regions (Fig.4.3).

Deep-sea trenches occur along the zones of convergence, where two plates move against each other. Originally they were believed to mark the location of underthrusting: the bottom of trenches was assumed to be a sliding junction between plates, where sediments from the oceanic plate would be scraped off and highly contorted. This picture hardly agrees with reality; instead, most trenches resemble deep troughs of oceanic crust downfaulted at both margins. The sediments within the trenches are layered flat and appear to be undisturbed. This indicates that the mechanism of interaction of lithospheric plates may involve tension and block faulting in the upper layers along the offshore zones of convergence.

The mechanism of extrusion in oceanic rises is imperfectly known. Divergence between adjoining plates may be episodic rather than continuous. The rise itself is not a continuous mountain chain, but is made up of segments set off by faults at right angles (Fig.4.4). These are the *transform faults*, where the plates slide past one another. Seismic

activity in oceanic rises is chiefly associated with these zones of transduction, rather than
with the actual zones of extrusion. The latter are the seats of volcanic activity and high
heat flow.

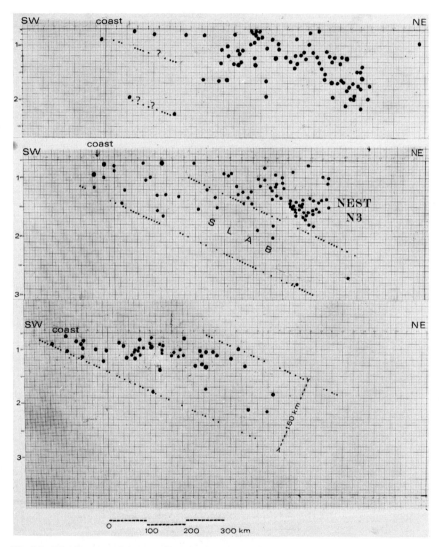

Fig.4.3. Distribution of intermediate-depth earthquakes in three successive north—south sections,
normal to the coast of Peru. Hypothetical "slabs" of lithosphere are indicated to show the lack of
agreement with distribution of hypocenters. Only the southernmost "slab" contains a majority of
shocks, but the location of this "slab" is not consistent with sea-floor spreading. Note the location of
intermediate nest *N3* (depths in hundreds of km).

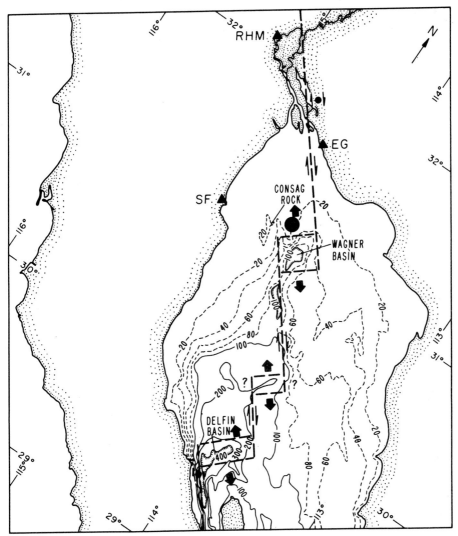

Fig.4.4. Structure under the Gulf of California. (After Lomnitz et al., 1970.)

STRESSES IN LITHOSPHERIC PLATES

In the early period of plate tectonics it was assumed that continental drift was caused by plates being pushed apart from the mid-ocean ridges. It was soon realized, however, that this is not mechanically feasible . The upwelling hot material cannot exert horizontal stresses on the lithosphere, and the aspect ratio of the plates themselves is so slender that they would buckle under axial compression rather than transmit stresses for thousands of kilometers. Nevertheless, the idea that most of the earth's crust is stressed in compression has persisted in the assumption of most authors.

This idea is now being revised. Elsasser (1971) has argued "that the low-latitude part of the lithosphere from the eastern coast of South America all the way to the eastern side of the Indian Ocean seems almost entirely tensile". One might add that the mechanism of ocean—continent interaction which prevails along the west coast of South and Central America, and which we have called "accretion" (p.60), is predominantly tensional in character.

It seems difficult to reconcile sea-floor spreading with horizontal tension until one realizes that the motions of lithospheric plates must be a part of the general circulation of the earth's mantle. Lithospheric material sinks into the mantle near the zones of convergence, and the gap is closed by the adjacent plates. Depending on the spreading rates and on the geometry of the plates, tensional stresses will arise in either or both of the plates. According to this view, compressional stresses across convergence zones would represent a special case, rather than the general norm.

For example, the westward advance of the Americas plate would require tensional stresses to exist along most of its Pacific edge. This implies that mountain building along such an edge must be explained by mechanisms other than horizontal compression.

The interior of the plates is essentially unstressed, as shown by the absence of earthquake activity. Deformation and seismic release occurs largely near the edges of plates. The underlying mechanism of these movements is unknown, but it seems plausible to assume that the convection cells tend to evolve toward a more stable global configuration. Thus, the exceedingly large Pacific cell would tend to shrink and the Americas cell would tend to grow at its expense. The stresses involved in changes of the aspect ratio of convection cells could be transmitted to the lithosphere, particularly in regions of upwelling and convergence.

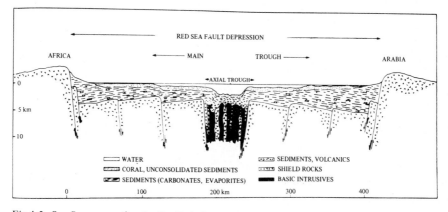

Fig.4.5. Sea-floor spreading in the Red Sea, an incipient ocean between Africa and Arabia. (From Girdler, 1967.)

The preceding interpretation of stresses and driving forces in the lithosphere is supported by the asymmetry of magnetic lineations, which cannot be explained by earlier theories. For example, the East Pacific Rise is spreading much faster toward South America than toward the Tonga Trench system. The Tonga Trench is a subduction zone, while western South America is largely a zone of accretion. Thus, the higher spreading velocity of the Nasca plate away from the East Pacific Rise is consistent with the tensional tectonics observed along the South American convergence. It is significant that the spreading rates are inversely proportional to the dimensions of the plate.

The tensional nature of extrusion mechanisms is well demonstrated in the Red Sea Rift, a spreading center of recent formation (Fig.4.5).

TRANSCURSION IN CALIFORNIA

In 1908 Andrew C. Lawson, then Chairman of the California State Earthquake Investigating Commission, suggested a geological interpretation of the mechanism of the San Francisco earthquake. Lawson's views were later translated into quantitative terms and given the form of a consistent theory by Harry Fielding Reid, an engineer who contributed greatly to the work of the Commission. Reid (1911) utilized for his basic data the results of geodetic surveys reported by J.F. Hayford and A.L. Baldwin, themselves members of the Commission.

The San Francisco Bay area had been surveyed by triangulation on three separate occasions: 1851—1866, 1874—1892 and 1906—1907. The relative position of the triangulation points changed considerably between each of these surveys, the exception being the line Mt. Diablo—Mt. Mocho which is nearly parallel to the San Andreas Fault and was used as a base line.

Between surveys II and III some further displacements were observed; but this time Mt. ft. to the northwest and its neighbor to the east (Mt. Tamalpais) had moved 5.4 ft. in the same direction. This motion was attributed to the 1868 Hayward earthquake by some, and to continuous fault creep by others.

Between surveys II and III some futher displacements were observed; but this time Mt. Tamalpais had moved 1.9 ft. in the *opposite* direction, while Farallon Lighthouse had continued to move 5.8 ft. to the north. The 1906 earthquake, which occurred prior to survey III, produced a displacement of 21 ft. along the San Andreas Fault, several miles north of the point where it crosses the Farallon—Tamalpais triangulation line. The remaining points showed displacements to the northwest or southeast, depending on whether the point was located on the ocean side or the continent side with respect to the San Andreas Fault.

The general inference at the time was that the two land masses on either side of the fault had been shifted by the earthquake. But Reid, following a suggestion by Lawson, went one step further: in lining up the average displacements across the fault (Fig. 4.6), he attributed the motion to elastic rebound of strains *assumed to have been pre-existent*

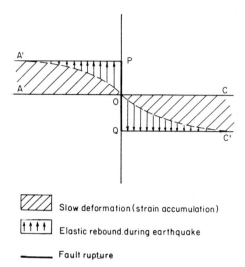

Slow deformation(strain accumulation)

Elastic rebound during earthquake

Fault rupture

Fig.4.6. H.F. Reid's reconstruction of deformations involved in the 1906 San Francisco earthquake. The maximum length PQ of the fault rupture was about 7 m at the earth's surface. AC = initial position of a base line across the fault; $A'P$, QC' = final position after the earthquake. (After Report of the State Earthquake Investigating Commission, 1908.)

in the rock at the time of the earthquake. "That the displacements gradually became less and less, as the distance from the fault line increased, seemed probable, because a thorough exploration of the region failed to discover any other line with offsets similar to those along the San Andreas Fault, and therefore *it was presumable that blocks of the earth's crust were not shifted as a whole*" (Reid, 1911).

With reference to Fig.4.6 Reid adds: "The line $A'C'$ represents a line which was straight at the time of the second survey. At the time of the earthquake this line was broken at the fault, and its two parts separated about 21 ft., taking the positions $A'P$ and $C'Q$. Three points and the distant Mount Diablo determine the right-hand curve; two points and the distant Farallon Lighthouse, together with the fact that PQ must be 21 ft., determine that on the left".

More recent triangulations in the San Francisco Bay area made in 1951, 1957, and 1963, throw some light on the question of slow strain accumulation. A new triangulation network of 20 stations covered much of the Counties of Alameda and San Francisco and parts of Contra Costa, Marin and San Mateo Counties. Unfortunately only one point was located to the west of the San Andreas Fault. The 1951–1957 vectors appear to indicate a general northward transcursion of the coast with respect to the continent, particularly west of the Hayward Fault. The 1963 survey, however, showed that "the 1957–1963 vectors are completely random in both size and direction". It was finally stated that "adverse atmospheric conditions during either survey could produce these effects" (Parkin, 1965).

In 1960 C.A. Whitten and C.N. Claire reported on surveys across the San Andreas Fault covering the period 1930–1951. In the vicinity of Hollister the fault had been displaced about 20 cm in a 20-year period; 75 miles to the southeast, in the vicinity of Cholame, the displacement was only about 5 cm in the same period. No major earthquakes could account for these differential displacements at the time; but the Parkfield earthquake of June 28, 1966 made up for the difference precisely in the Cholame area which Whitten and Claire had found anomalous.

Often no strain effects may be detected in the immediate vicinity of a fault prior to the earthquake. For example, geodetic measurements conducted for 30 years and until a few days before the San Fernando, California earthquake of February 9, 1971 failed to show any significant strain accumulation in the region connected with the earthquake. The overall displacement along the San Andreas system as a whole, about 5 cm/year, is fully consistent with the velocity of transcursion of the Pacific plate as obtained from sea-floor spreading measurements, however.

Strain accumulation occurs over large structures of the size of plate boundaries and may be obscured by complicated geology on a more detailed scale. This justifies Reid's procedure of obtaining the points in Fig.4.6 as group averages of geodetic displacements published by Hayford and Baldwin (1908) for a relatively large area around the San Andreas Fault. A careful analysis of Reid's papers reveals that Fig.4.6 was intended as an illustration of the *general trend* of regional deformations, rather than a reduced profile for the Farallon–Mt. Diablo line. In this sense, it can be said that the theory of elastic rebound has been vindicated by recent measurements in California and elsewhere, and that it must be understood in the context of sea-floor spreading and of transcursion between the American and Pacific plates.

VISCOELASTIC REBOUND AS AN EARTHQUAKE MECHANISM

In August 1950 Hugo Benioff reported on a sequence of earthquakes occurring since 1925 at 34° south 58° east, near the antipodes of Pasadena on the southwest Indian Ridge. By means of a cumulative plot of the square roots of the energy of these earthquakes, Benioff obtained a curve which stopped in 1933 (Fig.4.7). "If, since the last shock in this series," wrote Benioff "the strain has been accumulating in accordance with the curve there should now be stored enough energy for a shock of greater than 7.5 magnitude" (Benioff, 1951).

One year later (December 8, 1951), an earthquake of magnitude 7.6 occurred in the same epicentral region. Benioff concluded that the amount of available strain accumulated across the particular fault was indeed given by the curve of Fig.4.7, and that the maximum earthquake could be predicted for any given time. "This sequence provides convincing evidence that in a given region the accumulating strain may be relieved either by a large number of small shocks or by a small number of large shocks, in spite of the contrary conclusion expressed by others" (Benioff, 1955).

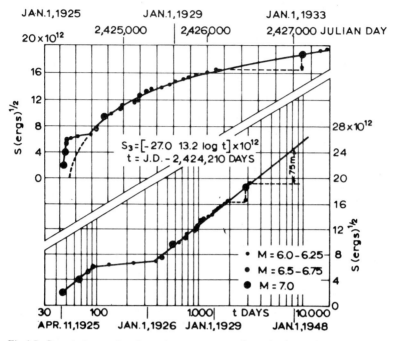

Fig.4.7. Cumulative strain release for the region 34°S 58°E in the Indian Ocean, and prediction of an earthquake of magnitude 7.5 (From Benioff, 1951.)

This reasoning stemmed directly from Reid's theory of elastic rebound, and is in agreement with plate tectonics. If we assume that the elastic strain accumulated prior to the earthquake was uniformly distributed in a volume V about the fault, the elastic energy stored in the rock would be given by:

$$E = \mu V \epsilon^2 / 2 \qquad\qquad\qquad\qquad [4.1]$$

where ϵ is the strain and μ is the elastic modulus of the rock. A certain fraction η of this earthquake energy is released in the form of seismic waves:

$$J = \eta \mu V \epsilon^2 / 2 \qquad\qquad\qquad\qquad [4.2]$$

the rest being consumed in heat and displacement work. Thus we may write:

$$\epsilon = k \sqrt{J} \qquad\qquad\qquad\qquad\qquad [4.3]$$

where k is some parameter which changes from earthquake to earthquake.

Benioff suggested that the parameter k *may be assumed to remain constant for a particular earthquake source.* This justified the summation of strains released in a given region by earthquakes of different magnitudes, as shown in Fig.4.7. If one takes the elastic modulus to be time-invariant this hypothesis implies, in the specified region:

$$\eta V = \text{constant} \qquad [4.4]$$

Perhaps the best-known application of Benioff's theory has been in aftershock sequences. If one plots a cumulative graph of the aftershock strains by eq.4.3 one finds that the process seems to follow a logarithmic trend in time (Fig.4.8). This has been interpreted in terms of an actual strain change in the rock, viz.

$$\epsilon(t) = A + B \log t \qquad [4.5]$$

which is of the form found in the laboratory for the creep behavior of rocks and other polycrystalline substances. Benioff inferred that aftershocks may be due to elastic after-working or recovery creep of the rock following the release of the purely elastic part of the strain in the main earthquake. He coined the term "elastic-strain rebound" for the mechanism described by eq.4.5. Among the advantages of extending Reid's theory to viscoelastic materials is the possibility of allowing for long-term creep effects in the earth's crust, independently of any earthquake strain accumulation that may be taking place.

The assumption of eq.4.4 is of doubtful validity, however. The earthquake volume V is an increasing function of the magnitude; thus, if [4.4] is true the efficiency of seismic

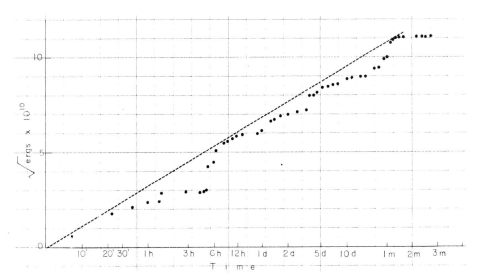

Fig.4.8. Cumulative strain release for the aftershock sequence of the 1970 Peru earthquake. Note that the strain release for the first 12 hours was the same as for the following 3 months.

energy conversion η should fall off with magnitude. Actually the opposite is more likely: if energy losses along the fault are mainly frictional the efficiency η should behave more or less as the ratio V/S between earthquake volume and the sliding surface S of the fault. King and Knopoff (1968) argued that η should be independent of magnitude. Hence the product ηV is most probably a steeply increasing function of magnitude, in contradiction with eq.4.4.

There are good reasons to believe that the decay curves of aftershock sequences (such as Fig.4.8) do not reflect a particular aftershock mechanism but are merely a result of the probability structure of the process in time. Most decay processes of physics yield similar logarithmic curves.

More recently, Mogi (1962) and Scholz (1968) have attempted to analyze the mechanism of earthquakes from the point of view of brittle fracture. By drawing on the analogy with microfractures produced in rock samples in the laboratory they have suggested that crustal earthquakes and microfractures are produced by a similar mechanism.

The ideas of viscoelastic rebound and brittle fracture have been applied primarily to transcursion in California. They have not succeeded in supplying new evidence on the mechanism of earthquakes in the continents but might well yield results in some simpler tectonic situations. The case of extrusion tectonics along ocean ridges is of particular interest as it supplied the initial (and so far the only) success of Benioff's prediction approach.

SUBDUCTION

The original idea of subduction sprang from Benioff's interpretation of earthquake foci as lying on a single fault plane, which was assumed to dip under the continental margins at an angle of $30-60°$. This large fault was initially conceived as a moving contact between two blocks: a continental block and an oceanic block.

After the advent of sea-floor spreading the Benioff "fault" became a plate of lithosphere thrusting into the mantle at a fairly steep angle. The continent was not seen as participating in the process and its location seemed unimportant, except to determine the edge of underthrusting.

At this stage it was fully expected that most earthquakes in a subduction zone were caused by some mechanism of jerky frictional sliding between the lithospheric slab and the mantle. It turned out, however, that the planes of faulting were not parallel to the inferred boundaries of plates, and could not be due to lithosphere-mantle interaction. Instead, most of the earthquakes appeared to take place *inside* the lithospheric slab. Oliver and Isacks (1967) proposed that the earthquakes were due to tension or compression pointing down-dip in the plane of the slabs themselves. Many papers have been written in elaboration of this theme, but relatively few concrete results have been produced so far.

The Tonga—Kermadec region may be cited as an example of subduction zone. This region accounts for 70% of the deep-focus earthquakes in the world. The dipping earthquake zone is less than 25 km thick, and very straight and flat. It starts to bend down-wards at the axis of the Tonga Trench and dips under the island arc at an angle of 45° down to depths of the order of 650 km. Earthquakes occur at all depths: there are no conspicuous gaps in seismic activity, as found under zones of accretion.

Fault-plane solutions have shown that the mechanism of shallow earthquakes behind the trench is dominantly thrust faulting towards and under the island arc. At greater depth the shocks indicate a mechanism of compression along the dip of the slab. This pattern appears to be characteristic of subduction; it is certainly true that most zones of accretion along continental margins exhibit down-dip tension along with a fragmentation of the slab into discrete sections or "nests" (Fig.4.9).

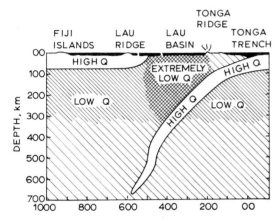

Fig.4.9. Subduction zone in the Fiji–Kermadec region, showing high Q (low attenuation) for the lithosphere, and low Q in the astenosphere. (After Barazangi and Isacks, 1971.)

The subduction zone has strikingly different mechanical properties from the sur-rounding mantle. Its attenuation coefficient Q is of the same order as in the lithosphere, and about one-seventh of its value in the mantle. This contrast is important enough to help define the boundaries of the downgoing slab: it now appears that the slab is almost 80 km thick and that the earthquakes tend to occur near the center of the slab.

Near the surface there is a certain amount of scatter in the epicenters, as might be expected. Earthquakes occur within the slab, along the slab boundaries, and in the ad-joining lithospheric plates. The volcanic islands behind the arc have no earthquakes, except for very local shallow events associated with the volcanoes themselves.

It is interesting that the zone of highest attenuation of seismic waves occurs in the mantle directly below the volcanic zone; this is also the region of high heat flow and high gravity. Everything seems to indicate that the source of volcanism in island arcs is in the upper mantle. The basaltic lavas erupted in Tonga–Kermadec and in other island arcs are chemically different from continental lavas in accretion zones. The continental basalts have a silica content in excess of 50% and have the same Ca/Alk ratio as the more acidic products (rhyolites, ignimbrites) which occur in these regions in great abundance. Hence continental basalts have more properly been called trachyte–andesites, derived from within the continental crust, while the true basalts from subduction zones are invariably more basic and have a lower calcium/alkali ratio.

The rising of magma from the upper mantle may be important enough to cause secondary spreading of the ocean floors behind the arc. A secondary trench may form inside the island arc, or the lithosphere under the island sea may become a small plate endowed with a spreading rate of its own.

In spite of the great contrasts between island arcs and continental borders, the mechanisms of accretion and subduction are far from clear-cut. In Pacific island arcs there is some evidence that accretion of crustal material occurs on the island side of the trench. Sedimentary rocks derived from the trench accumulate onshore and become metamorphosed into glaucophane schists and associated low-temperature metamorphic rocks. On the other hand, the existence of some deep-focus earthquake nests under the continents may be interpreted as evidence that subduction has occurred there until recently or may still be occurring locally. Hence, subduction and accretion may be regarded as mutually complementary forms of lithosphere consumption in the zones of convergence.

ACCRETION

The model of subduction, or absorption of oceanic plates into the upper mantle, seems to entail no energy transfer from one plate to another. A "conveyor belt" model appears to be fairly successful in describing the observations in areas where subduction occurs.

However, there are important areas initially assumed to be undergoing subduction, where the above model fits the data very poorly. This is notably the case of continental margins. The inclined "Benioff zone" of earthquakes was first described for such areas; hence the early theoreticians of sea-floor spreading assumed that the case for a descending slab under continental margins was especially strong. It appears now that this evidence has been overstated, and that other lines of evidence for "conveyor-belt" subduction under continental margins are equally weak.

Active continental margins, such as the west coast of South America, are zones of high tectonic activity, including faulting, vertical movements of the coast, and mountain-building. The source of the tectonic stresses involved in this activity cannot be derived from subduction, since the latter involves no deformation of the subducted plate.

We define "accretion" as a mechanism of interaction between two plates, such that one plate grows at the expense of the other. This will not necessarily involve an increase in the surface area of either plate, since the growth can occur as a vertical thickening rather than horizontal extension of the lithosphere.

The Elsasser model

It has been pointed out by Orowan and other authors that two plates cannot be pushed apart by a curtain of hot material rising from the mantle. Aside from fairly obvious mechanical considerations, any compressional model of sea-floor spreading is incompatible with the observed offsets of the spreading axis along ocean rises, and with the symmetry of magnetic lineations. In other words, it is difficult to justify a zigzagging vertical current rising from the mantle and pushing apart two plates of different sizes and configurations in perfectly symmetrical fashion. Also, the tectonic features found along oceanic rises indicate horizontal tension rather than compression.

These contradictions can be resolved if one assumes that the plates are being pulled apart by horizontal tension while they rest on an asthenosphere of relatively low viscosity. The lithosphere is brittle only in the crust; below the crust, it will draw out by "necking" in the hottest region, i.e. where hot mantle material has come up most recently. Hence the crust will tend to split again and again at the seam between two plates which are pulled apart, and the voids are replenished by hot material from below. This mechanism does not require the postulate of mantle currents rising exactly below the lines of active spreading (Elsasser, 1971).

In order to understand the origin of tensional forces in the oceanic lithosphere it is sufficient to accept that the oceans are *predominantly* regions of divergence in the convection pattern of the mantle, while continents are largely regions of convergence. The lithosphere acts as a horizontal stress guide and can transmit and redistribute stresses over considerable distances, even though the asthenosphere is too soft and yielding for the transmission of horizontal stress.

Now, if a cooling piece of lithosphere begins to sink into the mantle the motion of the adjacent lithosphere will be exactly the opposite as near a ridge. In fact, the lithosphere at both sides will move *toward* the void created by the sinking block of lithosphere. This

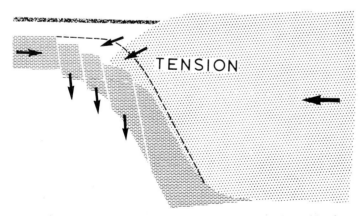

Fig.4.10. Origin of tensional stresses near an accreting continental border

Fig.4.11A. Apollo photograph of Atacama Desert (see Fig.4.11B).

mechanism is seen by Elsasser as creating a convection pattern: *convection originates at the surface*, because of gravitational sinking of cold segments of the lithosphere.

The horizontal motion of material flowing into the vacancy will cause tensile stresses in the lithosphere on both sides. These tensile stresses propagate in the lithosphere until they find a region of weakness where the crust can be split apart. Once the crust is split we have a region of divergence, which grows until the whole surface of the earth is divided into plates growing at one edge sinking at the opposite edge.

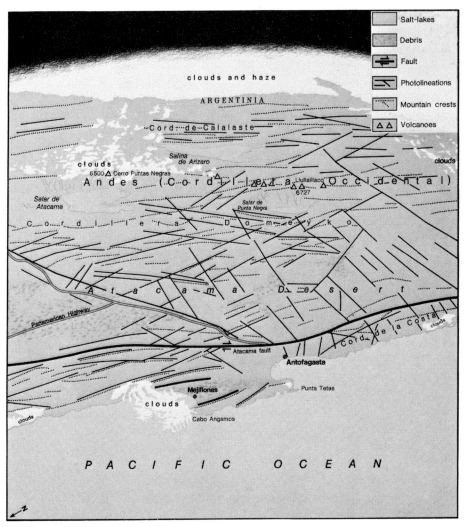

Fig. 4.11B. Block tectonics suggestive of tensional stresses in an active continental border (Atacama Desert, Chile). The long fault in the foreground represents a scar from a transcursion episode which lasted from Middle Cretaceous to about 20 million years ago. All features are preserved by the extreme aridity of the climate. (From Bodechtel and Gierloff-Emden, 1969.)

If the convection currents created by this mechanism are stable the zone of convergence comes to resemble a conveyor belt. The cool plate sinks at a slant below the adjoining plate, which is kept afloat by heating due to rising chemical differentiates from the submerged slab. Volcanism and high heat flow are two indicators of this process, which has been described in the preceding section. On the other hand, if the adjoining convection currents are strongly asymmetrical the zone of convergence will tend to shift toward a more stable configuration. Under these conditions, the net motion of a cold piece of lithosphere may be more vertical than would be required in the conveyor-belt model (Fig.4.10). The hotter plate will move bodily into the void, and the region of convergence will be translated from right to left.

This scheme provides a mechanism for what we have termed "accretion". The Elsasser model yields (1) a plausible cause of tensional stresses in the lithosphere; (2) a simple model for a zone of convergence which moves out as it sinks, drawing the other plate along in its wake.

What happens to the slabs of lithosphere that have already sunk? These are obviously no longer connected with the oceanic plate. We submit that the process begins when the leading edge of a continent is drawn into the sink. At this point the position reverses and the opposite slab sinks under the continent (Fig.4.10). Retrograde motion now involves segments of sinking lithosphere which become attached to the underside of the continental border, thus causing mountain building, volcanism, and other tectonic processes, as the continent advances into the receding oceanic plate.

THE SOUTH AMERICAN WEST COAST

Accretion in South America may have started in the Upper Jurassic. The initial phase of underthrusting and gravity sliding was followed first by compressional folding, then by peneplanation and transcurrent faulting, and finally by tensional block faulting. This tectonic evolution is not consistent with the assumption that there has been continuous underthrusting of the Pacific plate since the Triassic or the Permian. It agrees with observations by geologists who have had extensive field experience in this area, and who have shown that old inverse faults are being reactivated as normal faults since the Plio-Pleistocene. At present the tectonics is tensional, as exemplified by Atacama Province (Fig.4.11). The Atacama Fault, shown here as a long arcuate structure parallel to the coast, is a former transcurrent fault which is not seismically active any longer.

In central Peru Wilson and others have described a succession of tectonic provinces with gravity sliding to the east and reactivation of old normal faults in the coastal area. There has been a reversal of tectonic stress since the Plio-Pleistocene, as elsewhere on the west coast of South America. These trends appear to be connected with observed changes in the pattern of magnetic lineations in the Nasca plate during the past 10 million years (Herron, 1972).

An earthquake of magnitude 7 3/4 occurred off the coast of central Peru on May 31, 1970 (Fig.4.12). Damage and loss of life extended over a coastal strip including the city of Chimbote, and throughout the Valley of the Santa River, located in a graben trending parallel to the coast. No major earthquake had struck this area since 1725, though avalanches from the unstable slopes of the Cordillera Blanca have been frequent. Seismic effects of the 1970 earthquake included a minor tsunami which caused no flooding and no damage. Triggering of an avalanche of mud and ice was responsible for more than half the total loss of life in the earthquake. The avalanche was caused by a fall of rock and ice

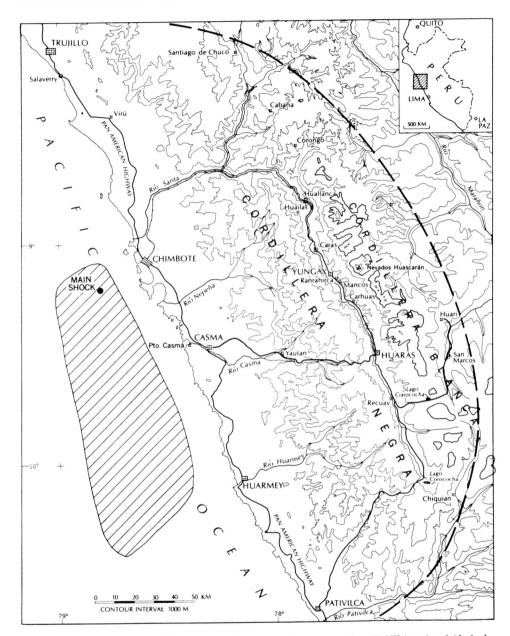

Fig.4.12. Map of the Peru, 1970 aftershock area (shaded), and the Mercalli VII isoseismal (dashed line). (From Plafker et al., 1971.)

Fig.4.13. Two views of the town of Yungay, Peru, before and after the 1970 avalanche of seismic origin. (Lower photograph, courtesy of Lloyd S. Cluff.)

starting from an elevation of 6,400 m on the North Peak of Mt. Huascarán. This avalanche gathered incredible momentum as it raced down the slope and buried the town of Yungay by dynamic sloshing over a 200-m high ridge. This is considered the most severe seismic disaster in the history of the Western Hemisphere (Fig.4.13).

In Peru and along the South American border with the Nasca plate shallow and intermediate earthquakes make up about 60% of the total seismicity. Epicenters extend continuously along the continental border but much of the intermediate and all of the deep-focus activity is concentrated in so-called "nests". A more detailed study of recent activity (Fig.4.14) shows the intermediate nests and one deep-focus nest (cross-hatched).

For an analysis of activity vs. depth we have used recent epicenters: relatively accurate focal depths have only become available within the last few years. We divide Peru into three approximately equal strips normal to the coast and we project the focal depths onto

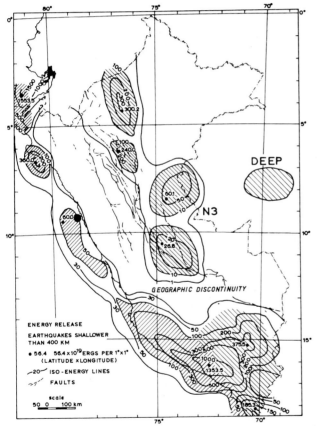

Fig.4.14. Intermediate and deep-focus nests in Peru, after an energy release map by Ocola (1966). The nest shown as *N3* was first described by Santo (1969). Small shocks occur at all depths between 70–200 km (see Fig.4.3.), but the energy release in the nests is much higher so that they appear isolated from the normal-focus areas along the coast. No earthquakes are known between *N3* and the deep-focus nest under western Brazil.

a vertical plane (Fig.4.3). The sections show that earthquake activity cannot be associated with a single descending slab of 50 km thickness as suggested by earlier investigators. Even a plate 150 km thick is not adequate to contain all the foci; in the case of southern Peru, the plate would emerge right at the coast. The Benioff zone is discontinuous; we may distinguish particularly nest N-3, first described by Santo (1969). Multiple events are frequent. The mechanism of intermediate shocks is opposite to that of deep-focus events.

Thus the entire continental margin is active over a wide range of depths. In one case, near Arequipa, a seismic source of small horizontal dimensions was found to be active from the surface down to a depth of 200 km. In conclusion, the activity is not confined

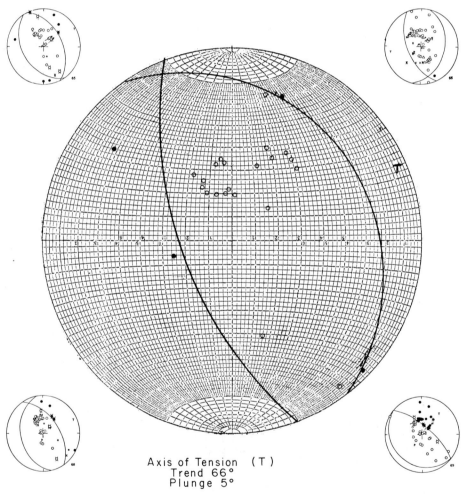

Axis of Tension (T)
Trend 66°
Plunge 5°

Fig.4.15. Focal plane solution for the 1970 Peru earthquake, and four solutions for other earthquakes in the same area (Isacks and Molnar, 1971). All mechanisms are suggestive of normal faulting in a sinking plate (as in Fig.4.10), or in the continental border.

to a single slab sloping from the trench inland; rather, it is distributed along near-vertical structures which transect the continental margin. The trench itself is affected by block faulting: it appears to be sinking.

The focal mechanism of the 1970 earthquake indicates normal faulting along a near-vertical plane, striking parallel to the coast. The axis of tension plunges slightly inland. This mechanism agrees with those found in Peru by Isacks and Molnar (1971), being nearly identical to their shock no. 68 in the same region (Fig.4.15).

We found that the main shock was a composite event, due perhaps to block faulting along more than one fault plane. A number of aftershocks also had opposite first motions, interpreted as normal faulting dipping away from the continent. This would be expected for a mechanism of tensional tectonics involving block faulting with a near-horizontal axis of tension. The focal depth of all events was between 35–70 km. The aftershock sequence was quite regular (Fig.4.8), indicating that shocks of opposite mechanisms belong to the same seismic process. In fact we are looking at a seismic process on two sets of normal faults, dipping toward and away from the continent.

The bulk of data can be reconciled with a mechanism of accretion. The slab sinks by segmentation rather than underthrusting, and produces normal faulting and earthquakes with tensional mechanism. The continent grows into the vacancy left by the sinking trench; eventually the trench moves out to the west and the continent accretes at the expense of the ocean. The deep-focus nests may be interpreted as remnants of former subduction zones, which are still in the process of sinking into the earth's mantle.

PART II

EARTHQUAKE RISK

*"The relationship is not analogous
to that of broth to beef but rather
to that of wardrobe check number to
overcoat."*

A. Einstein

CHAPTER 5

Stochastic Processes

INTRODUCTION

A stochastic process is a mathematical model of a given physical system that changes in accordance with the laws of probability. Although there is a one-to-one correspondence between the states of the stochastic process and those of the physical system, they are two essentially different things altogether. As Einstein put it, their relationship is one "of wardrobe check number to overcoat".

The conversion of stationary energy inputs into discrete jumps or bursts is modelled by a family of stochastic processes known as "point processes". The physical process is sometimes known as "gating", since the size and frequency of the energy bursts depends on some physical threshold, or "gate". The cumulative number of jumps, jointly with the cumulative energy released, define the "state" of the system. Any individual state transition is called an "event".

It is evident that earthquakes are events in some kind of gating process, the mechanics of which are hidden to us. A control engineer might say that we are looking at the output from a black box. This is a baffling situation to statisticians, accustomed as they are to dealing with stochastic processes whose underlying mechanics are known in detail. As a result, very few statisticians have ventured into the field of earthquake processes.

There are two different approaches to the understanding of point processes. One possibility is to simulate the gating mechanism by means of some physical or mathematical analog, and to study its behavior in time. This approach was followed by Burridge and Knopoff (1967), who constructed a mechanical model of sliding masses connected by springs. The masses rest on a rough level surface. As one of the weights is dragged along the surface at a constant velocity the other weights begin to follow at irregular jumps. Such models yield some insight into the mechanics of the process at a low level of complexity, where any changes of state of the system are quasi-deterministic.

Another approach consists in analyzing the regularities of the process on a purely random basis. One might assume that such a study would be highly indeterminate, but actually the reverse is true. The number of different mechanical models that may be constructed to simulate the earthquake process is very large, whereas the number of distinct stochastic processes that occur in nature is relatively small. This explains why the mathematical distribution functions found in statistical practice are so remarkably few. For example, Vere-Jones (1966, 1970a, b) was able to discuss earthquake models based on leaking reservoirs, an analogy which bears no mechanical resemblance to a set of sliding block but which may be just as realistic in terms of its mathematical behavior.

STATISTICS

Reality is structured from an infinite array of interacting variables. In theory any small event, such as the fall of a sparrow, influences the course of satellites and may be used to improve their orbital predictions. Since this would make scientific work a practical impossibility, the primary task of statistics consists in deciding which variables are *relevant* to a given process.

A certain degree of arbitrariness in this choice cannot be avoided. Consider the problem of predicting the time of occurrence of a lunar eclipse. Experience tells us that the orbital parameters which enter into this process can be reduced to a very few, which can be obtained from differential equations containing single-valued functions of time only. This is a "deterministic" problem, provided that no extreme accuracy is required.

On the other hand, if it were a matter of predicting earthquakes with the same approach it now seems almost certain that such a prediction cannot be achieved. Even if we knew the mechanism of earthquakes in great detail (which we do not), the number of relevant variables and the complexity of their interaction would be such as to rule out any "deterministic" prediction at once. Alternatively, if we decide to isolate only a few variables as potential predictors, the statistical fluctuations in these variables will be large in terms of an expected accuracy such as we have become accustomed to from astronomical phenomena.

Prediction is the extrapolation of a process in time. For a "deterministic" process, prediction is a single-valued function of time; for a stochastic process it is a distribution function which contains time as a parameter. This is the essential difference between both types of processes.

We define *statistics* as the art of applying probability theory to the understanding of a process. The art of statistics (like other arts) is pragmatic and performance-oriented. Statistics, like surgery, can be exploratory, corrective, or merely cosmetic[1]. A knowledge of its techniques, applications and limitations is indispensable to any field of research in experimental physics and engineering.

A process can be described in two equivalent ways: (a) by its history, and (b) by its dynamics. If a process has an invariant measure (for example, a quasi-stationary mean), it can be shown that any complete realization of the process contains its dynamics in full. Thus, if the earthquake process has an invariant measure it is a matter of indifference, for the purpose of prediction, whether we know the set of past earthquakes, or whether we succeed in obtaining a complete mechanical and thermodynamical description of the

---

[1] The frequent use of statistics to conceal the blemishes of reality may be reponsible for an attitude of defensive ignorance which is still shared by some scientists. Cf. the recent comment of a well-known geophysicist: "I never use statistics, I only deal with facts."

system. A complete set of data points makes knowledge of the mechanism redundant (Wiener, 1956).

BAYESIAN STATISTICS

In an important class of cases one has neither a complete set of data points nor a complete knowledge of the mechanism. Can one use *partial* knowledge of the mechanism to complement the data in such a way as to improve the prediction of the process? Bayesian statistics maintains that one can.

Let H be a hypothesis having some predictive relevance to the process, and let $[A]$ be our body of data. In conventional statistics we may use $[A]$ to determine whether or not H is probably correct. In order to do this, we select a dummy hypothesis H_0, called the "null hypothesis", such that Prob $\{H \cap H_0\}$ =0. In all fairness, H_0 ought to be more general, and perhaps at least as reasonably likely, as H. The test consists in determining the probability that $[A]$ fits the null hypothesis H_0. If p is the experimental probability that H_0 is true, we say that H_0 is accepted (or rejected) at the p *significance level*. By inference, if H and H_0 are mutually exclusive (such that Prob $\{H\}$ + Prob $\{H_0\}$= 1), we may conclude that H has been rejected (or accepted) at the same significance level p; otherwise, a further null hypothesis H_0 may be required until all logical possibilities have been exhausted.

In Bayesian statistics the hypothesis H is not tested but *modified* by the data $[A]$. Let $[H_j]$ be the complete set of alternative hypotheses, and let Pr $\{H\}$ be the "*prior probability*" that H is true; this prior probability must be assigned on the basis of our theoretical and practical knowledge of the mechanism of the process. Then application of Bayes' Theorem yields (Rosenblueth, 1964; Newmark and Rosenblueth, 1971):

$$\text{Pr} \{H|A\} = \frac{\text{Pr} \{A|H\} \, \text{Pr} \{H\}}{\Sigma \, \text{Pr} \{A|H_j\} \, \text{Pr} \{H_j\}} \qquad [5.1]$$

where Pr $\{H|A\}$ is the *new*, or modified, probability of H as conditioned by the data set $[A]$. For example, $[A]$ might be an earthquake catalog and $[H_j]$ might be a set of maps of earthquake risk, based on different geological interpretations.

The obvious advantage of the Bayesian approach lies in the possibility of modifying existing predictions through the incorporation of new data. The particular hypothesis which maximizes Pr $\{H|A\}$ will be preferred at any given step. The drawback of the approach is equally obvious: prediction depends to a considerable extent on initial assumptions concerning the prior probabilities Pr $\{H_j\}$. Where the knowledge of the mechanism of the process is weak, these prior probabilities may be little better than wild guesses.

The usefulness of Bayesian methods for earthquake risk estimation has been greatly enhanced by the availability of new results from global tectonics, which make it possible to assign more realistic values to the strain rates within a given region. This, together with an improved knowledge of tectonic deformation in the field should be conducive to more refined estimates of prior probabilities for use in Bayes' formula (Newmark and Rosenblueth, 1971).

INDEPENDENCE

Two events A and B are *independent* if their joint probability is the product of their marginal probabilities:

$$\Pr \{A \cap B\} = \Pr \{A\} \Pr \{B\} \qquad\qquad [5.2]$$

Another way of putting this is "the probability of occurrence of either event is not conditioned by the occurrence of the other event", e.g.:

$$\Pr \{A|B\} = \Pr \{A\} \qquad\qquad [5.3]$$

Consider a multidimensional continuum divided into regions called *states* of the process; for instance, the variables "energy", "number of earthquakes", "latitude", "longitude", "depth", and "time" define a 6-dimensional space which we may call the earthquake *state space*. The process jumps from one state to the other in state space.

If the state space is crowded with events the likelihood of a dependence between successive states of the system will be correspondingly greater than if the events are widely spaced. Let us assume that the spacing of events is such that each state depends only on the preceding state, and the earlier history of the process can be neglected. This is called a *Markov process*, and it is fully described by the transition matrix $[p_{ij}]$, where p_{ij} is the transition probability from state i to state j.

If the events become more and more rare, the interactions are finally weakened to the point where:

$$p_{ij} = p_{.j} = \lambda_j \qquad\qquad [5.4]$$

so that all the columns of $[p_{ij}]$ become identical. This means that condition [5.3] is fulfilled, and all events are independent.

Strictly independent processes do not occur in nature, but it is useful to consider independence as a limiting condition when the interaction between successive events can be neglected. For example, we may model the time series of large earthquakes after a simple Poisson process, even though the occurrence of aftershocks proves that the process is not independent. The validity of such an approximation depends on the context and requires careful testing for each and every application.

STATIONARITY

Consider a stochastic process with variables a_1, a_2, a_3,... in the time domain. The state of the process may be expressed as a function $S(a_1, a_2, a_3, ..., t)$. We say that the process is strictly stationary when:

$$\partial s/\partial t = \text{constant} \tag{5.5}$$

Of course, this condition can only be realized if the process is "deterministic"; otherwise, $\partial S/\partial t$ is itself a stochastic process. However, stationarity in a wider sense can be applied to stochastic processes, where it means that $\partial S/\partial t$ is not a function of time *in the mean*. Thus, if we sample the process at any arbitrary time t the state of the process will be independent of t.

A further generalization consists in allowing that $\partial S/\partial t$ may be a function of time, but that the mean of $\partial S/\partial t$ varies about a constant value in time. For example, the process might involve periodic or quasi-periodic fluctuations about some average set of values $\bar{a}_1$, $\bar{a}_2$, $\bar{a}_3$, ...) which does not depend on time. This case is sometimes referred to as weak stationarity, or *quasi-stationarity*.

True stationarity does not occur in nature, any more than does statistical independence. All systems have entropy, and cannot be kept running indefinitely at a constant level. However, there is a definition of quasi-stationarity which has a very specific physical meaning. In any thermodynamic system, "steady-state" is defined as *the condition of minimum entropy production*. For example, in the case of a pot of water sitting on an open flame, stationarity is reached when the rate of convection is just sufficient to dissipate any excess heat energy after conduction and radiation. Since all systems seek their level of minimum entropy production, external forces which do not permanently change the energy balance of the system may be treated as transient perturbations of stationarity.

This thermodynamical definition of stationarity requires that the system has a saddle-point in entropy production. It does no require that the entropy production be constant in time, but merely that it be minimal at all times. Thus, the statistical definition of stationarity is merely the limiting case of thermodynamic stationarity for infinitely slow changes in the energy balance of the system.

HOMOGENEITY

In general, a stochastic process is intended to model a physical process occurring in real time, such as the earthquake process. But stochastic processes can also be used in a heuristic fashion, to provide a theoretical basis for statistical observations not in the time domain.

Consider the distribution of incomes in a given nation. It is a well-known fact that it resembles the lognormal distribution, which happens to be positively skewed. The fact that a small percentage of the population enjoys the highest incomes, while the bulk of the population has an income slightly below the mean, is a property of this distribution which is psychologically perceived as "unjust". Yet no amount of social reform (short of abolishing private property altogether) can succeed in eliminating the skew of the lognormal distribution. Hence it appears of more than routine interest to investigate the random mechanism which originates the income partition in a society; this mechanism can be modeled after a simple stochastic process, in which the gross national product is subdivided at random into a large number of individual portions. We shall later use the same process in order to derive the magnitude partition of earthquakes (cf. Chapter 11).

Such processes do not explicity contain the time variable, but they can be treated much like time series. Usually one of the variables, say v, plays the role of criterion variable; thus, the state of the process may be represented as a function $S(a_1, a_2, a_3, . . ., v)$. Then the condition:

$$\partial S/\partial v = K \tag{5.6}$$

where K is a random variable having a distribution which is independent of v, is called *homogeneity*. This condition is analogous to stationarity, except that it is a static rather than a dynamical condition. Speaking in terms of thermodynamics, homogeneity maximizes the entropy, while stationarity minimizes the entropy flow. For example, in the case of the distribution of incomes in a population the condition of homogeneity means that the parameters of the distribution are the same for any arbitrary subset of the population. This is notoriously untrue, as the mean income changes markedly, not only from one region to another but also from neighborhood to neighborhood within any given locality.

A point process which transcurs in real (three-dimensional) space may be called a space series. Some of the properties of space series were studied by Mathéron (1970), who has provided a general theory for their estimation and prediction.

CHAPTER 6

Point Processes

DEFINITION

There are two kinds of stochastic processes: continuous and discrete. In a discrete process the variable changes discontinuously in time. Each change in the variable is called an event.

Let us consider a discrete process, whose realizations consist of a series of point events. We may look at such a process in two different ways: (a) by concentrating on the number of events which have occurred up to any arbitrary time t; (b) by concentrating on the individual occurrence times t_i of each of the events. An example of the former is a birth process, in which we are interested in the *number of individuals* alive at any given time, rather than the dates of the individual births. An example of the latter is the earthquake process.

Discrete stochastic processes which describe the positions of the events in time are called *point processes*. The prototype of all point processes is the Poisson process. Any point process may be viewed as a generalization of the Poisson process.

THE POISSON PROCESS

Let $N(t, t + \Delta t)$ be the number of events which occur from time t to time $(t + \Delta t)$, Δt being a small time interval. The pure Poisson process is defined by three basic properties:

(a) *Independence:* $N(t, t + \Delta t)$ is independent of $N(\tau, \tau + \Delta \tau)$ for any time τ prior to t.

(b) *Orderliness:*

The events are widely spaced so that the probability of two or more simultaneous events is infinitesimally small:

$$\lim_{\Delta t \to 0} \text{Prob } [N(t, t + \Delta t) > 1] = o(\Delta t) \tag{6.1}$$

(c) *Stationarity:*

Let λ be the *rate* of the process, i.e. the mean number of occurrences per unit time:

$$\text{Prob } \{N(t, t + \Delta t) = 1\} = \lambda \, \Delta t \tag{6.2}$$

The process is stationary if λ is not a function of time. In other words, the probability of occurrence of an event is exactly the same for any elementary interval along the time axis.

The probability density function of n, the number of events per unit time, is the well-known *Poisson distribution*:

$$f(n) = (\lambda^n/n!)\, e^{-\lambda} \qquad\qquad\qquad [6.3]$$

Equivalently, the distribution of the time intervals T between events is the *negative exponential distribution*:

$$f(T) = \lambda e^{-\lambda T} \qquad\qquad\qquad\qquad [6.4]$$

The mean of n is λ, and the variance of n is λ^2. Similarly, the mean of T is λ^{-1}, and the variance of T is λ^{-2}.

Because of the independence and stationarity of the process, the time T may be measured from any arbitrary point on the time axis. Thus, if the occurrence of large earthquakes is a Poisson process an interval of 50 years measured from the last earthquake is as likely as an interval of 50 years measured from today, since the next event "does not know" when the previous event has occurred.

Of course this does not mean that all intervals are equally likely. Fig.6.1 shows the distribution of intervals according to eq.6.4. Notice that short intervals are more probable than long ones. This means that the events tend to cluster together in small groups, separated by longer spacings (Fig.6.2). This apparent clustering does not indicate any greater dependence between the closer-spaced events than between the more distant ones.

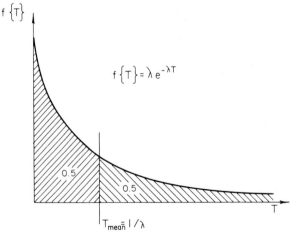

Fig.6.1. The exponential distribution of time intervals, as found in pure Poisson processes and in Markov processes with independent increments. The mean number of events per unit time is λ.

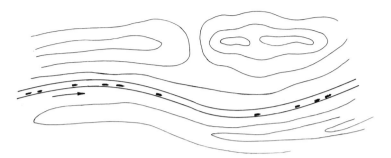

Fig.6.2. A realization of the process described by Fig.6.1 (car traffic on a one-way road). Apparent clustering is caused by the fact that short intervals are more probable than long ones.

The common intuitive assumption that randomness in time should lead to uniform spacing of events is erroneous.

If instead of considering the variable n (number of events per unit time), we chose the variable $m(t) = \Sigma n$, the *cumulative* number of events up to time t, the process is Markovian and is called a *pure birth process*.

MARKOV PROCESSES

A Markov process is a stochastic process in which each state depends exclusively on the immediately preceding state. Thus, if a variable x forms an independent process its cumulative Σx necessarily forms a Markov process.

Continuous Markov processes are called "diffusion processes"; they may be of importance in understanding the underlying process of earthquake generation. *Discrete* Markov processes are of two types: (a) discrete in space and time; (b) discrete in space and continuous in time.

All Poisson-type processes are of the second type. Usually the process consists in counting the number of events. If the number of events increases steadily we have a *birth process*; otherwise it is a *birth and death* process. If the birth rate is much different from the death rate we may speak of an *immigration or emigration process*. When the events occur independently of each other the inter-occurrence times T are distributed as in the pure Poisson process, namely:

$$f(T) = \lambda e^{-\lambda T} \tag{6.5}$$

were λ is the mean number of events per unit time.

RENEWAL PROCESSES

A renewal process is a general point process for which the interoccurrence time distribution $f(T)$ can have any form. The Poisson process is a special case of renewal process. In the general case, however, renewal processes are non-Markovian.

The expected number of events up to time t is called the *renewal function $H(t)$*. The renewal function for an arbitrary process has been derived by Cox (1962) in terms of the Laplace transforms of the interoccurrence time distributions. In the special case of a stationary renewal process we have:

$$H(t) = t/\mu \qquad\qquad [6.6]$$

where μ is the mean interval between events.

Instead of having a unique interval distribution $f(T)$ we may construct a renewal process such that the interval from event i to event j is distributed as $f_{ij}(T)$. When all T are mutually independent we obtain a so-called *semi-Markov process*. The sequence of transitions from events of type i to events of type j forms a Markov chain.

For example, we might wish to analyze seismic events as belonging to n different regions, and assume that the sequence of events from region to region forms an n-state Markov chain. This means that the probability of an event occurring in region k depends on the region where the previous event has occurred.

Let us now define n^2 interval time distributions. If the time interval of occurrence between an event in region i and an event in region j is distributed as $f_{ij}(T)$, then the resulting renewal process is semi-Markov. The theory of such processes may become fairly complex, but simple results have been obtained for the case $n = 2$, and for the case when the distribution functions f_{ij} have simple rational Laplace transforms (Pyke, 1961).

GENERALIZED POISSON PROCESSES; SUPERPOSITION

An alternative way of analyzing renewal processes is by considering them as generalizations of a simple Poisson process.

Suppose, for example, that we have k seismic regions that are intermittently active, and let p_i be the proportion of time that region i is active. If each region when active generates earthquakes according to a Poisson process of rate λ_i, and if all processes are mutually independent, the pooled output of the system may be obtained by superposition:

$$\text{Prob}\ \{n\} = \frac{1}{kn!} \sum_{i=1}^{k} p_i \lambda_i^n e^{-\lambda_i} \qquad\qquad [6.7]$$

which is called a *compound Poisson distribution*[1]. This distribution has been observed to provide a reasonably good fit to local earthquake data.

Another possible generalization of the Poisson process consists in assuming that the rate λ of the process is not a constant. Two major cases have been analyzed:

(a) If the rate is a function of time $\lambda(t)$ the process may be nonstationary, weakly stationary, or oscillatory (quasi-stationary). In these cases the probability of obtaining n events per unit time is obviously:

$$\text{Prob}\,\{\,n\,\} = \frac{[\lambda(t)]^n}{n!}\,e^{-\lambda(t)} \qquad [6.8]$$

It can be shown that the number of events $N(t)$ from time 0 up to time t has a Poisson distribution of mean:

$$E\,[N(t)] = \int_0^t \lambda(u)\,du \qquad [6.9]$$

If we introduce a non-linear transformation of the time scale, such that the new time parameter τ is related to real time by:

$$d\tau = \lambda(t)\,dt \qquad [6.10]$$

we may transform the time-dependent Poisson process into a pure Poisson process of unit rate. This technique has been successfully applied to the analysis of aftershock sequences, where the rate decays hyperbolically with time (Lomnitz and Hax, 1966).

(b) If the rate λ is a random variable with distribution $f(\lambda)$ we have a *doubly stochastic Poisson process*. The process is stationary when $f(\lambda)$ does not depend on time.

By combining the generalizations (a) and (b) we may produce almost any kind of renewal process. There is a limited usefulness to such generalizations from Poisson theory, in the case of earthquakes, because we know that the events are not really independent. Perhaps the most important result to be obtained from Poisson theory is the superposition property found by Khintchine (1960):

If we have an array of generalized Poisson processes generated by a single system, such as the earth, we may expect that the parameters of these processes will be identically distributed throughout the system. For example, the mean rate of earthquake production will have some worldwide distribution function. In this case it is possible to show that the superposition of all these individual processes tends asymptotically to a pure Poisson process.

Thus, even if the local processes of earthquake generation deviate markedly from a Poisson process, their *superposition* on a broad regional or worldwide scale can be treated as if the events were perfectly independent. This is a result in earthquake statistics, which has been confirmed by many investigators.

---

[1] Also called "Stuttering Poisson distribution" (Lomnitz, 1966b).

CHAPTER 7

Modelling the Earthquake Process

INTRODUCTION

Stochastic models are mathematical analogies which purport to exhibit the same statistical properties as the process being modelled. For many years earthquakes were thought to be a response of the earth to periodic stresses. The following periodicities in earthquake occurrence have been proposed at one time or another: 42 min, 1 day, 14.8 days, 29.6 days , 6 months, 1 year, 11 years, and 19 years. Most of these periodicities will be recognized as connected with orbital frequencies of the sun–earth–moon system.

The gravitational attractions of the sun and moon represent by far the largest external stresses on the earth. Yet a Fourier analysis of earthquake time series fails to detect significant spectral lines corresponding to lunisolar periods (Fig.7.1). This is a surprising result and one which still awaits a detailed explanation. Sir Harold Jeffreys has suggested that earthquakes are triggered by random elastoplastic yielding due to a gradual accumulation of strains. If they were caused by brittle failure at a specific strength, he argued, the lunisolar periodicities would become so dominant as to require no Fourier analysis to bring them out.

Statistical models for sequences of large earthquakes are relatively easy to produce. A successful model, which has been adopted by engineers and statisticians, consists of two assumptions: (a) the number of earthquakes in a year is a Poisson random variable with mean λ; (b) M, the earthquake magnitude, is a random variable distributed with cumulative distribution function:

$$F(M) = 1 - e^{-\beta M} \quad (M \geqslant 0) \tag{7.1}$$

This model, which we may call the "*Large-Earthquake Model*", is especially useful when one has access only to a list of *largest* earthquakes in a region. It affords adequate predictions of mean return periods, modal earthquake maxima, and the expected number of earthquakes exceeding a given magnitude (Epstein and Lomnitz, 1966).

A more sophisticated model requires the incorporation of non-Markovian effects (aftershock sequences). Attempts to model aftershock sequences after a simple Markov process have generally met with failure. Such attempts were made by Aki (1956), and by Vere-Jones (1966), but they predicted a decay in the expected magnitude of aftershocks with time.

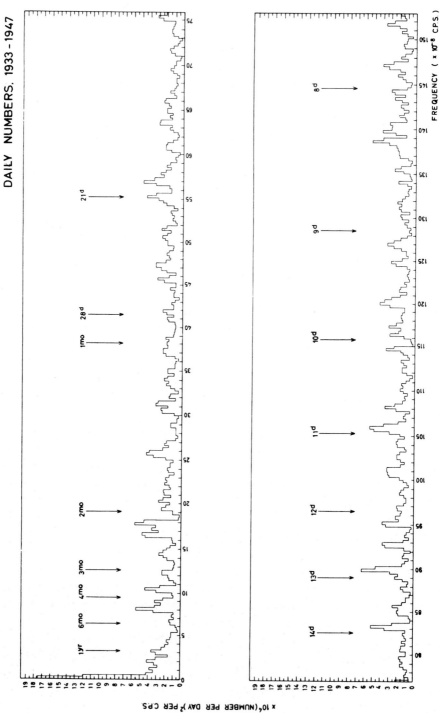

Fig. 7.1. Fourier power spectrum of the series of world earthquakes. Notice the absence of significant peaks corresponding to absence of lunisolar periods, proving that the effects arising from attraction of the sun or moon are not in phase, presumably because of the random orientation of earthquake faults with respect to lunisolar forces. (From Lomnitz, 1964.)

A HEURISTIC MODEL FOR THE EARTHQUAKE PROCESS

Imagine that gold has been discovered in the Klondike and that we wish to describe gold discoveries as a point process. Each discovery will be termed a "strike" and will be assigned a time t as well as geographical coordinates (l, φ) and a magnitude M, indicative of the amount of gold associated with each strike.

Obviously, there is information between the prospectors, so that successful strikes will attract swarms of prospectors to the same area; these will comb the countryside until every nugget in that area has been discovered. We may call this phenomenon an "after-strike sequence".

Let us now turn our attention to $f(M)$, the distribution of the magnitude of strikes. The distribution of gold deposits depends on geologic factors and not on the interaction between the prospectors. It is entirely independent of the rate of discoveries. Whether the prospectors dig up a given claim in one month or in ten years they will find the same amount of gold.

There is another property of $f(M)$ which has an important bearing on the earthquake process. This is the fact that gold deposits are distributed in "lodes" or "fields". In other words, the mean magnitude is correlated as a function of distance on an (l, φ)-grid. Stochastic variables such as M were discussed extensively by Mathéron (1970), who has called them "regionalized variables"; they play a central role in geostatistics.

The process formed by a regionalized variable may be treated as a space series, i.e. an assemblage of random variables which transcurs in space rather than in time. The ore content of a mineral deposit is described by a space series. Many of the familiar concepts of time series (smoothing, filtering, aliasing, etc.) can be applied to space series.

In the present model, which we shall call a "Klondike model", there is a clear-cut distinction between the underlying space series (the distribution of gold), and the time series of strikes, which may be viewed as a sampling process operating on that space series. We may say that the latter process is imbedded in the former. As a first approximation, neglecting the depletion of the lodes, the underlying space series is independent of the sampling process. Thus, we may consider the *local mean sample content* as an estimator of the ore content of the region. This, of course, is precisely what one does in mining practice. Once the underlying space series is known at a sufficient number of points we may predict the probable ore content of any sample by interpolation and extrapolation.

The "afterstrike sequence", then, is merely an effect of the randomness of strikes, and of the dependence between successive strikes. It has nothing to do with the structure of gold deposits. If there were a dependence between the two processes (e.g., if the prospectors were given access to advance information about the location of the lodes), there would be no afterstrike sequences, but rather a systematic and orderly sequence of finds by decreasing magnitude.

THE KLONDIKE MODEL IN EARTHQUAKE THEORY

In order to apply the preceding model to earthquakes it is necessary to prove that the earthquake process can be unfolded into two independent processes, one of which is imbedded in the other.

In an analysis of the 1958 Maipo Valley, Chile aftershock sequence it was found that the mean magnitude of earthquakes remained constant while the sequence was petering out (Lomnitz, 1960). Similar observations were later made in California (Lomnitz, 1966a), Japan (Hamada and Hagiwara, 1967), Greece (Drakopoulos, 1971), New Zealand (Hamilton, 1966) and the Azores–Gibraltar Ridge (López-Arroyo and Udías, 1972). Thus, if $f(M, t)$ is the joint distribution of magnitudes and times of occurrence in an aftershock sequence we may write:

$$f(M,t) = f_1 (M) \ f_2(t) \tag{7.2}$$

which says that the magnitude is independent of the time of occurrence (cf. eq.5.2).

We may propose the following hypothesis ("Magnitude stability"): In any given realization of the earthquake process the magnitude distribution is (a) stationary, (b) independent of the rate of occurrence of earthquakes.

This hypothesis implies that the magnitude of earthquakes is a regionalized variable, and that the process of magnitude distribution may be described by a space series which is independent of time. A sequence of earthquakes could therefore be described as a random sampling process of this underlying space series.

The magnitude distribution in space is fully determined, with good approximation, by the distribution in space of the mean magnitude $\overline{M}$. This is due to the fact that the magnitude distribution for any given region can be represented by the negative exponential distribution (cf.eq.7.1):

$$F(M) = 1 - e^{-\beta M} \tag{7.3}$$

where $\beta = 1/\overline{M}$. Since the distribution of M contains no other parameter except β, the distribution of β in space automatically determines the distribution of M in space. As an example, Fig.7.2 shows the distribution of $\overline{M}$ with depth for several subduction zones around the Pacific Ocean. The two subduction zones which exhibit seismic activity at all depths (Tonga–Fiji and Japan) have the same magnitude distribution from the surface down to depths of 700 km. On the other hand, those subduction zones which contain notorious gaps in seismicity at depths of 250–400 km, such as the New Hebrides, the Solomon Islands, and the Andes of South America reveal appreciable differences in mean magnitudes above and below the seismicity gap. This observation may be interpreted in support of the assumption that lithospheric plates which exhibit a lack of seismicity at some intermediate depth are actually discontinuous, and should not be described in terms of a single descending geological unit.

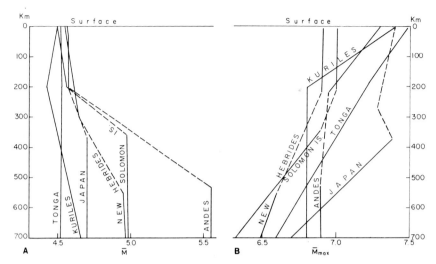

Fig.7.2. Variation of (A) mean, and (B) maximum magnitudes with depth. Continuous subduction zones like Tonga tend to have constant mean magnitudes, suggesting that the structure of the lithospheric slab is not altered as it intrudes the mantle. Zones of accretion, like the Andes, exhibit major discontinuities (dashed lines) where no earthquakes occur. Maximum magnitudes always decrease with depth.

A physical interpretation of the mean local magnitude $\overline{M}$ involves a discussion of several unrelated variables, particularly the mean fault area $\overline{A}$ and the mean tectonic stress $\overline{\sigma}$. In the case of an aftershock sequence, there is no reason to assume that $\overline{A}$ changes during the sequence; hence, the observed stability of $\overline{M}$ implies stationarity of stresses. This can be explained by noting that the energy drain due to aftershocks is small as compared to the energy of the main shock; also, the flow of recovery energy into the region (described in pp.39–41) tends to balance the cumulative stress drop due to aftershocks.

On the other hand, the stationary of $\overline{\sigma}$ cannot in general be assumed. Suyehiro (1966) has noted, for instance, that the β-value in eq.7.3 rises suddenly after a large earthquake in a region. In other words, the mean magnitude $\overline{M}$ drops to a lower value after a large strain decrement. This effect can reasonably be attributed to a step decrease in the mean regional stress $\overline{\sigma}$. Thus, we are now faced with the necessity of modifying our original assumption of magnitude stability, to take into account the phenomenon of stress depletion by large earthquakes. Apparently, the time process of earthquake occurrence cannot be simply decoupled from the underlying space series of magnitude distribution, since the latter is influenced by the former through the variations in regional stress.

The solution of this difficulty is quite simple. We know that the mean local magnitude is not merely a constant during brief aftershock sequences; it is also stationary during periods of time of decades, each of which includes a representative number of large shocks. This observation was the one which induced Gutenberg, Evernden, Duda, Karnik, and numerous other authors to postulate that β was a regional invariant. This means that the mean local magnitude exhibits long-term stationarity. In other words, the variations in $\overline{M}$ after the occurrence of large earthquakes must be treated as transients superimposed on the stationary mean value of $\overline{M}$ for the region.

But this leads us to a conclusion, which plays an important role in the estimation of earthquake risk. Since a considerable proportion of earthquakes corresponds to after-shocks, any random sample of earthquakes is actually more representative of *low-stress conditions in the region* than of the normal state of stress. Hence the use of β-values systematically underestimates the mean magnitude of earthquakes which the region can produce under normal, stationary conditions. But it is precisely this set of conditions which is relevant to the estimation of earthquake risk.

There is yet another reason why $\overline{M}$ underestimates the average size of earthquakes in a region. By definition, the magnitude is roughly proportional to the logarithm of the energy of an earthquake. But the mean of the logarithm of a variable is nothing but the

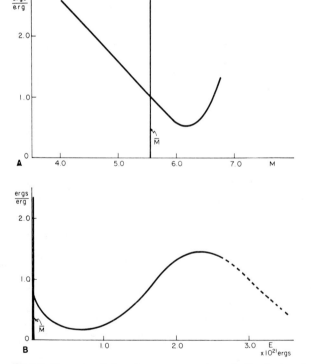

Fig.7.3. The rate of deep-focus energy release in South America (below 500 km) has a peak above magnitude 6.5. A conventional magnitude–frequency graph (A) leads to an estimate of mean magnitude at least one order smaller than a spectrum (B), which gives the amount of energy released per unit energy interval.

logarithm of the geometric mean:

$$E[\log x] = \sum_n \log x_i/n = \log \prod_n x_i^{1/n} \qquad [7.4]$$

Therefore, the energy corresponding to $\overline{M}$ will be the *geometric* mean of all the energies in the sample, which is always smaller than the arithmetic mean. An example of such an underestimation may be seen from Fig.7.3, which represents the energy spectrum and the magnitude distribution for deep-focus earthquakes in the Andes of South America. The energy spectrum shows a pronounced maximum of energy release in the 6.5–7.0 magnitude range. Yet the β-value (or, alternatively, the direct estimation of $\overline{M}$) leads to a value of the mean local magnitude in the range of 5.0–5.5 only. Such inconsistencies cannot be overcome by any refinements in the method of estimation for β or $\overline{M}$, as they are inherent in the use of the magnitude scale as a measure of earthquake size.

In conclusion, the use of a Klondike-type model of earthquake occurrence leads to valuable insights into the structure of the earthquake process, which can be used for predictive purposes provided that the variables used to describe earthquake size are well understood. In many cases the mean seismic moment $\overline{M}_0$ might yield a more consistent estimation of average stress conditions in the region, than the mean magnitude $\overline{M}$. Another way of preventing an earthquake sample to be swamped by low-stress aftershocks is the use of extremal methods, which will be discussed in Chapter 8.

THE KOLMOGOROV PROCESS

In the early 1940's, separated by a raging war, Japanese and American seismologists almost simultaneously made a momentous discovery. They found that the number of earthquakes in a region decreased exponentially with their magnitudes. This relationship is usually expressed by the so-called "magnitude–frequency equation" (Ishimoto and Iida, 1939; Gutenberg and Richter, 1944):

$$\log_{10} N(M) = a - b M \qquad [7.5]$$

where $N(M)$ is the number of earthquakes greater than M, and a and b are constant parameters. This equation may easily be normalized to yield the frequency distribution of magnitudes in a region.

Thus, we observe that $a = \log_{10} N(0)$, the logarithm of the number of earthquakes greater than $M = 0$. Normalization is achieved by dividing through by $N(0)$:

$$\log_{10}[1 - F(M)] = \log_{10} \frac{N(M)}{N(0)} = bM \qquad [7.6]$$

which yields:

$$1 - F(M) = e^{-\beta M} \qquad (M \geqslant 0) \tag{7.7}$$

where $\beta = b/\log_{10} e = 1/\overline{M}$, and $F(M)$ is the cumulative probability distribution of earthquake magnitudes. The frequency distribution $f(M)$ is the first derivative of $F(M)$:

$$f(M) = \beta e^{-\beta M} \qquad (M \geqslant 0) \tag{7.8}$$

Problem: In California it was found that $\beta = 2.0$ and $a = 4.97$ per year. Estimate the mean magnitude and mean sample size of earthquakes above magnitude 4.0 in any given year.

Answer: The mean magnitude is

$$\overline{M} = 1/\beta = 0.5 \qquad (M \geqslant 0)$$

For changes in origin the exponential distribution does not change; e.g., if one uses a base magnitude M_{min} instead of zero the frequency distribution [7.8] becomes:

$$f(M) = \beta \exp\,[-\beta\,(M - M_{min})] \qquad (M \geqslant M_{min}) \tag{7.9}$$

Therefore the mean magnitude becomes:

$$\overline{M} = M_{min} + \beta^{-1} \qquad (M \geqslant M_{min}) \tag{7.10}$$

Since $M_{min} = 4.0$ we find $\overline{M} = 4.5$ for California. Similarly, the estimated number of earthquakes per year is:

$$N(0) = 10^a = 10^{4.97}$$

In order to find $N(4.0)$, the number of shocks above magnitude 4.0, we note that:

$$N(4.0) \div N(0) = [1 - F(4.0)] \div [1 - F(0)]$$

since the cumulative distribution expresses the proportion of shocks *below* a given magnitude. Since $F(0) = 0$ by definition we find:

$$N(4.0) = 10^{4.97}\,e^{-2\times4} = 31$$

This answer checks well with the observed magnitudes and numbers of earthquakes in California.

Now, the energy E of an earthquake can be represented as a product of the size A of a fault, times the mean energy released per unit area. The mean energy is proportional to the stress drop, which is of order 100 bars in shallow earthquakes.

The distribution of fault areas may be derived by means of a model first proposed in its most general form by Kolmogorov (1941). Consider the total area of the earth's crust, broken up by successive stages into smaller and smaller areas. Let y be the stressed area which is tributary to a fault of size A (proportional to some power of y). If the breakup process is random and homogeneous we may write for any stage j:

$$f_j(y) = T_j f_{j-1}(y) \qquad [7.11]$$

where T_j is a positive, identically distributed random variable. Treating this as a recurrence equation we obtain:

$$f_n(y) = f_0(y) \prod_{j=1}^{n} T_j \qquad [7.12]$$

Now, taking logarithms of both sides and applying the Central Limit Theorem we find:

$$\lim_{n \to \infty} F_n(y) = \text{Erf}\left[\log(y/\bar{y})/\sigma^2\right] \qquad [7.13]$$

where $F(y)$ is the cumulative distribution of y. The error function of the logarithm of a variable is called "lognormal" distribution. It has the same importance in the theory of non-negative variables than the normal distribution has for zero-mean variables.

Because of a theorem on the reproductive properties of lognormality, it is found that any power of a lognormal variable is also a lognormal variable. Hence, if the stress-tributary areas of the earth's surface are lognormal and if the fault surfaces are related to these areas by a power law, it follows that the fault surface A is also a lognormal variable. And, if the mean stress drop is stationary, the distribution of earthquake energies should also be lognormal (Lomnitz, 1964a).

This model of the earthquake-energy partition is based on broad assumptions of homogeneity and stationarity. By inference, however, its conclusions may be extended to any system of non-homogeneous, quasi-stationary partition, provided that the driving mechanism remains the same and that the local factors which affect homogeneity are very numerous. For example, the lognormality of a crushed aggregate is not affected by inhomogeneities in the rock, provided that all the rock comes from the same quarry and that the same crusher is used throughout.

Aitchison and Brown (1957) have given numerous examples of lognormal variables: grain sizes or contents of various chemical elements in a rock, watershed areas and stream lengths in hydrology, sieve fractions in sands by weight (because the grain weight is a power of the grain size), star sizes in the universe, incomes in a population, and many others. The number of entries in a Chinese dictionary is a lognormal variable, because Chinese ideograms are classified by number of strokes: the whole language can be regarded as the result of a random subdivision into characters having $1, 2, \ldots, n$ strokes.

In view of the great generality of the lognormal distribution the excellent fit of earthquake energies to this distribution comes as no surprise (Fig.7.4). Since the magnitude M is proportional to the logarithm of the energy, it is concluded that M should be normally distributed:

$$F(M) = \text{Erf}(M - \bar{M}/\sigma^2) \qquad [7.14]$$

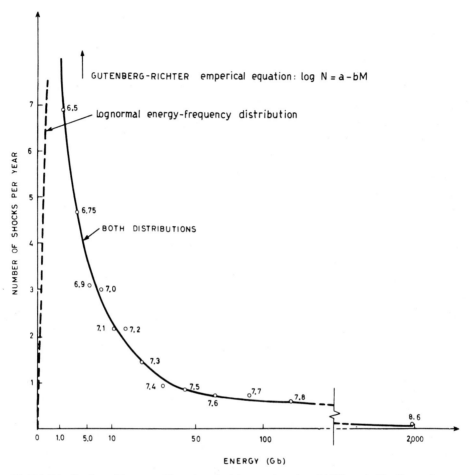

Fig.7.4. Distribution of large world earthquakes (energy in units of 10^{21} ergs). The fit to a lognormal distribution is excellent.

For historical reasons, and principally because of the lack of earthquake data ranging from very small to very large magnitudes, the exponential distribution is used instead of the normal:

$$F(M) = 1 - e^{-\beta M} \qquad\qquad [7.15]$$

where $\beta = 1/\overline{M}$. This function fits the tail of any normal distribution, with the advantage that it has but a single parameter instead of two. Its main theoretical drawback is the fact that it requires the introduction of artificial magnitude cutoffs at both ends of the range: otherwise the energy distribution will diverge.

It has been argued against the lognormal energy distribution, that there should not be a downturn in the distribution for small earthquakes. Indeed, the empirical distribution of micro-earthquakes, in the magnitude range +2 to −2, exhibits the same general distribution as do larger earthquakes. This reasoning is fallacious, however, as a sample of small shocks cannot be used to make inferences about the distribution of large shocks. Let us suppose that we take a handful of sand from a conglomerate which contains large boulders. The sample of sand is likely to have the same type of grain-size distribution as the conglomerate; yet this observation lacks any relevance in terms of the proportion of sand vs boulders, or the size of the boulders in the conglomerate. This example serves to highlight the fallacy of extrapolating micro-earthquake surveys to predict the large-scale seismicity of a region.

Actually, a downturn in the frequency distribution at small magnitudes has often been observed in earthquake data. This downturn is always attributed to lack of data for small earthquakes. Be that as it may, the fact remains that a decrease in the sample frequency of earthquakes is expected on theoretical grounds as the energy of the shock approaches zero. A very considerable number of extremely small events are generated during and near a large earthquake; but these events are not part of an ordinary seismicity sample, just as the dust generated in the process of rock crushing is not a normal part of an aggregate.

In conclusion, the Kolmogorov Process of random fragmentation represents probably an adequate model for the observed distribution of energies in earthquakes. From the point of view of earthquake risk it is immaterial whether earthquake magnitudes obey the exponential or the normal law. Both have the same extreme-value distribution (Chapter 8):

$$F(z) = \exp\left(-\alpha n e^{-\beta z}\right) \qquad\qquad [7.16]$$

where z is the magnitude of the largest earthquakes in n years, and α is the mean number of shocks per year.

In this book, and for risk applications generally, the exponential form [7.15] will be preferred to the normal form of the magnitude distribution, because a single-parameter distribution affords a more economical description of seismicity without any loss of generality, in the range of large magnitudes.

BOLTZMANN PROCESSES

The Klondike process proposed in this chapter is an example of a generalized non-Markovian process, where each event depends on all preceding events. Another example of such a process is the generalized birth process, where the probability of a birth depends on the age of all individuals in a population .

When the effect of each event may be superposed on the cumulative effects of all preceding events, we obtain a class of linear non-Markovian processes which we may call *Boltzmann processes*, because the prototype of such models was first proposed by Ludwig Boltzmann in 1876. This was the model for the "elastic aftereffect" ("*elastische*

Nachwirkung"), whereby all strain effects are taken to be linearly additive for all preceding stress inputs:

$$\dot{\epsilon}(t) = \sum_i \Delta\sigma_i \, \dot{\varphi}(t - t_i) \qquad\qquad [7.17]$$

Here $\varphi(t)$ is a memory function called the "creep function" (cf. Chapter 3). The Boltzmann process describes a broad class of rate processes in physics. The rate of the process normally decays in time.

Consider the probability $\lambda(t)$ of occurrence of an earthquake at time t. In the Klondike model $\lambda(t)$ depends on the occurrence and magnitude of all previous shocks. Assuming the dependence to be a function of magnitude only we may write, in analogy with [7.17]:

$$\lambda(t) = \sum_i \gamma_i(t - t_i) \qquad\qquad [7.18]$$

where γ_i is the rate function associated with the i-th earthquake.

Now, a large earthquake at $t = 0$ releases a near-simultaneous burst of shocks of all sizes in the vicinity of the fault. If the rate function may be expressed as $\gamma_i(t) =$ constant $\cdot$ exp $(-\alpha_i t)$, where α_i depends on the magnitude M_i, we may write the rate of the aftershock process at time t as:

$$\lambda(t) = \text{constant} \cdot \sum_i e^{-\alpha_i t} \qquad\qquad [7.19]$$

Now, the magnitudes M_i are exponentially distributed. We may assume that the α_i are also exponentially distributed:

$$f(\alpha) = k \, e^{-k\alpha} \qquad\qquad [7.20]$$

Hence [7.19] may be written, for a burst containing the entire magnitude spectrum:

$$\lambda(t) = \text{constant} \cdot \int_0^{\infty} f(\alpha) \, e^{-\alpha t} \, d\alpha \qquad\qquad [7.21]$$

Since the distribution $f(\alpha)$ is exponential we may integrate the preceding expression as follows:

$$\lambda(t) = \text{constant}/(t + k) \qquad\qquad [7.22]$$

This is known as Omori's Law. By deriving Omori's Law of aftershock occurrence as an envelope of exponential decay functions we have proved a result of great generality, which is applicable to all rate processes generated by a step input (relaxation processes).

By integrating [7.22] we find:

$$\int_0^t \lambda(t)\,dt = \text{constant} \cdot \log(t + k) \qquad\qquad [7.23]$$

i.e., the cumulative number of aftershocks is logarithmic in time. If the mean magnitude of aftershocks is stationary in time, so is the mean strain release per shock. Hence the well-known result by Benioff (1951), that the cumulative strain release in aftershocks is logarithmic in time.

The preceding derivation explains why logarithmic decay processes are so common. At the elementary level they may be reduced to the envelope of a very large number of randomly distributed exponential decay mechanisms. This applies to the logarithmic creep function ("Lomnitz law"), as well as to rate processes of chemistry and physics.

THE TAGGED SELF-EXCITING PROCESS

Let us now return to the Boltzmann formulation. We assume that we have introduced a change of variable:

$$\chi = x(M) \qquad\qquad [7.24]$$

such that the relation between the rate λ and the variable χ is linear. Twice the value of χ will produce twice the value of λ. Variables such as χ are known as "marks" or "tags", and the process becomes a "tagged" process.

Let $\gamma(t)$ be the influence function. Then we may write:

$$\lambda(t) = \lambda_0 + \sum \chi_i\, \gamma(t - t_i) \qquad\qquad [7.25]$$

where λ_0 is a base rate, which prevents the process from dying out. In other words, there is always a small positive probability $\lambda_0\,dt$ of occurrence of an event, even if no earlier event has occurred for a very long time.

The model described by [7.25] is suitable not merely for aftershocks but for the earthquake process as a whole. In fact, the model will automatically produce an aftershock sequence after every large earthquake, even if the tag χ is independently distributed and stationary in time.

The model has been used chiefly in biological applications, where it is called a "tagged self-exciting process" (Hawkes, 1971a, b). The mean rate of activity of the process is given by:

$$\lambda_{mean} = \lambda_0 / [1 - \int_0^\infty \gamma(t) \, dt] \qquad [7.26]$$

If, as suggested in the preceding section, we use:

$$\gamma(t) = k \, e^{-\alpha t} \qquad [7.27]$$

we may write:

$$\lambda_{mean} = \lambda_0 / (1 - k/\alpha) \qquad [7.28]$$

We may note that Omori's Law would be unsuitable as an influence function in eq.7.26, since its integral does not converge.

If we write the earthquake process in terms of a time series $\chi(t)$ we may obtain the rate function as a convolution integral:

$$\lambda(t) = \lambda_0 + \int_0^\infty \chi(\tau) \, \dot\gamma(t - \tau) d\tau \qquad [7.29]$$

or, introducing [7.27]:

$$\lambda(t) = \lambda_0 - \alpha k \int_0^\infty \chi(\tau) \, e^{-\alpha(t - \tau)} \, d\tau \qquad [7.30]$$

This process is quite amenable to simulation, and it even admits some closed predictors. For example, the probability of obtaining no earthquakes in a time interval $(t, t + \tau)$ is:

$$P_0(t, t + \tau) = \exp[-\int_t^{t+\tau} \lambda(x) \, dx] \qquad [7.31]$$

Hence the cumulative probability distribution of the forward return period τ (given an event at time t) is:

$$F_t(\tau) = 1 - \exp[-\int_t^{t+\tau} \lambda(x) \, dx] \qquad [7.32]$$

and so on. The influence of the older terms in $\lambda(t)$ decreases rapidly and it is possible to introduce a cutoff in the computer program which keeps only a finite number of terms in the sum. The number of terms in $\lambda(t)$ will tend to become stationary after a suitable number of iterations. This makes the Boltzmann process a very effective model for computer simulation of earthquake time series.

A TOPOLOGICAL MODEL

The energy partition of earthquakes has been derived in a general way by means of the Kolmogorov model. But this model provided no insight into the *spatial* distribution or pattern which might be expected from such a process. We shall now attempt to provide such an insight, by using a hydrological analogy.

Mathematically speaking, the problem of deriving the distribution of stream lengths in a watershed is entirely analogous to the problem of fault sizes as discussed on pp. 92–94. If the system is homogeneous both distributions are lognormal. We shall assume that fault systems behave like stream systems in topological respects.

(1) Then each region will have one main fault, and an ordered array of tributary, or subsidiary faults.

(2) All stress energy accumulated in the region will drain through the main fault and its system of tributary faults.

(3) If n is the number of faults in the region up to some arbitrary order, there are: .

$$N(n) = \binom{l}{n} / l \qquad\qquad [7.33]$$

topologically different configurations which can be constructed, where $l = 2n-1$ (Fig.7.5).

(4) The order of the network is a slowly-varying function of the number of branches. Thus, in a network consisting of 100 individual faults the highest possible order is 6, but the most probable maximum order is 4. Table 7.1 shows the probability of occurrence of a network of given order, as a function of the total number of branches.

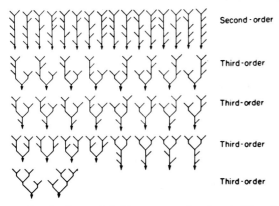

Second-order

Third-order

Third-order

Third-order

Third-order

Fig.7.5. Random subdivision patterns for six subsidiary faults "draining" a stress region (from stream topology after Shreve, 1966). Note that the highest order for a given configuration is three.

TABLE 7.1

Number of topologically distinct configurations N for a network of n subsidiary faults
(After Shreve, 1966)

n	N	Order number	
		most probable	highest possible
6	42	3	3
16	10^7	3	5
25	10^{12}	4	5
50	$5 \cdot 10^{26}$	4	6
75	$3 \cdot 10^{41}$	4	8
100	$2 \cdot 10^{56}$	5	10

(5) Let us assume that the region is divided into tributary stress fields, one to each fault. Naturally, the stress fields corresponding to faults of different order may overlap. Let $\bar{A}_j$ be the mean area of all stress fields of order j. Then, within any given region:

$$\bar{A}_{j-1}/\bar{A}_j = R \tag{7.34}$$

and:

$$\bar{A}_{j-i}/\bar{A}_j = R^i \tag{7.35}$$

where the constant ratio R can have values between 2 and 5 depending on the shape of the stress regions. For square stress fields $R = 4$.

Another consequence of this property, called *scale invariance*, is the fact that the ratio between the number of faults of different order is constant:

$$N_j/N_{j-1} = Q \tag{7.36}$$

where the ratio Q again varies between 2 and 5, with an average of 4.

Scale invariance is a direct result of the Kolmogorov breakage process (cf.eq.7.11) and means that any part of the region is topologically homologous to the region as a whole. Ratios such as R are called *scale factors*. The scale invariance relations can be extended to fault lengths, and possibly to stress gradients. In other words, the tectonic pattern in any given sector is identical (except for a scale factor) to the tectonic pattern in the region as a whole.

CHAPTER 8

Extreme-Value Methods

INTRODUCTION

Consider an arbitrary stochastic process $F(x, t)$, where x is some variable relevant to engineering design. For example, x may be the flow in a river that needs to be dammed. Frequently the design hinges not so much on an accurate knowledge of $F(x, t)$ as on the *largest* (or *smallest*) values that the variable x can assume in a given design period.

Of course, a complete knowledge of the process $F(x, t)$ also includes its maxima and minima. But the complete data are always cumbersome to process, and sometimes unavailable. Let us divide the time scale into equally-spaced intervals and consider the *extreme value y* which the variable x reaches within each interval. Thus, if x is the flow in a river, y might be the maximum annual flood. The variable y, called the *extreme value*, forms a regular point process imbedded in the original process $F(x, t)$. The properties of extreme values have been extensively discussed by Gumbel (1958).

EARTHQUAKE MAXIMA

The central result found by Gumbel (1958) is the following: there are only four major mathematically distinct distributions of y. For example, the first distribution (also called "Type I") is

$$G(y) = \exp(-\alpha e^{-\beta y}) \qquad (y \geqslant 0) \qquad\qquad [8.1]$$

Gumbel's result is explained by the fact that $G(y)$ depends only on the *tail* of the distribution of x. Certain important distributions behave in a similar way at large values: the normal, the exponential and the lognormal, for example. Thus, Gumbel's "Type I" distribution holds for extreme values derived from both normal and exponential populations.

Let us now consider the problem of predicting maximum earthquake magnitudes. The question of whether the magnitude distribution is exponential or normal (cf. Chapter 7) now becomes irrelevant, since both distributions yield identical tails.

Also, only large events will be used. This enables us to apply the Large-Earthquake Model defined in p.85.

We consider a seismic region defined by a main fault with its tributaries, and we assume a homogenous earthquake process with a cumulative magnitude distribution

$$F(x) = 1 - e^{-\beta x} \qquad (x \geqslant 0) \tag{8.2}$$

Let α be the mean number of earthquakes per year above magnitude zero. Then y, the maximum annual earthquake magnitude, will be distributed as in eq.8.1.

In order to estimate the parameters α and β one takes the largest yearly earthquake magnitudes $y_1, y_2, \ldots, y_n$ in a sample of n consecutive years. These magnitudes are arranged in order of increasing size, so that $y_{(1)} \leqslant y_{(2)} \leqslant \ldots \leqslant y_{(n)}$. Then one estimates the values of $G(y)$ by:

$$G(y_{(j)}) = j/(n+1) \tag{8.3}$$

Finally, the values of α and β are estimated from a least-square fit to eq. 8.1.

$$\log[-\log G(y)] = \log \alpha - \beta y \tag{8.4}$$

Special extremal probability paper is available for linearizing eq.8.4.

Once the parameters α and β have been determined, all other questions can be easily answered. The following quantities are of frequent use in problems of earthquake risk estimation (Epstein and Lomnitz, 1966):

(a) *Mean magnitude of earthquakes in a region.*

If M_{min} is the magnitude threshold of an earthquake sample over the region, the mean magnitude is estimated by:

$$\bar{M} = M_{min} + \beta^{-1} \tag{8.5}$$

(b) *Number of shocks above magnitude M_{min}.*

The yearly number of earthquakes above magnitude zero is α. Hence the expected number of shocks above magnitude M_{min} in D years is:

$$DN_y = D \alpha \exp(-\beta M_{min}) \tag{8.6}$$

(c) *Mean return period.*

If N is the expected number of earthquakes per year, $T = 1/N$ is the mean return period in years.

For example, the mean return period for shocks exceeding magnitude y is:

$$T_y = 1/N_y = \exp(\beta y)/\alpha \tag{8.7}$$

(d) *Modal maxima.*

The modal annual maximum $\tilde{y}$ is that maximum which is most frequently observed. It is not the mean of all maxima, but rather that maximum which has the highest probability of occurrence, i.e. which makes dG/dy a maximum:

$$\tilde{y} = \frac{\log\alpha}{\beta} \qquad [8.8]$$

The mean return period of an earthquake of magnitude $\tilde{y}$ is exactly one year.

(e) *Exceedance probability.*

The probability that a given magnitude y be exceeded during any given year is:

$$\text{Prob } \{ Y \geqslant y \} = 1 - G(y) \qquad [8.9]$$

The probability that the modal earthquake $\tilde{y}$ be exceeded in a given year is:

$$\text{Prob } \{Y \geqslant \tilde{y}\} = 1 - e^{-1} = 0.633 \qquad [8.10]$$

Hence, the modal earthquake is, more often than not, overtopped in an average year.

(f) *Occurrences with specified probability.*

The value of the earthquake magnitude which is exceeded with probability p in a D year period is given by:

$$y_p(D) = y_p + \beta^{-1} \log D \qquad [8.11]$$

where y_p, the *annual* maximum exceeded with probability p, is:

$$y_p = \tilde{y} - \beta^{-1} \log [- \log (1 - p)] \qquad [8.12]$$

(g) *Probability of an arbitrary return period.*

For a given design earthquake y, the mean return period T_y is given by eq.8.7. The probability of exceedance of an arbitrary return period T will be:

$$\text{Prob } \{ t \geqslant T \} = \exp (- T/T_y) \qquad [8.13]$$

(h) *Earthquake risk*

The earthquake risk $R_D(y)$, that is, the probability of occurrence of an earthquake of magnitude y or more in a D year period, is (cf. pp.130–133):

$$R_D(y) = 1 - \exp (- \alpha D e^{-\beta y}) \qquad [8.14]$$

AN APPLICATION TO CALIFORNIA

The seismicity of the State of California has been investigated in more detail than any other region. Independent estimates of α and β are available. California therefore affords an opportunity to compare different estimates of seismicity with those obtained by extreme-value methods.

We use a published catalogue of earthquakes in excess of magnitude 4.0 in California and we select the largest event in every year for the period 1932–1962. This yields 31 yearly maxima, which may be ordered by increasing magnitude (Table 8.1). The corresponding values of $G(y)$ were computed according to eq.8.3.

TABLE 8.1

California yearly maximum earthquakes, for period 1932–1962
(After Epstein and Lomnitz, 1966)

y	$G(y)$	y	$G(y)$
4.9	0.0312	6.0	0.500
5.3	0.0625	6.0	0.531
5.3	0.0937	6.0	0.562
5.5	0.125	6.0	0.594
5.5	0.156	6.0	0.625
5.5	0.187	6.2	0.656
5.5	0.219	6.2	0.687
5.6	0.250	6.3	0.719
5.6	0.281	6.3	0.750
5.6	0.312	6.4	0.781
5.8	0.344	6.4	0.812
5.8	0.375	6.5	0.844
5.8	0.406	6.5	0.875
5.9	0.437	6.5 ·	0.906
6.0	0.469	7.1	0.937
		7.7	0.969

The values of $G(y)$ may be graphed on extremal probability paper (Fig.8.1). The slope of the least-square fit gives $\beta = 2.00$ and the intercept yields log $\alpha = 11.43$.

Let us now compute the expected numbers of earthquakes per year, and the corresponding mean return periods, for earthquakes of various magnitudes in California. For this purpose we may use eq.8.6 and eq.8.7. Table 8.2 shows that an earthquake of magnitude 5 occurs every three months, while a shock of magnitude 6 is to be expected roughly every two years. These estimates, as well as the values of α and β, check extremely well with the values obtained by Gutenberg and Richter.

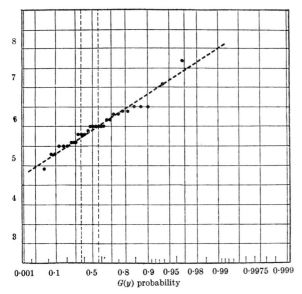

Fig.8.1. Data of Table 8.1 plotted on extremal probability paper for the estimation of parameters in the extremal magnitude distribution. (From Epstein and Lomnitz, 1966.)

What about a possible extrapolation of the method? Table 8.2 predicts a mean return period of 100.0 years for an earthquake of magnitude 8 or greater. This return period exceeds the range of the period of record, which was only 31 years. Hence there is no statistical basis for any estimates which exceed 31 years.

Yet a case can be made for utilizing such extrapolations from short-term data. Firstly, there are no available magnitude data in California spanning a continuous interval of 100 years or more. Secondly, the estimate derived from our 31-year run is likely to be conservative, as it neglects the downturn in the frequency curve of occurrence of earth-

TABLE 8.2

Predicted yearly numbers N and mean return periods T for California earthquakes
(After Epstein and Lomnitz, 1966)

Magnitude	N	T
3	228	1.6 days
4	31	11.8 days
5	4.18	87.3 days
6	0.57	1.8 years
7	0.076	13.2 years
8	0.010	100.0 years
9	0.0014	720. years

quakes at large magnitudes. Thus, the extreme-value approach predicts an earthquake of magnitude 9 in California every 720 years, which is probably unrealistic.

The assumption $T_{8.0} = 100$ years leads to the following conclusions, which are worth pondering:

(a) The probability of occurrence of an event of magnitude 8 or over in any given year is about 1%.

(b) The probability of at least one such event occurring in a century is 63.3%.

(c) The probability of at least two such events occurring in a century is 26.6%. This will occur in one out of four centuries, approximately.

(d) The probability of an interval of less than 50 years is 39% while the probability of an interval of more than 50 years is 61%.

(e) The median return period is 70 years. Half of all intervals will be above 70 years and half will be below it.

(f) The earthquake risk in California for an earthquake of magnitude 8 or larger is about 9% in a decade, and about 39% in a 50-year period.

The above estimates are based on the assumption that California can be considered as a single homogeneous region. Actually there are local differences in β-values, with pronounced lows along the San Andreas Fault where the major earthquakes have occurred in the past. Such inhomogeneities serve to determine the probable location of future large earthquakes; whether they make a substantial difference in the regionwide estimates of earthquake incidence is a moot question.

Some cautionary remarks about the uncritical use of extreme-value methods are included in Chapter 10. There are specific instances in which extreme-value predictions may be grossly misleading. For instance, if the major source of earthquake risk in a given region is a fault which has not been active during the period of record, the extreme-value distribution for that period will be meaningless in terms of the probable activity of that fault. Thus, an analysis of the Agadir, Morocco region prior to the 1960 earthquake might easily have led an incautious user of extreme-value methods to the conclusion that the probability of a destructive earthquake was negligible.

As a rule, the lower the seismicity of the region, the larger is the minimum safe period of observation for application of extreme-value methods. These methods are most reliable where a high incidence of large shocks suggests that a sample of a few decades may be representative of the long-term regional seismicity.

THE MAXIMUM MAGNITUDE IN A REGION

In the previous chapter we have proposed several mutually compatible models for deriving the magnitude distribution of earthquakes. In these models the energy distribution of earthquakes was generated by random partition, starting out from some finite total. We know that this total is of the order of 10^{26} ergs/year and that it fluctuates about a quasi-stationary mean.

How is this fact reconciled with the use of distributions such as the exponential, which are in fact unbounded? Is there actually a finite probability for an earthquake of magnitude 10 in every region of the earth, no matter how small?

The problem is quite general and is by no means exclusive to earthquakes. Most statisticians are interested in the central tendencies of distributions, rather than in their extremes. Even Gumbel (1958) failed to acknowledge the full implications of using mathematical distributions in a range of extremely rare events, where the Law of Large Numbers obviously ceases to be valid.

Let us return for a moment to the Kolmogorov model of energy partition (Chapter 7). Let X_0 be the size of the largest fault in the region. Then at stage 0 we have exactly *one* fault in the region, and the probability of occurrence of fault sizes $x > X_0$ is nil. Now, at stage 1 there will be Q_1 tributary faults of size $P_1 X_0$; and so forth. In general, P_i and Q_i will be random variables, and we know that $F(x)$ tends to lognormality.

However, in the special case where P_i and Q_i are *constant* we obtain an apparently different distribution known as the Pareto distribution (Steindl, 1965):

$$f(x) = (\delta - 1)\, k^{\delta - 1}\, x^{-\delta} \qquad (x > k) \tag{8.15}$$

This distribution is uniformly decreasing from a lower bound k (Fig.8.2).

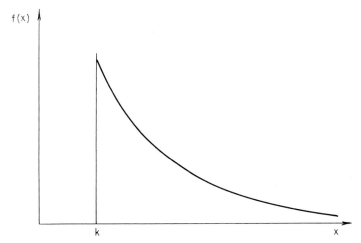

Fig.8.2. The Pareto distribution.

The classical process used to generate a Pareto distribution is shown in Fig.8.3. The variables X are represented by the areas of triangles; X_0 is the large triangle at the center. Each stage of subdivision produces three times as many triangles as the preceding stage; hence $Q = 3$. In the figure the scale factor for areas from stage to stage is $P = 1/4$.

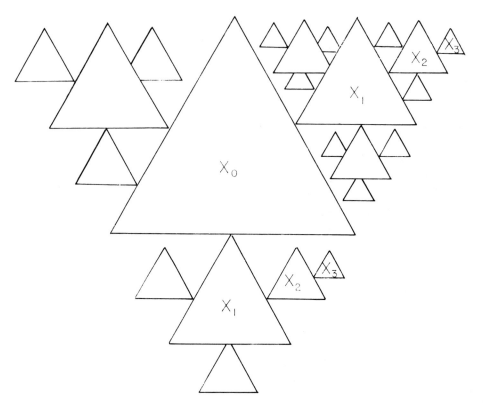

Fig.8.3. A geometrical algorithm for generating a Pareto distribution of variable X. The pattern is scale-invariant, i.e. any arbitrary sector is homologous to the whole (as suggested in Vere-Jones, 1970). The initial area X_0 represents the maximum value of X.

Now, the Pareto distribution has the advantage over the lognormal distribution that it explicitly contains the β-factor:

$$\beta = 3.45\ \delta \qquad\qquad\qquad\qquad\qquad\qquad\qquad\qquad [8.16]$$

a relation which can be easily checked by replacing x by $10^{1.5M+11.4}$ in eq.8.15. In a process of subdivision without remainders, if P and Q are constants we should have $PQ= 1$ and $\delta= 1$. In other words, the size of units at each stage times the number of units should give the size of units at the preceding stage. However, if P and Q are positive random variables which have a distribution their mean product PQ will normally be smaller than unity. For example, if the distribution of P is lognormal, gamma, or Pareto and if the distribution of Q is Poisson or binomial the modes of both distributions are smaller than their means, and $\delta \neq 1$ in general. Thus, the factor $\beta = 3.45\ \delta$ may be interpreted as a measure of randomness of the mechanism of subdivision. The more different from 3.45, the more random is the mechanism.

A computer program has been designed to simulate a generalized Pareto process, letting P and Q be random variables having, respectively, lognormal and Poisson distributions. The logarithm of fault areas X was assumed to be proportional to $1.5\,M$, where M is the magnitude. Hence, if M_{max} is the maximum magnitude in the region all other magnitudes may be scaled down from M_{max} by:

$$M = M_{max} - (\log_{10} X_0 - \log_{10} X)/1.5 \qquad\qquad [8.18]$$

The value of β was preset to 2.0 by adjusting the means of the distributions of P and Q. Because of the scaling law [8.18] the actual value of M_{max} is irrelevant, but for the sake of realism we have used $M_{max} = 8.9$. Some of the computer results are shown in Fig.8.4; they clearly show the downturn of the magnitude—frequency curve, as the maximum magnitude is approached. The levelling-off at smaller magnitudes is due to the fact that the program was terminated after a finite number of stages of subdivision. Note also that the experimental β-value fluctuates slightly about the preset value of 2.0.

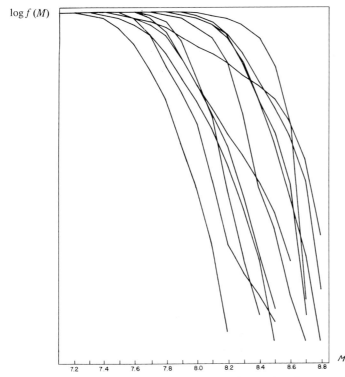

Fig.8.4. Monte Carlo computer output for twelve earthquake sequences $(M_{max} = 8.9,\ \beta = 2.0)$, simulated by means of an algorithm modified from Fig.8.3, by randomizing the number and size ratio of triangles at each step. The distortion at small magnitudes is due to a programmed cutoff in the number of iterations. Longer runs develop perfectly straight lines of slope 2.0 in the lower magnitude ranges.

In the region of the downturn of the magnitude—frequency relation all statistical predictions cease to be valid, since the number of events is very small. Predictions based on extreme-value theory are conservative, however, since they assume a straight-line extrapolation of the magnitude—frequency relation leading to more pessimistic estimates of the recurrence of large earthquakes.

On a purely empirical basis I have found that the following procedure yields an approximate estimate of M_{max} for the above model:

(1) Compute $N(M)$, the cumulative number of earthquakes greater or equal to M, in the range of magnitudes where the downturn is noticeable.

(2) Plot $N(M)$ against $(M_{max} - M)$ on a log-log graph. Since M_{max} is unknown, use trial values of M_{max} until a straight line is obtained.

(3) To the value of M_{max} which makes the plot a straight line add a correction for incompleteness of sample. The correction may range from +0.1 for long-term samples to 0.6 for relatively short-term samples (less than 10% of the return period of M_{max}).

If a maximum earthquake is included in the sample there is a possibility of seriously overestimating M_{max} by this method. Hence it is advisable to repeat the above procedure, omitting the largest shock in the sample, to check for consistency. This should lower the estimate of M_{max} by not more than 0.2 units of magnitude.

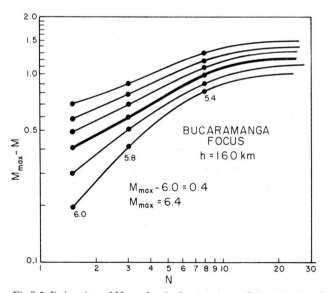

Fig.8.5. Estimation of M_{max} for the Bucaramanga, Colombia, deep-focus earthquake nest.

Fig.8.5 shows an example of estimation of M_{max} for the Bucaramanga, Colombia intermediate focus. If we assume an incompleteness correction of 0.1 we find $M_{max} = 6.5$ for this focus, in good agreement with historical evidence.

CHAPTER 9

Earthquake Zoning

WHY SEISMIC ZONING?

There is probably no inhabited area on earth where earthquakes can be said to be totally unknown. Damaging earthquakes have occurred in England, in central Australia, in Siberia, and in other regions of low tectonic activity. In recent centuries, the casualty rate from earthquakes has been higher in Italy than in Japan.

Yet there is an evident correlation between the frequency of large earthquakes and the risk of casualties and damage. Within a given country, or within a relatively homogeneous cultural area such as Latin America, high risk is asssociated with high earthquake incidence. Higher safety factors are warranted when designing a building or a dam in a region of frequent large earthquakes. The higher cost of earthquake-resistant construction should balance the seismic risk in such areas. Seismic zoning is not a problem for the earth scientist alone: it involves an assessment of the social cost of earthquakes and of the amount the community is prepared to pay for protection from earthquake risk.

SOVIET CONCEPTS OF ZONING

The first earthquake zoning maps for the Soviet Union were proposed by the Moscow Institute of Physics of the Earth in 1937. These maps were first incorporated into the building code for the Russian Federative Republic. Later, the Institute of Physics of the Earth prepared more detailed maps, which were incorporated in the 1957 Zoning (*Rayonirovanye*) of the Soviet Union. These maps became an official part of the Earthquake Building Code SN8-57 of the U.S.S.R. (Fig.9.1).

The zones considered seismically active comprise 20.9% of the territory of the Soviet Union: these are the areas affected by earthquakes of Mercalli intensity 6 and above. More than forty million people live in these areas, with a mean population density of 9 inhabitants per square kilometer. The capitals of nine Soviet republics (Moldavian S.S.R., Georgian S.S.R., Armenian S.S.R., Azerbayan S.S.R., Turkmen S.S.R., Uzbek S.S.R., Tadjik S.S.R., Kirghiz S.S.R. and Kazakh S.S.R.) are within the seismic zone. However, by far the largest seismic area is included within the Russian S.F.S.R. (Northern Caucasus, Altai, Baikal, Verkhoyansk, Chukot Peninsula, Kamchatka, and the margins of the Sea of Okhotsk).

The procedure used in producing the Soviet zoning maps consists of two steps:

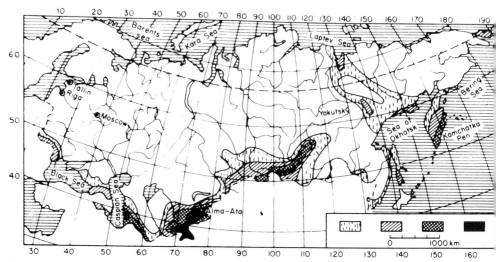

Fig.9.1. Earthquake zoning map of the U.S.S.R. (Normy i pravila stroitel' stva v seismicheskikh raionakh SN8–57, Stroiizdat, 1958).

(a) Compilation of seismicity maps, i.e. maps showing the incidence of earthquake epicenters in different regions. These seismicity maps combine plots of epicentral locations with geological data on recent faulting and other crustal movements.

(b) Mapping of soil conditions affecting seismic intensity; such mapping is usually done through the study of isoseismals of past earthquakes, plus geologic evidence.

The combination of these two steps cannot be done as yet in a rigorous way. Specific regional conditions which are taken into account include local peculiarities of the seismic process, relations between geology and seismicity, uncertainty factors which involve the relative availability of data, and "other factors" such as economic and human considerations (Medvedev). The final zoning maps show the areas where intensities of 6, 7, 8, and 9 on the Mercalli Scale (or on the roughly equivalent GOST 6249-52 scale) may be expected to occur. In some instances these zoning maps are superposed on geotectonic maps. They may contain information about the relative frequency of earthquakes, e.g. "low" (once every 150–200 years), "moderate" (once every 50 years), or "high" (once every 15 years).

EARTHQUAKE ZONING IN THE U.S.A.

The development of zoning concepts in the United States has been closely connected with the development of building codes. As long as each city or district has its own building regulations there is little incentive for zoning. In California, statewide rules on earthquake design existed only for school buildings, as a result of the Field Act of 1933. After considerable efforts by the engineering profession a conference of Pacific Coast building officials approved the 1958 Uniform Building Code, which has exerted some unifying influence. However, most major cities retained their own codes. The earthquake provisions of the Los Angeles County 1968 Building Code are reproduced in Appendix 1.

The practice of estimating earthquake risk and design factors separately for each locality has led American engineers to regard wholesale regionalization schemes with mistrust. A provisional regionalization of the United States proposed by the U.S. Coast and Geodetic Survey around 1957 was promptly withdrawn, under strong criticism. Later, a tentative regionalization map incorporating Soviet concepts was published by Richter (1959). It is interesting that this map (Fig.9.2) was criticized as being excessively conservative, by the Soviet expert Medvedev (1965).

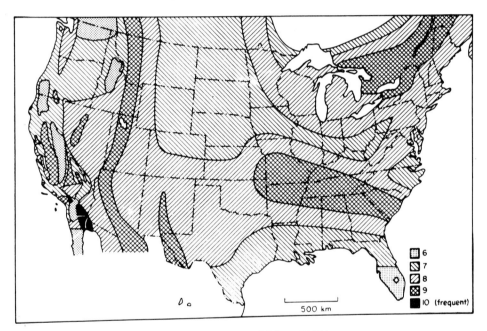

Fig.9.2. Earthquake zoning map of the U.S.A. (From Richter, 1959.)

Richter's projected intensities for the southeastern states (Missouri to South Carolina) are largely based on two events: the New Madrid earthquakes of 1811 and the Charleston earthquake of 1886. Medvedev (1965) has observed in this connection that earthquakes in this area "are comparatively rare and less strong than on the Pacific coast". This argument casts some light on the Soviet procedures since it is known that intensities of order 9 were observed twice in this region, (which proves that such intensities can and do occur). The matter is far from trivial, because of the potentially high cost of raising the code requirements to California levels in a vast region of the United States.

RISK MAPPING

Earthquake risk has been defined as the probability of occurrence of a critical earth-quake during a specified design period (Lomnitz, 1964b). The critical earthquake is called the "design earthquake", and its magnitude M_D the "design magnitude".

Let D be the design period for the region or locality. Then the earthquake risk R_D may be written approximately:

$$R_D = 1 - \exp\left(- \alpha D e^{-\beta M_D}\right) \qquad [9.1]$$

where α is the mean rate of occurrence and β is the parameter of the magnitude frequency distribution (cf. Chapter 8). If the region is sufficiently homogeneous to assume constancy of β it becomes possible to map the earthquake risk R_D for a given design earthquake.

Usually we select as our design earthquake a shock capable of producing horizontal accelerations in excess of 0.1 g at a given locality. The procedure is as follows: (a) take a list of m epicenters in the region over a period $T>D$; (b) define a grid of m x n points covering the region; (c) for each grid point compute:

$$p_{ij} = 1 - \exp\left(- \beta x_j\right) \qquad [9.2]$$

where x_j is the magnitude which, if released at the j-th epicenter, will produce an acceleration of 0.1 g at grid point i.

It is easy to see that p_{ij} represents the probability that the design earthquake will *not* occur at epicenter j during a period of T years. Hence the earthquake risk at grid point i may be written:

$$R_T(i) = 1 - \prod_j p_{ij} \qquad [9.3]$$

Finally, the earthquake risk R_D for the design period D is given by:

$$\log(1 - R_D) = \frac{D}{T} \log(1 - R_T) \qquad [9.4]$$

which can be derived from eq (9.1).

An example of an earthquake risk map obtained by this procedure is shown in Fig.9.3. It is of some interest to discuss the errors involved in the assumption of homogeneity of the region. Thus, anyone familiar with the seismicity of California will recognize that the risk map is weighed toward areas of frequent earthquakes (such as the Hollister area), rather than areas of rare but large shocks. It has been argued that the sections of *low* apparent risk (i.e. the saddles in Fig.9.3) along the major active faults may be precisely the most likely spots for a great earthquake, since they show little evidence of strain release. In this connection, it is significant that the 1971 San Fernando earthquake

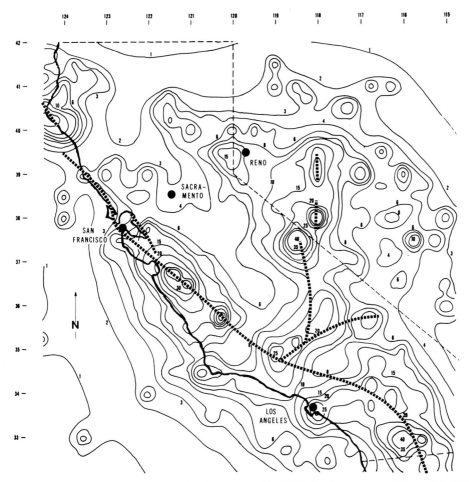

Fig.9.3. Earthquake risk map of California, computed in 1966. Contours represent the probability (in percent) of occurrence of an earthquake of minimum acceleration 0.1 *g* during a design period of 30 years (see text for assumptions). The sectors of *lowest* predicted risk along the San Andreas Fault have since ruptured in the damaging Parkfield and San Fernando earthquakes.

occurred precisely in a saddle between two "high" areas on the San Andreas system. The same is true for the 1966 Parkfield earthquake, which was not included in Fig.9.3.

In conclusion, risk mapping indicates chiefly the areas of high-level, medium-sized earthquake activity along an active structure. Saddles or gaps in the risk contours do not necessarily indicate an absence of risk. Quite the opposite, in the case of continuous structures such as the San Andreas system they may serve to pinpoint the areas where potentially damaging earthquakes will next occur.

A more generalized version of risk mapping, utilizing historical earthquake data, has been used in an attempt to provide general guidelines for earthquake zoning in Chile (Fig.9.4).

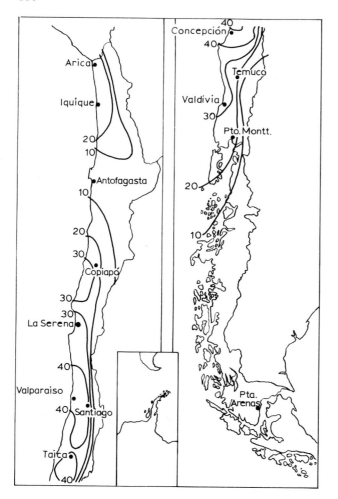

Fig.9.4. Earthquake-risk map for Chile. Contours represent the estimated probability (in percent) of occurrence of an earthquake of minimum acceleration 0.1 *g* during a design period of 30 years. (From Lomnitz, 1969a.)

APPROACHES TO EARTHQUAKE PREDICTION

Many criteria of seismicity and earthquake risk have been proposed in the past. Complete references will be found in Kárník (1971). A more specialized bibliography, oriented primarily toward earthquake prediction, and including a number of Soviet references, is given by Schmidt (1971).

In this book we shall merely mention the recent development of methods of risk estimation by V.I. Keilis-Borok and some of his students, particularly G.M. Molchan with the active cooperation of specialists in decision theory. These methods fall in the category of composition methods (cf. Chapter 10), and attempt to include economic factors such as cost, depreciation, and insurance premiums. The basic statistical model is notable for its bare and simple assumptions (Kantorovich et al., 1970). More recent work has not yet become available in translation.

A review of Soviet experiments in earthquake prediction (Sadovski, 1971) mentions the following parameters which undergo consistent observable changes before large earthquakes: (a) frequency of occurrence of minor shocks; (b) surface tilt; (c) ratio v_P / v_S of seismic velocities of P and S waves; (d) electrical conductivity; (e) telluric currents. In the case of changes in the seismic velocity ratio a forecast accuracy of 5–15 days is claimed; the anomaly preceding the earthquake sets in about 1–3 months before the event.

At present only two or three examples of successful predictions are available for each method. The number of unsuccessful predictions is not generally available. Similar observations, with equally inconclusive results, are being conducted in Japan (Rikitake, 1972) and in the United States. Measurements of micro-earthquakes and fault creep have not shown any clear causal connection between these phenomena and the occurrence of large earthquakes.

Much of the material presented in support of specific forecasting methods is not only statistically insignificant but plagued by experimental errors. Repeated seismic velocity measurements along the San Andreas Fault had to be given up because the variations in the vicinity of the shot points proved larger than the effects being measured. Soviet experimenters have used repeated offshore explosions, but the control of shot locations and depth of charges may have been inadequate, judging from published seismograms.

In view of the fact that all proposed methods are directly or indirectly related to monitoring the state of stress in the earth, it will take long-term observations under controlled conditions and over a variety of tectonic configurations before such effects can be properly discussed and thoroughly understood.

CHAPTER 10

Estimation Procedures for Earthquake Risk

INTRODUCTION

In recent years an increasing amount of attention has been paid to economic questions and questions of public safety as related to natural hazards. The systematic application of statistical methods to the estimation or prediction of such hazards offers the hope of reducing the loss of life and the damage caused by natural disasters. As long as earthquake risk remains quantitatively unknown it defies any efforts at planning or prevention; it affords no rational basis for design criteria or insurance premiums.

Most authors distinguish between questions of public safety (loss of life and limb) and questions of economic loss. This is reasonable since the factors involved are different, and so are the protective measures and the types of insurance coverage. It is commonly held that loss of life represents the primary risk and that the economic losses are secondary. A serious account of loss of life in earthquakes is difficult to find. The engineering design factors used in building codes are supposed to provide "adequate" protection for the occupants of a building; but there is seldom any objective evidence to support such criteria of "adequacy".

In the following we shall assume that risk of life in earthquakes is closely correlated with risk of structural failure.

This is not strictly correct; for example, the evidence on a correlation between number of casualties and time of day (Fig.10.1) suggests that non-structural factors may be equally important as structural ones. In Chile, the well-ingrained habit of running out of doors at the onset of an earthquake has possibly saved more lives than all other preventive measures combined (Lomnitz, 1970a).

APPROACHES OF ANALYSIS

There is no unique method for the estimation of earthquake risk. Two basic levels of approach may be distinguished in all types of analysis:

(1) According to the depth of statistical treatment: descriptive statistics, or statistical inference.

(2) According to the degree of interaction with physical descriptions of the underlying process: stochastic models, or models which incorporate geophysical results of a deterministic nature.

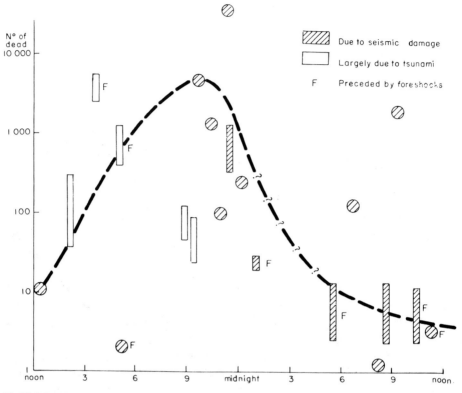

Fig.10.1 Incidence of casualties in Chilean earthquakes, vs. local time. There is a significant correlation with dwelling occupancy. (From Lomnitz, 1970a.)

Each of these levels represents a stage of sophistication in the analysis, rather than a true difference in approach. Lacking both adequate data and an adequate model of the physical mechanism, the statistician will clutch at straws, so to speak, in his attempt to extract a maximum of information from all available sources. In the words of a UNESCO (1972) report, "the amount of relevant data concerning natural hazards is inadequate for the immediate application of standard methods of statistical inference".

The methods in current use may be classified as follows:

(A)   Extreme-value methods.
(B)   Bayesian methods.
(C)   Optimization methods.
(D)   Composition methods.
(E)   Zoning methods.
(F)   Simulation methods.

These methods may either be used singly, or more often in combination. Each of them has advantages and disadvantages, and their use depends on the circumstances of each problem.[1]

EXTREME-VALUE METHODS

The basic techniques of extreme-value methods have been discussed in Chapter 8. These techniques represent a logical first choice whenever one is concerned with the extremes of a statistical variable, such as wind velocity, stream flow, and earthquake ground acceleration.

Some of the more important practical advantages of extreme-value methods are the following:

(a) The extreme values of a geophysical variable are better known, more homogeneous in time, and more accurately determined than the average events in a time series of data.

(b) The method does not require a detailed knowledge of the parent distribution.

(c) The method is simple to use and to understand. It involves few assumptions; hence its uncertainties are relatively easy to discuss.

Of course, each of these advantages has its own dangers. The great ease of application of extreme-value methods has led to their over-sanguine use, particularly by extrapolation beyond the range of values for which data is available. Perhaps the earliest widespread use of extreme-value methods occurred in the prediction of maximum floods in a river. These predictions have proved reliable in most cases, but there is an important group of cases where the method proved totally inadequate. The extreme annual floods in some basins may be caused by several different mechanisms: snowmelting, stream runoff, or the rupture of natural dams. One of these mechanisms (e.g. the rupture of natural dams) may be so infrequent that the available data contains not a single example of such an event, whether large or small. Yet this may be just the type of event which should be taken as critical for the design of a protective structure.

In addition, geophysical variables are subject to secular variations, such as climatic changes and fluctuations in seismic activity. These variations are not well-observed and are poorly understood at present. They tend to invalidate any statistical predictions based on assumptions of stationarity; this includes extreme-value methods as well as most other methods that have been proposed.

Long-term correlations in the data, including secular effects, introduce non-conservative errors in extreme-value estimates. Thus, the predicted maxima tend to be positively correlated with the period of observation: the longer the data run, the larger the inferred maximum event for any given return period. This is an awkward effect, which had already been observed in floods and might well be present in earthquakes.

Nevertheless, extreme-value methods will continue to play an essential role in

---

[1] I should like to thank UNESCO for permission to extract Section 5 of the *Report on Statistics of Natural Hazards* (1972), for which I acted as reporter.

earthquake-risk estimation, in combination with other methods. For example, Plafker (1965) has found from geomorphological evidence that large earthquakes in Alaska ($M = 8\frac{1}{2}$ +) occur at intervals of the order of 1,000 years. This kind of evidence, which may be extremely valuable for the estimation of earthquake risk, is easily incorporated into extreme-value procedures, and should greatly improve the reliability of extrapolations from limited data runs.

BAYESIAN METHODS

Bayesian methods for the estimation of earthquake risk were originally developed in Mexico by the earthquake engineering research group headed by E. Rosenblueth and L. Esteva. The usefulness of these methods depends on assumptions of similitude or mechanism underlying the initial hypothesis used.

The basic procedure has been briefly outlined in Chapter 5. The idea is to use all kinds of relevant information to complement the body of hard data, that is felt to be inadequate. For example, data runs from neighboring or analogous system may provide the basis for an initial hypothesis. Also, geophysical models may be used in the same manner, e.g., estimates of secular strain rates from observations of sea-floor spreading. The data are then used to modify the initial hypothesis by Bayes' Theorem.

The advantage of Bayesian methods lies in their flexibility. New data may be used to improve estimates at any time, i.e. the results of a Bayesian estimation may serve as initial hypothesis for future estimations. This open-ended character of the Bayesian approach is particularly attractive in a time of great change and rapid development in the earth sciences.

On the other hand, the assignment of prior probabilities to any initial hypothesis may involve an arbitrary decision on the part of the user. For example, it may be tempting to use regional data on small earthquakes as an initial input for the Bayesian estimation of the recurrence of large shocks in a region. Clearly, the prior probability to be attached to such a hypothesis would vary greatly among different seismologists.

The amount of personal judgment which goes into a Bayesian procedure is not always easy to pin down. With the increased use of these methods a consensus on prior probabilities may be expected to emerge. Such a consensus will greatly enhance the usefulness of Bayesian methods in supplementing data runs of limited length, by taking into account all heterogeneous factors which may be relevant to the estimation of earthquake risk.

OPTIMIZATION METHODS

By optimization methods we mean all techniques of systems analysis and decision theory, including game theory, linear and dynamic programming, and related techniques of operations research. The most immediate applications of such methods are in relation to optimal siting with respect to potential sources of seismic hazard.

Why are these well-known techniques so rarely applied in connection with earthquake risk? The answer seems to be that other factors of a deterministic nature have overruled seismic considerations in the initial stages of siting. Thus, the location of a large dam or even of a nuclear reactor is determined by factors other than seismic safety. The earthquake risk is estimated a posteriori, for purposes of design. This situation is changing in respect to nuclear reactors, and perhaps to other important structures as well.

Game theory is applicable wherever human decisions play a role in determining the long-range cost of earthquake hazards. Undoubtedly, public policies concerning building codes, seismic zoning, and earthquake insurance have a tremendous influence on the losses resulting from earthquakes. Too often, regulations are tightened just after a large loss has occurred: a rather unsatisfactory strategy from the game-theoretical point of view.

Alternative decisions on earthquake policies can be analyzed as strategies in a game against nature. Such an approach could have a healthy effect on official policies, by bringing to light some aspects of the problem which had not been sufficiently explored until that time; e.g., what is the potential for reducing earthquake losses through insurance?

Optimization of earthquake risk may also be applied to the design of single structures. In many cases, buildings are underdesigned in terms of mean probable damage, i.e. an increase in the seismic design factor could mean a probable saving in excess of the increase in the initial cost.

The development of strategies in the presence of information gaps is a common feature of game theory, which makes it particularly suited to the optimization of earthquake policies. In the course of transferring such policies to a game matrix it becomes possible to define all missing elements of information which may affect the decision process in a critical way, and which might otherwise have been overlooked.

COMPOSITION METHODS

Let A be the location at which some estimate of earthquake risk is required. In favorable cases we may have a record of maximum ground accelerations at A over a suitable period of years, which can be used as input in some prediction scheme derived from one of the preceding methods.

More often, though, the site A lacks any relevant data on local accelerations or other seismic observations. In this case, a list of past accelerations at A may be computed on the basis of the magnitudes and epicentral distances of all shocks previously determined in the region, by using some general formula which connects these variables to estimated ground acceleration.

Such indirect methods of estimation will be refered to as "composition methods". Their accuracy obviously depends on the assumptions involved and the formulas used. Local factors (geology, soils) can rarely be taken into account in a satisfactory way. Nevertheless, composition methods often represent the only practical way of dealing with problems of earthquake risk in locations where no instrumental data is available.

Let a (M, Δ) be the estimated acceleration as a function of magnitude M and epicentral distance Δ. Some well-known expressions for this function have been discussed in Chapter 3. If the function a (M, Δ) were linear in M and Δ one could obtain the distribution $f(a)$ of accelerations at the site as a convolution of the distributions of M and Δ with the function a. Indeed, a suitable change of variables may succeed in linearizing the function a for the purpose of making the problem tractable by convolution techniques.

In general, however, this represents no substantial improvement, since the distribution of Δ varies from site to site. Among several roughly equivalent techniques, the following appears to give consistent results: Let $f_i(M)$ be the distribution of magnitudes at the i-th epicenter. Then the probability of occurrence of an earthquake of magnitude less than M_c may be written:

$$p_i = 1 - \exp(-\beta_i M_c) \qquad [10.1]$$

If we define M_c as the magnitude which produces a critical acceleration a_c at a distance Δ_i, the quantity p_i represents the probability that an earthquake at epicenter i will not produce an acceleration in excess of a_c at the given locality.

Now, we may use the given function a (M, Δ) to compute the critical magnitudes M_{critical} for all events in the earthquake list. If the list is homogeneous and has a threshold magnitude M_{min} we should use $M_c = M_{\text{critical}} - M_{\text{min}}$ in order to normalize the probabilities p_i. Hence the composition of probabilities for all epicenters in the list is:

$$P = \prod_i p_i \qquad [10.2]$$

and the probability that the given critical acceleration will be exceeded is $(1-P)$.

This technique assumes that the period of record is sufficiently long, so that the distribution of epicenters is representative for the region. In practice the magnitude distribution f_i (M) cannot be determined for each individual epicenter; instead, it is assumed that $f(M)$ varies slowly over the region, so that we can adopt characteristic values of β for different geologic provinces or ranges of focal depths.

The composition approach offers a wide spectrum of experimental variations, and its adaptability to the computer represents a distinct advantage. Techniques of parameter variation have been successfully used to test different assumptions. For example, it was found that the distribution of ground accelerations is relatively insensitive to changes in the form of the distribution of seismic sources in space.

Composition methods would be greatly improved if local factors such as soil response could be effectively incorporated into the estimation procedure. At present little progress has been made in this direction.

ZONING METHODS

A general discussion of zoning has been provided in Chapter 9. In principle the subdivision of land areas into zones of different earthquake incidence is an essential objective of risk estimation. Unfortunately, many so-called seismotectonic maps are based solely on the occurrence of past events, and contain no information on local geology or soil conditions.

The most useful zoning schemes are either very broad or very detailed. *Broad* zoning maps can be objectively based on qualitative differences in earthquake incidence, e.g., between the Gulf Coast and the Pacific seaboard of Mexico. Such regionalization is of prime importance in matters involving legislation, insurance, and building codes. Too fine a subdivision tends to be self-defeating, however, as the borders between adjoining zones become more debatable. Contention and litigation are apt to increase in inverse proportion to the amount of confidence attached to a given zoning scheme.

Small-scale zoning, which incorporates realistic information on local soil conditions, is called microzonation. This type of zoning should always be based on actual data, rather than on computed response inferred from composition methods. A great deal of laborious and exacting data gathering and processing is involved. In spite of the increasing need for microzonation in many parts of the world the actual amount of research done in this field has been disappointingly small.

SIMULATION METHODS

Earthquake processes may be simulated in many different ways. A number of varieties of stochastic processes have been discussed in preceding chapters; these may be used as tools to explore the actual process underlying the occurrence of earthquakes.

Physical models of earthquake mechanisms have also been used. The best-known of these models consists of an assemblage of sliding blocks connected by springs, and was constructed by Burridge and Knopoff (1967). This model reproduces some clustering properties observed in aftershock sequences.

Computer simulation includes the use of Monte Carlo methods, in order to study the behavior of complex stochastic processes through actual numerical realizations. The technique of computer simulation is simple: an example will suffice. Suppose that we wish to simulate a stochastic process corresponding to the "Large-Earthquake Model" (Chapter 7). In this model the events are independently distributed according to a stationary Poisson process, and the magnitudes are independently distributed according to an exponential process.

The simulation uses a subroutine RANDOM, which generates a pseudo-random number with a uniform distribution in the range (0,1). The program proceeds in two steps:

(a) generate a Poisson-distributed sequence of events with mean λ. This can be done most efficiently by generating a sequence of time intervals TINTVL which are exponentially distributed:

TINTVL = − ALOG(1. − RANDOM)/LAMBDA

(b) Associate with each event a magnitude MAG, which will be exponentially distributed with mean $1/\beta$:

MAG = − ALOG(1. − RANDOM) * BETA

This will generate a sequence of events having magnitudes greater or equal to zero. If one wishes to simulate an earthquake catalogue having a threshold magnitude MAGMIN one may write instead:

MAG = MAGMIN − ALOG(1. − RANDOM) * BETA

Using similar techniques it is possible to simulate stochastic processes of great complexity, including non-Markovian processes such as the linear self-exciting process (Boltzmann process) and others. An example of a result obtained by computer simulation is given in Fig.8.4.

It is not difficult to simulate sequences of pseudo-earthquakes on a computer; the data runs generated by different models can only be distinguished from each other or from real date by means of sophisticated statistical testing.

The inverse problem, viz. inferring the stochastic process on the basis of a limited data run, is highly indeterminate. Some early attempts have used techniques of goodness of fit to various theoretical distributions, in order to compare one stochastic model to another; since the number of possible models is very large, the power of such tests is correspondingly low. The main use of simulation techniques is in constructing a serviceable working hypothesis for a specific purpose. Table 10.1 lists some of the models which have been used in simulation techniques for some typical applications.

TABLE 10.1

Simulation techniques

Model	Applications
1. Large-earthquake model	return periods of extreme events
2. Boltzmann process	regional seismicity, aftershock sequences
3. Kolmogorov process	magnitude distribution
4. Pareto process	largest magnitude in a region
5. Neyman−Scott process	time-space clustering of aftershocks

A CASE HISTORY

Spot estimates of earthquake risk are part of the preliminary design stage for practically all structures and engineering works in known earthquake zones. In the great majority of cases these estimates are based on "engineering judgment", which means that no quantitative elements of decision are involved in them.

Where zoning maps exist the task of the engineer is facilitated, because of the availability of maximum intensities or their equivalent. However, the period of recurrence of such "maximum" events may be of critical importance to design; and this information is not normally supplied with zoning maps. For example, according to the proposed zoning map of the United States contained in the 1950 Uniform Building Code, western California and southeast Missouri receive the same rating, even though the incidence of damaging earthquakes in California is much higher than it is in Missouri (Fig.10.2).

Zero-risk design is extremely rare, because of its high cost; but it is quite simple to achieve. According to computations by Brune (1968) the highest acceleration that can be impressed on the sides of a fault during an earthquake is 2 g. Any structure designed to withstand loads of 2 g in any direction, both statically and dynamically, would be absolutely earthquake-proof. Obviously, such a massive construction can only be considered when the cost is no object.

Normal engineering structures are built to stand up under their own weight, as a minimum. Hence an acceleration of at least 1 g is standard in the vertical direction. However, design against horizontal forces is not standard, and every provision to resist such forces tends to be regarded as an extra expense tagged onto the "normal" price of the structure: this seismic overprice may range from 10% to 20% in most structures, depending on design requirements.

The following case history has been developed in some detail, to afford an example of an actual application of earthquake risk concepts to engineering design.

PROJECT DESCRIPTION

The project is located at 14°39'N 90°32'W, near the northwest boundary of Guatemala City, in the Republic of Guatemala. A six-lane highway bridge is to be built over a deep ravine. Elevation of the road surface above the bottom of the ravine will be about 440 ft., and the length of the bridge will be less than half a mile.[1]

A monolithic reinforced concrete structure supported on six hollow rectangular piles has been proposed. The City of Guatemala has no special provisions for horizontal forces in the building code; however, because of a history of destructive earthquakes a special study of seismic risk is included in the design requirements.

---

[1] Case history reproduced by permission of the Municipality of Guatemala and of Comex, Inc., Consulting Engineers, Mexico, 1972. This case history does not describe the final project which was adopted.

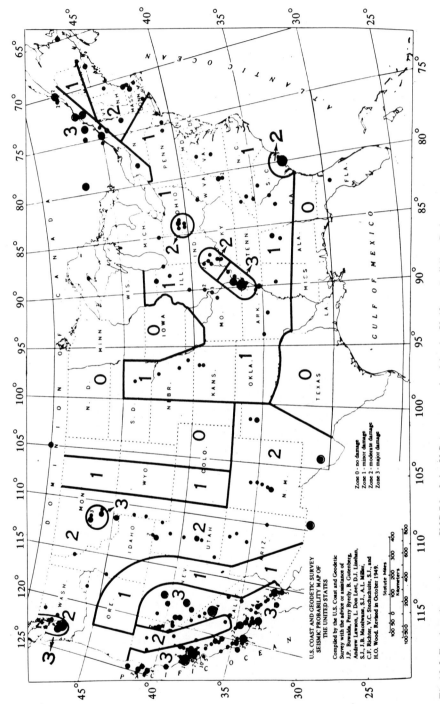

Fig.10.2 Earthquake zoning map SMC-76 of the U.S.A., as contained in the Uniform Building Code (1950). Withdrawn by the U.S. Coast and Geodetic Survey in 1952.

GEOLOGIC SITUATION

Guatemala City lies at an altitude of less than 5,000 ft., on the continental divide between the Atlantic and Pacific Oceans. It is underlain by a volcanic fill of ash flows of indeterminate thickness. The city is located 27 km from the nearest active volcano (Mt. Pacaya). The ash flows may be described as fine, welded tuffs (nuées ardentes), containing abundant white pumice and little else. The flows were deposited by gravity under dry conditions; there is very little evidence of alluvial redeposition.

The topography resembles a flat plain, which is being dissected by gullies advancing from the Atlantic direction towards the northern outskirts of the city. One of these gullies, the Río La Barranca, forms the western boundary of the city and is used as a convenient channel to drain a large part of the urban area. Storm sewers and sewage drains empty near the upstream end of the gully. The proposed bridge will cross this gully near the northern city limits, towards an isolated western suburb called Bethania (Fig.10.3).

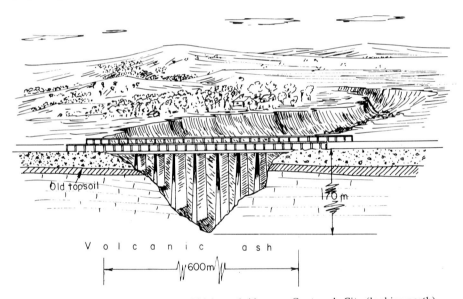

Fig.10.3. Geologic setting of a proposed highway bridge near Guatemala City (looking north).

SEISMOTECTONIC SETTING,

According to the seismicity maps found in Part III of this volume, most of the seismic activity occurs offshore between the coast and the Mid-American Trench.

Actually, the large-scale seismicity does not afford an accurate estimate of earthquake risk. A study of local records reveals that practically all the damage from earthquakes in

Guatemala has been caused by inland epicenters. The destructive earthquakes that have affected the region of the capital are shallow events located at distances of 10–50 km from the city, close to the volcanic belt. These shocks rarely exceed a magnitude of six, and their radius of perceptibility is relatively small. However, they can be severely damaging within epicentral distances of the order of 50 km.

Because of their shallow focus and their frequent occurrence in swarms these local earthquakes are similar to those which affect the Median Trough of El Salvador and Nicaragua. They are probably connected with tensional tectonics along the volcanic axis of Central America, even though the known local grabens in Guatemala are normal to the trend of this axis.

The offshore events and the intermediate shocks associated with the Mid-American convergence zone are believed to result from the interaction between the Cocos plate and the continental block of Yucatán–Guatemala, of Paleozoic age. These earthquakes may reach large magnitudes, but their effects in Guatemala City are only critical for structures of large natural periods.

SEISMIC HISTORY

Some of the major seismic events in the history of Guatemala are listed in Part III, under Region 5.

An important item of information concerns the old structures that have withstood historical earthquakes. The first building erected in 1620 on the present site of Guatemala City was the chapel known as Ermita del Carmen. The original building stood for three centuries, and was demolished by a local earthquake on January 3, 1918. This is indirect evidence for the absence of earthquakes of intensity exceeding the 1918 shock during the preceding 300 years. Of course, the cumulative effect of previous shocks which had affected the building cannot be assessed; it is entirely possible that the building was ready to collapse at the slightest external provocation. Hence, extreme caution is required in the use of such circumstantial evidence.

However, a thorough study of the seismic history appears to confirm that the 1918 shock was probably the largest earthquake during the 360 years of recorded history of the settlement.

ESTIMATION OF EARTHQUAKE RISK

Suppose that the 1918 earthquake is accepted as our critical design earthquake, i.e. that the bridge will be designed to withstand a seismic event of the same size.

If we assume that the mean return period of this event is T_c = 360 years we may estimate the earthquake risk for different design periods, using the Large-Earthquake Model (Chapter 8). Thus, if the bridge is designed for an effective period of service of 50 years the earthquake risk is:

$R_{50}(360) = 1 - \exp(-50/360) = 0.13$

meaning that there is a probability of 13% that the bridge will be subjected to a design earthquake during its projected period of operation.

If the design period is lengthened to 100 years we have:

$R_{100}(360) = 1 - \exp(-100/360) = 0.24$

On the other hand, if the design earthquake had a different mean return period, say T_c = 100 years, the risk would go up appreciably. Thus, for D = 50 years we have:

$R_{50}(100) = 1 - \exp(-50/100) = 0.39$

If the design period is lengthened to D = 100 years, equal to the mean return period, we obviously have $R_T(T) = 1 - e^{-1} = 0.633$. In this case there is more than an even chance that the bridge will be subjected at least once to a design earthquake.

The above preliminary considerations provide the necessary quantitative background information for "engineering judgment". How much of a gamble is the designer willing to take? How good is the historical evidence, including the fact that the Ermita del Carmen remained standing until 1918 and that there has been no larger shock since 1918? How representative is the 360-year period of historical record?

The bridge will have a volume of traffic of several million cars per year. Even if the bridge resists the earthquake with only minor damage, the interruption of traffic may be costly. At this point the designer may decide that a more detailed study of the earthquake risk is warranted.

"PESSIMISTIC" EARTHQUAKE RISK

In order to compute the risk from available intrumental data we list all Guatemalan epicenters for the last 60 years, as determined by the U.S. Coast and Geodetic Survey (NOAA). We make the tentative assumption that each epicenter is the source of a Poisson process of rate unity. If any epicenter has been active more than once the effect of two or more Poisson processes of rate unity is the same as one Poisson process of rate two or more. Further we assume one magnitude distribution for shallow inland epicenters and another for offshore and intermediate shocks, with β-values of 1.8 and 1.9 (determined experimentally).

As a next step, we associate each epicenter with a critical magnitude as a function of its epicentral distance to the site of the bridge. For this purpose we may use any of a number of empirical attenuation functions, such as [3.7]. Hence, for a given critical acceleration a_c at the site we may compute the set of critical magnitudes $[M_i]$ corresponding to the set of epicentral distance $[\Delta_i]$ in the sample.

Finally, for each epicenter we compute the probability p_i that the magnitude M_i not be exceeded during a unit time interval (the unit here is the total timespan covered by the data):

$$p_i = 1 - \exp(-\beta M_i)$$

where β is 1.9 or 1.8, depending on whether the i-th epicenter is offshore or inland. The computer program used for this purpose has a special "region tag" which can be preset for sorting the earthquakes by regions with different β-values. The β-values for each region are computed in the same run, using the relationship $\beta = 1/\overline{M}$.

The earthquake risk is estimated by summing the logarithms of the p_i (cf. eq.9.4):

$$\log(1 - R_D) = D \sum_i \log p_i \qquad\qquad [10.3]$$

where R_D is the earthquake risk for a design period of D units (each time unit being equal to the data period of record). In the present case our time unit is 70 years and the design period is 50 years; hence $D = 50/70 = 0.714$.

The result of this computation for different critical accelerations a_c is shown of Fig.10.4. The resulting curve is labelled "compound risk" because of the use of a composition method in its estimation. This curve is conservative, since it assigns all epicenters

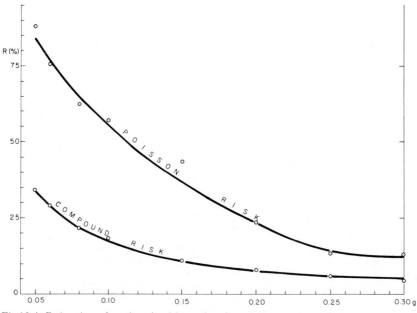

Fig.10.4. Estimation of earthquake risk per decade vs. design acceleration, for two sets of assumptions.

an equal chance of generating a large earthquake. Since the sample contains earthquakes of different magnitudes, a majority of which are smaller than the critical magnitude M_i, an unknown proportion of the epicenters will have maximum magnitudes below M_i and thus will never be able to generate a shock as large as M_i. This unknown proportion will increase with M_i, so that the estimate becomes increasingly more conservative for higher values of a_c.

"POISSONIAN" RISK

A further estimate of earthquake risk may be obtained as follows. Let a_c be the critical acceleration at the site; then, from the previous computation we may easily obtain the number of times n that the acceleration has been exceeded during the period of record, assuming that the transfer function [3.7] is correct. Then, if each exceedance is an independent, Poisson-distributed event we may write:

$$R_T = \text{Prob}\ \{n \geqslant 1\} = 1 - e^{-n} \tag{10.4}$$

or, if D is the design period:

$$R_D = 1 - \exp\left(-n\,D/T\right) \tag{10.5}$$

On account of the peculiar distribution of epicenters and magnitudes in Guatemala it turns out that the Poissonian estimate is consistently higher than the compound estimate. In other words, the critical acceleration of, say, $0.1\,g$ should have been exceeded 12 times during the past 70 years.

INCORPORATION OF HISTORICAL DATA

The preceding estimate seems unrealistic, since there are at most two documented instances (1917 and 1918) of exceedance of $0.1\,g$ in Guatemala City since 1902. What is the source of the discrepancy between the estimate and the historical record? This discrepancy must be due to local soil conditions in Guatemala City.

Unfortunately, data on soil response are very scarce. However, an accelerometer has functioned at the Guatemala National Observatory since 1947, with a very delicate trigger setting, so that about ten records have fortunately been obtained. These records consistently show about half the acceleration that would be expected from the Esteva—Rosenblueth (1964) formula for hard ground. For the 1950 earthquake ($M = 7$) the recorded peak acceleration was $0.037\,g$ while the computed acceleration was $0.08\,g$. Similarly, the National Observatory utilized local observations to estimate an acceleration of $0.07\,g$ for the 1942 earthquake, largest since 1917; but the computed Esteva—Rosenblueth value was $0.16\,g$.

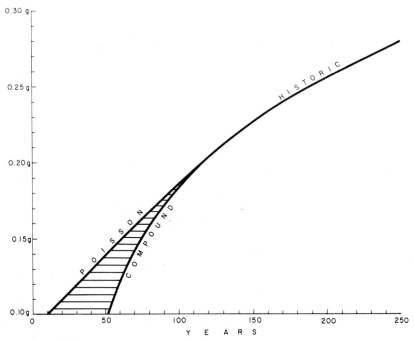

Fig.10.5. Estimation of mean return periods vs. design acceleration, for two sets of assumptions discussed in the text. The shaded region was recommended for design.

In conclusion, local soil conditions in Guatemala City indicate a 50% reduction in the predicted accelerations for hard ground from eq. 3.7.

We may now plot the expected return periods for the two original methods of estimation (Fig.10.5). The right-hand branch is obtained by assuming a return period of 160 years (half the total historic record) to the 1918 earthquake with estimated acceleration of 0.25 *g*. In this fashion, we have incorporated a safety factor of at least two, at every critical point in the estimation.

SUMMARY OF RISK ESTIMATES

The object of this exercise is not so much to reach an estimate with any pretense of accuracy (this is ruled out by the limitations of the data), as to gain some insight into the effect of various assumptions on the probabilities of earthquake occurrence.

We may summarize our discussion of earthquake risk for Guatemala City in graph 10.5. This graph shows the estimated mean return periods for various design accelerations. We have found this type of presentation to be effective in terms of engineering decision-making.

What can we say about the shaded area in Fig.10.5? Certainly, it represents a conservative estimate of earthquake risk in terms of exceedances during the past 70 years. It is conservative with respect to the Esteva–Rosenblueth (1964) formula for hard ground, which in turn appears to be conservative for soil conditions in Guatemala City. Finally, it appears to be conservative in terms of the 360-year historical record.

Is it too conservative? A design period of 50 years for the bridge would yield a seismic design factor of 0.10 g, while a design period of 100 years will yield 0.20 g. These figures represent an acceptable range for a basis of design; they already contain a factor of safety whose exact size is unknown, but which we hope is at least of the order of two. In view of the history of damaging earthquakes at the site, no lesser criterion would be acceptable for an engineering project of this magnitude and importance.

The 1918 earthquake attained an acceleration of 0.20–0.25 g, which exceeds the proposed design acceleration. In the case of nuclear reactors, designing for the maximum credible earthquake would be mandatory. This means that a design acceleration of at least 0.25 g would be required if the structure to be erected were a nuclear reactor. This is because the negative value assigned to the eventuality of failure of a nuclear reactor is extremely high, much higher than the negative value assigned to the failure of a highway bridge.

CHAPTER 11

Strategies for Control of Earthquake Hazard

INTRODUCTION

Between 1965 and 1968 there was a considerable resurgence of interest in earthquake prediction, particularly in the United States. In May, 1965 the Panel on Earthquake Prediction appointed by the President's Office of Science and Technology recommended a national program of ten years towards the development of practical methods for predicting earthquakes. On June 11, 1965 the U.S. Coast and Geodetic Survey was asked to prepare a "management plan" for such a national program. This request apparently was one of the factors which accelerated the formation of the new Environmental Science Services Administration (ESSA), incorporating the former Coast and Geodetic Survey. On April 26, 1966 an inter-agency Working Group for Earthquake Research was established with the participation of representatives of ESSA, NASA, the National Science Foundation, the Geological Survey, the Advanced Research Projects Agency, the Atomic Energy Commission, the Bureau of Reclamation, the Army Corps of Engineers, the Department of Agriculture and the Department of Housing and Urban Development. This working Group produced a proposal in June, 1967 recommending a budget of 218 million dollars for a 10-year period. In addition, the report noted, "the National Academy of Engineering formed a Committee on Earthquake Engineering in 1966 to formulate an earthquake engineering program and that Committee has advised our Working Group that they will recommend a program substantially greater than presented here."

Two years later the National Earthquake Prediction Program was quietly shelved, and has not been heard of since.

INITIAL STRATEGIES

Whatever the reasons for this apparent reversal of national policy, its implications went deeper than a mere tactical retreat. The prestige of the academic community had been thrown behind the project. Failure to muster support in Congress meant, in some ways, a disavowal of U.S. scientific leadership. It was perhaps the earliest indication of a massive retreat from the high levels of public support which scientific research had enjoyed during the decade of the 1960's.

This occurred at a time of exceptional renovation and productivity in the earth sciences. New ideas were being generated at a fantastic rate. Seen from the scientist's point of view, the public apathy and antagonism appeared incomprehensible. Many scientists were convinced that a 10-year "crash program" of earthquake prediction was not only exciting but timely, and should catch the fancy of the public.

Did the strategy fail because it was unsound to begin with? It was not the first of its kind. In 1961 a group for earthquake prediction research was formed in Japan. This group proposed a "Blueprint" for future research, which succeeded in obtaining support from the Science Council of Japan. After the Niigata Earthquake of 1964 a Government program for five years was proposed, and was finally approved and funded for more than 10 million dollars.

The Japanese program involved the following points:

I. *Coastal deformation*
    a. Tide-gage stations.
    b. Geodetic measurements.
    c. Continuous recording of ground deformation.

II. *Seismicity*
    a. Observatory studies.
    b. Micro-earthquakes.
    c. Changes in seismic velocities.
    d. Active faulting and folding.

III. *Geothermal and rock mechanics studies*
    a. Heat flow measurements.
    b. Rock deformation in the laboratory.

IV. *Magnetism and telluric currents*
    a. Magnetic surveys.
    b. Secular variations.
    c. Differential magnetometer observations.
    d. Conductivity anomalies.

V. *Data processing center*

It is interesting to compare this outline with the project prepared by the U.S. Working Group for Earthquake Prediction. The American project was not only much larger but also more comprehensive, apparently including all scientific aspects related to earthquake research. The project was divided into five categories, as follows:

I. *Field Studies*
    a. Detailed geologic mapping.
    b. Rates of deformation.

    c.   Tectonic mechanisms.
    d.   Gravity surveys.
    e.   Aeromagnetic surveys.
    f.   Seismic profiles.
    g.   Miscellaneous geophysical studies.
    h.   Aftershock studies.
    i.   Geodetic surveys.

II   *Instrumentation of seismic zones*
    a.   Micro-earthquake arrays.
    b.   Other "cluster" instruments.
    c.   Special survey devices.
    d.   Deep hole instruments.
    e.   Telemetry.
    f.   Systems operation and management.
    g.   Moveable "clusters".
    h.   Central analysis system.

III.   *Physical basis of earthquakes*
    a.   Theoretical studies.
    b.   Experiments in fracture and flow.
    c.   Field measurements.
    d.   Seismic source studies.
    e.   Seismic propagation studies.

IV.   *Earthquake engineering*
    a.   Seismic zoning.
    b.   Soil mechanics and foundation engineering.
    c.   Structural dynamics.
    d.   Design techniques.
    e.   Economic studies.

V.   *Miscellaneous projects*
    a.   Tsunami studies.
    b.   Heat flow.
    c.   Tide gages.
    d.   Psychological and practical aspects.
    e.   Analysis and prediction.
    f.   Earthquakes and fluid injection.

The most notable contribution of the program was the idea of "seismic clusters", or arrays of instruments to be assembled in certain active earthquake areas for the purpose of monitoring all kinds of geophysical variables simultaneously. The most specific part of the program concerned earthquake engineering; this part was ultimately successful in obtaining support.

It is interesting that the Working Group attached to its report a section entitled "Alternatives", which begins as follows:

"Using existing knowledge, without a major research program much could be done to reduce the potential loss of life and property from future earthquakes . . ."

ALTERNATIVE STRATEGIES

The report proceeded to outline the following alternatives:

(A) If the requested amount of 218 million dollars is granted, the "probable potential loss" of a great earthquake in the United States (estimated at around 20 billion dollars) could be reduced by at least 25% by the end of the decade.

(B) If the budget is cut to 73 million dollars in 10 years, the 25% reduction in earthquake damage would probably be delayed 50 years or more.

(C) If the budget is held at a level of 100 million dollars the 25% objective could be achieved in 30 years. The program states the belief that "if a 30-year program is adopted, there is greater than a 50-% chance that a great earthquake will occur before the program accomplishes its objectives".

It appears that none of these proposed strategies appealed particularly to the legislators, since none was adopted. In retrospect, the alternatives simply lacked credibility. As guesses go, they may well have been correct; but guesses they undoubtedly were. In that case, how much guesswork was involved in the more technical aspects of the proposal?

The lessons to be derived from this exercise are simple and straightforward. A scientific strategy must be based on knowledge already acquired and securely held, not on knowledge hopefully to be gained in the future.We cannot tell how, or by what means, future knowledge may (or may not) be generated. While the Working Group on Earthquake Prediction was making projections at a range of 30—50 years the concept of plate tectonics was being developed; and this concept has had a considerable impact on the estimation of earthquake risk, which was unforeseen by the planners.

The only sound strategy appears to consist in the support of existing research groups, without attempting to set deadlines on the production of any specific discoveries. Scientific history shows that important results were often produced simultaneously by independent investigators; this indicates that the major advances in research are critical events, which happen according to an internal logic of their own.

PREDICTION VERSUS PREVENTION?

How important is it actually to predict earthquakes? Indeed, if the great 1964 Alaska earthquake could have been predicted about a hundred people killed in that disaster might be alive today; but perhaps twice as many might be dead as a consequence of traffic disruptions and other dislocations caused by the prediction itself. As for damage, it would be difficult to show how a warning could have made much of a difference, even if it had come a week or two in advance of the earthquake. Any savings due to preventive measures would have been offset by the economic consequences of an evacuation of cities and coastal towns.

This argument presupposes that prediction of earthquakes (in the sense of forecasting their date, location and magnitude) can be achieved to any useful degree of accuracy. But even this is by no means certain. The idea of earthquake forecasting hinges on the eventual discovery of some premonitory effect, such as ground tilt, small foreshocks, changes in seismic velocities, electromagnetic effects, and so on. Such premonitory effects do exist; but they either produce too small and ambiguous signatures, or the signal begins too early or too late for effective utilization. The great 1960 Chile earthquake was preceded by large foreshocks for a period of 33 hours; yet there appears to be no indication during that time that the earth "knew" a much larger shock was still coming.

In conclusion, on the basis of current knowledge there is a definite possibility that deterministic forecasting of earthquakes is not feasible. An analogy with weather forecasting seems probably valid in the sense that regional increases in seismicity could be predicted if the stresses in and around the region could be effectively monitored. For example, Turkey is suffering from unusual earthquake activity since 1939, while northern Chile has been relatively quiescent since about 1880; such periods of abnormal seismicity could probably be correlated with regional stress anomalies.

Yet forecasting the time and place of a specific earthquake is another matter. Even the best weather forecasting system cannot predict the place where lightning is going to strike. Protection against lightning must rely on other methods.

AN EARTHQUAKE STRATEGY

Table 11.1 shows the incidence of damaging earthquakes throughout the world for a period of 20 years. The following countries have suffered catastrophic earthquakes (in excess of 1,000 dead) during this particular period: Argentina, Burma, Chile, China, Colombia, Ecuador, Greece, India, Iran, Italy, Japan, Nepal, Pakistan, Peru, Taiwan, Turkey and U.S.S.R.

Thus, the seismic history (cf. Part III) seems to afford a reasonably good projection of where major damaging earthquakes are going to occur, even for the relatively short period of 20 years. In most of these countries the net earthquake risk has increased in recent decades, as a result of the accelerating trend of population growth and urbanization.

TABLE 11.1

Earthquake casualties[1], and number of damaging earthquakes, by country, during a 20-year period from January 1, 1949 to January 1, 1969

Country	No. of persons believed killed	Total no. of damaging earthquakes[2]
Afghanistan	15	2
Aleutian Islands	240	–
Albania	33	6
Algeria	280	14
Argentina	5,100	8
Australia	–	4
Austria	–	2
Azores Islands	18	–·
Belgium	3	–
Bolivia	12	3
Brazil	–	1
Bulgaria	100	–
Burma	6,000	1
Canada	34	2
Cape Verde Islands	–	1
Caroline Islands	–	1
Chile	28,000	32
China (mainland)	156,000	5
Colombia	1,200	15
Costa Rica	–	4
Cuba	15	–
Cyprus	–	3
Dominican Republic	73	1
Ecuador	5,500	11
Egypt	–	1
Ethiopia	–	3
Fiji	–	1
France	–	1
Germany	–	1
Ghana	16	–
Greece (inc. Aegean Is., Crete)	1,500	47
Guatemala	–	6
Haiti	–	4
Hawaii	–	4
Honduras	53	–
Hungary	–	2
India (excl. Kashmir)	6,500	6
Indonesia	220	11
Iran	7,500	29
Iraq	6	–
Israel	250	–
Italy	1,800	15
Jamaica	–	1
Japan (excl. Ryukyu Islands)	15,800	35

TABLE 11.1 (continued)

Country	No. of persons believed killed	Total no. of damaging earthquakes[2]
Kashmir	−	1
Lebanon	−	2
Lesser Antilles	1	−
Libya	−	1
Malagasy Republic	−	1
Malaysia	−	1
Manchuria	58	−
Mexico	460	29
Mongolia	−	1
Morocco	−	2
Nepal	2,000	1
New Zealand	1,000	4
Nicaragua	500	2
Oceania	17	−
Oman	500	−
Pakistan	40,000	5
Panama	1	−
Papua and New Guinea	−	3
Peru	2,200	18
Philippines	36	6
Puerto Rico	70	−
Rumania	1,100	−
Ryukyu Islands	−	1
El Salvador	410	5
Solomon Islands	−	2
South Africa	6	−
Spain	−	3
Sudan	−	1
Switzerland	4	−
Syria	−	1
Taiwan	3,300	12
Tibet	50	1
Trinidad	−	2
Tunisia	−	2
Turkey	46,400	54
Uganda	−	2
USA.	160	38
U.S.S.R.	15,000	2
Venezuela	400	8
Yugoslavia	1	20
Zaire	−	3
Total	349,942 (350,000)	521

[1] According to Montandon.
[2] The dashes in the last column mean "not known" or "not exactly known".

Because of rural—urban migration large belts of substandard housing have formed around many cities. The progress achieved in engineering design and construction techniques is not adequately reflected in the quality of the average dwelling unit throughout the world. In some countries the standards of housing are actually lower than they have ever been before.

This situation is an obvious cause of the wariness with which the insurance profession has approached the problem of earthquake hazard. Earthquake coverage is largely inexistent, and the victims of seismic damage must rely on measures of national and international relief. Each new earthquake is treated as a separate emergency, and the relief and reconstruction measures tend to be improvised anew in every case, leading to costly and ineffective solutions.

A modern earthquake strategy must begin with the prevention of earthquake losses. This may perhaps be achieved most efficiently through insurance techniques. The insurance profession is familiar with these techniques; it alone can propose incentives for preventive measures which the individuals or countries (because of the remoteness of the risk) are often reluctant to adopt on their own.

Protection costs money; but the absence of protection spells disaster. This is the classical situation where spreading the risk evenly will lessen the burden, not only for the affected country but also for the world community at large. Earthquake insurance premiums may be made to vary according to the construction: this provides a tangible, immediate incentive for improving the quality of substandard housing, and for stimulating new research on earthquake risk.

One should remember that the Congress of the United States was unimpressed with a relatively modest proposal for research, which promised to reduce substantially the earthquake hazard in that country. Other countries of smaller resources cannot be expected to invest in long-range earthquake programs either. Under these circumstances, the insistence on earthquake prediction as a first-priority objective is both scientifically unsound and tactically wrong.

In this book we have presented some preliminary methods of estimating earthquake risk, on the basis of available data. Earthquake engineering tells how to diagnose and prevent earthquake hazards; on the whole, the proven record of earthquake-designed buildings under actual earthquake conditions has been excellent. Risk estimation plus structural guidelines imply the possibility of effective design against seismic forces. Nevertheless, it seems likely that no real progress will be made towards the control of earthquake hazards until the creation of broad regional or international systems of earthquake insurance. Such systems are urgently needed to provide a rational basis of coordination for future seismological research, and for all other efforts in the long fight against natural disasters. To a large proportion of humanity earthquakes mean an ever-present, growing threat. We cannot know when the next large shock will strike: the ground under our feet is less solid than we think.

PART III

WORLD SEISMICITY

*'Tis since the earthquake now
eleven years.*

Romeo and Juliet

CHAPTER 12

The Data

SEISMOGRAPHS

The seismograph is an instrument which measures the motion of the ground. Ideally, this requires a fixed reference point. As such a reference point is unavailable, it is replaced by an inertial reference system, such as the mass of a pendulum.

When the ground moves under a pendulum, the mass of the pendulum stays behind. This is equivalent to moving the center of gravity of the pendulum from its rest position. The pendulum starts swinging according to the well-known differential equation of motion (Richter, 1958):

$$\ddot{u} + 2h\omega\dot{u} + \omega^2 u = -\ddot{x} \qquad [12.1]$$

where u is the displacement of the ground. The deflection x of the pendulum can be recorded by means of a variety of transducers, including mechanical levers, light beams, moving coils in a magnetic field, moving condenser plates, variable transformers, and so on.

Strain meters

A strain meter is a pendulum of infinite period (Fig.12.1). It consists of a rigid bar suspended from one point. The relative displacement between the bar and the ground is measured by means of a variable condenser. The original design is due to Benioff, who obtained a sensitivity of 10^{-9} radian with a quartz bar of 25 m length.

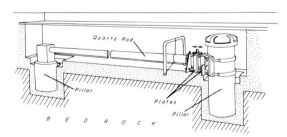

Fig.12.1 A drawing of the original Benioff rod extensometer. In the standard design the tube is 25 m long and is made of sections of fused quartz pipe cemented together. The transducer may be of the variable capacitance type.

Accelerometers

The properties of a seismograph depend primarily on the period T_0 of the pendulum. If T_0 is short as compared to the period of ground motion, eq. 12.1 shows that the deflection x of the instrument will be roughly proportional to the ground acceleration $\ddot{u}$. Hence the name "accelerometers" given to seismometers of very short period (Fig.12.2).

Accelerometer records are of particular interest to earthquake engineers, since the ground acceleration is proportional to the force transmitted to structures during earthquakes. A low-gain accelerometer record is called a "strong-motion accelerogram". The

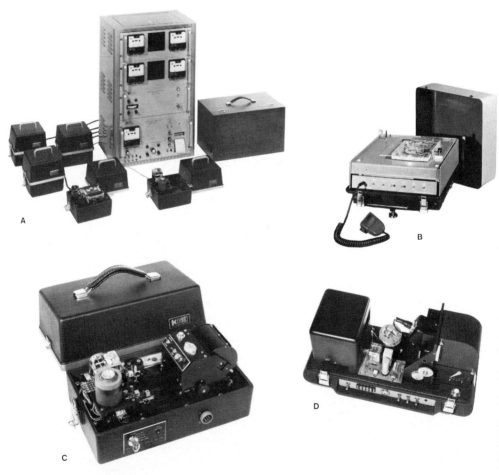

Fig.12.2. Some commercial strong-motion instruments. A. Kinemetrics SMA-3 central recording and playback unit, with 4 remote units and trigger. B. Teledyne/Geotech MTS-200 cartridge Accelecorder. C. Teledyne/Geotech RFT-250 strong-motion accelerograph. D. Kinemetrics SMA-1 strong-motion accelerograph with two-component trigger. (Courtesy of Kinemetrics, Inc. and Teledyne/Geotech.)

first such accelerogram was obtained for the Long Beach, California earthquake of 1933. During the El Centro, California earthquake of 1940 a set of accelerograms was recorded which served as a model of near-field ground motion for many years.

Accelerograms are used by engineers to compute the theoretical response of a one-degree of freedom structure with variable amounts of damping. The response spectra of such ideal structures provide some information about predicting the behavior of real buildings in earthquakes.

Velocity and displacement seismographs

If the period T_0 of the seismograph is very long as compared to the period of ground motion, the instrument response will be approximately proportional to ground displacement u. This is intuitively clear, as the pendulum has no time to react to the ground

Fig. 12.3. Portable "backpack" seismograph. The instrument has an internal clock and can operate up to 7 days without recharging. (Courtesy of Kinemetrics, Inc.)

motion; hence the net deflections are equal to the displacement of the ground.[1]

On the other hand, if the period is of the same order as the period of ground motion the response of the instrument will be intermediate between an acceleration response and a displacement response. It can be shown that such an instrument records a signal proportional to *ground velocity* $\dot{u}$. Velocity seismographs typically have their peak response in the vicinity of 1 Hz and are particularly suited for detecting body waves in the far field. For this purpose, high gains (50,000–500,000) are desirable (Fig.12.3).

Displacement seismographs of the pendulum type have periods $T_0 = 20$–200 sec and are used principally to record surface waves. They are usually operated at low gains (1,000–2,000), since the surface waves of earthquakes may attain large amplitudes. Mantle Rayleigh waves from the 1964 Alaska earthquake attained amplitudes of 30 cm at distances of more than 5,000 km. The earliest instance of record of such large surface waves was during the 1868 Chile earthquake, which was observed on the zenithal telescope at Pulkovo Observatory, Russia.

Exploration seismographs

Ordinary seismographs and accelerographs are pendulums constrained to move in a fixed plane. Hence three separate instruments are required in order to record the particle motion of the ground in all three Cartesian coordinates.

In the case of exploration seismology, only one component of ground motion (the vertical) is commonly used. Short-period seismographs (called *geophones*) are strung out on a recording line at equal spacing intervals. The finished seismogram contains both the instant of the explosion (cap break), and the traces of arrival of seismic waves at each channel. Hence the travel times can be directly read off and plotted.

This method has been in use for about 40 years, principally in mapping subsurface sedimentary layers for purposes of oil exploration. The basic methods (refraction and reflection) have not changed appreciably. Most of the advances have been in data processing. Magnetic tape recording is used in combination with various analog and digital filtering and playback techniques, in order to facilitate the interpretation and plotting of geological sections from the seismograms. Deep seismic sounding is used to explore the structure of the earth's crust, in conjunction with laboratory simulation techniques (Fig.12.4).

EARTHQUAKE DATA PROCESSING

A seismograph records the arrival time of a seismic wave front at some station located on the earth's surface. It cannot record the location or the instant of initiation of the

---

[1] Many rigorous developments of seismometer theory are available. For an introductory discussion see Richter (1958).

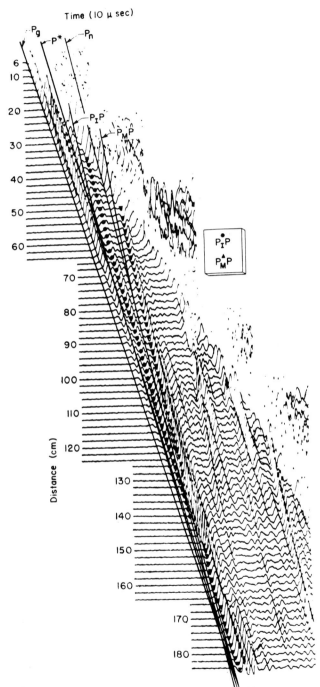

Fig.12.4. Model seismogram for a two-layer crust, showing the cross-over between the direct wave (*Pg*), the first refraction (*P**) and the refracted wave in the top of the mantle (*Pn*), all between 170 and 180 cm. Two deep reflections are also shown (Healy, 1967).

actual earthquake at a distance. These parameters must be inferred by comparing seismograms written at many stations, preferably well-distributed all around the epicenter. In
other words, the location process of earthquakes is a statistical process.

The location procedure in current use was largely developed by Jeffreys (1936); the
Jeffreys-Bullen tables, giving values of travel-time vs. distance, have been in continuous
use since 1935. Controlled experiments using explosive sources have since revealed the
existence of systematic errors in current procedures, largely due to the presence of
incorrect assumptions about the structure of the data. But it turns out that the scatter in
travel times in the real earth is quite large, so that the Jeffreys-Bullen error (though
probably real) is within the noise of the data.

Worldwide epicenter determination services are maintained by NOAA (National
Oceanic and Atmospheric Administration) of the United States, and by the International
Seismological Centre in Scotland. The latter also publishes a yearly catalogue of earth-
quake readings reported from stations throughout the world.

Large earthquakes ($M \geqslant 6$) prior to 1954 were located by Gutenberg and Richter
(1954), whose numbered yellow working pads are still kept on file at the Seismological
Laboratory in Pasadena. Gutenberg devised an ingeniously simple improvement on location procedures: instead of applying a least-square solution to travel times he plotted the
station residuals as a function of azimuth, and adjusted a sine curve to them (Fig.12.5).
The amplitude of the sine curve is the latitude correction, and the phase is the longitude
correction. This method, which tends to eliminate the bias due to inhomogeneous geo-

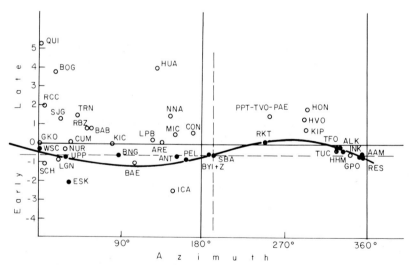

Fig.12.5. Sine-wave adjustment of the epicenter for the 1970 Peru earthquake, by the Gutenberg
method (travel-time residuals in seconds). This method permits a selective improvement over the
least-square solution, as early arrivals are given a greater weight than late one. The indicated epicentral
shift is 22 km toward the coast and the origin time shift is -0.6 sec.

graphical distribution of stations, has yet to be adopted by the international agencies. As a result, spurious azimuthal error terms are introduced, which are sometimes mistaken for sinusoidal "source corrections" and "station corrections" (Lomnitz, 1971).

The total epicentral error in an earthquake location is generally unknown; it tends to be larger than the "standard errors" given by the reporting agencies. For well-controlled artificial sources, such as the LONG SHOT nuclear explosion in 1965, "blind" location procedures were in error by about a quarter of a degree. The error may be as much as half a degree for less well-recorded shocks, particularly in the Southern Hemisphere.

When the earthquake occurs within a tight local network the epicenter may usually be located to within 5–10 km, and exceptionally to the nearest kilometer, if there is a station at close range and if the region has been "calibrated" by means of artificial explosions.

The computed origin time of an earthquake is not independent of the computed epicenter: errors in either one will cause errors in the other. The mean standard deviation of travel times of controlled explosion sources is of order 2 sec, and their range of effective fluctuations is about 9 sec at all distances.

Magnitude determinations are less standardized than are epicenter determinations, though a great deal has been written on the subject and there have been sporadic attempts at uniformity. The international agencies tend to use body-wave magnitude m, but the majority of users (including the engineering profession) still abides with the surface-wave magnitude M as originally defined by Richter. Conversion formulas exist, but the two measures are not physically equivalent.

In either case, azimuthal variations may easily exceed half a magnitude unit. Averaging the reported magnitudes from several stations will be helpful, but will not guarantee a consistent estimate. Body-wave magnitudes from large earthquakes recorded at near stations are sometimes grossly underestimated, when a small foreshock is mistaken for the main shock.

Local earthquakes which occur within a tight network of stations may usually be determined to the nearest tenth of magnitude. In all other cases, Gutenberg and Richter (1954) adopted the practice of reporting to the nearest quarter-magnitude. Computer processing has done away with this practice without improving on the precision of magnitude determinations, with the result that one can no longer tell at a glance how accurate a reported magnitude is meant to be.

ARRAY TECHNOLOGY

The most important advance in seismic data processing since the days of Gutenberg and Richter has been in the field of seismic arrays. The use of such arrays has caused a spectacular rise in the seismic detection level, to the point where events of magnitude 4 can be routinely detected anywhere in the world.

The principle of an array is the simultaneous central processing of several detectors on-line, as had been done years before in oil prospecting. Obviously, the scale of earth-quake arrays is much larger than a line of geophones in geophysical prospecting. The LASA array of Montana (Fig.12.6) has a diameter of 200 km; the Berkeley array spans a length of 250 km along the San Andreas Fault.

Fig.12.6. Aerial view of one of the 21 subarrays in LASA. Each subarray has a diameter of 7 km and contains 25 buried seismometers. (Courtesy of LASA.)

In some cases the arrays are simply used as telemetry facilities, and no special signal conditioning or processing is done. The more sophisticated arrays have on-line lags and signal cross-correlation, so that the array may be "steered" and sharply focused in a given downward direction. Ideally this system should produce phenomenal gains in signal/noise ratio as well as resolution; the theory is analogous to that of the radio telescope. In actual practice there are severe limitations, due to the shallow and crustal inhomogeneities across the array.

Space technology has had an increasing impact on seismology. The old problem of local timekeeping and mail handling of undeveloped photographic records is being solved by inexpensive telemetry units. Self-contained seismographic stations, powered by solar panels, are successfully operating around the Gulf of California, Mexico (Fig.12.7). Low-

Fig.12.7. Solar-powered autonomous seismic station of the Baja California, Mexico network (cooperative program Univ. of Mexico–Univ. of California–Caltech; Photograph by C.R. Allen). .

cost, printed-circuit amplifiers are replacing the old mechanical or optical lever systems in the recording room. Even the old problem of local timekeeping, which haunts the national seismographic services in many countries, is being solved through the increased availability of time-signal broadcasts at various frequencies. The ultra-low frequency American station WWVB, which broadcasts continuous date-time code on 60 kHz, can be recorded around the clock in a wide geographic area including most of Mexico.

CHAPTER 13

Seismic Regions of the World

INTRODUCTION

The regional nature of earthquakes has been recognized very slowly. In classical times and up to the nineteenth Century it was assumed that earthquakes were about equally likely to happen most anywhere. The Basle earthquake of 1356, the Lisbon disaster of 1755 and British shocks such as gave rise to Shakespeare's seismological references contributed to this early opinion.

The first thorough study of world seismicity from a modern point of view was undertaken by Montessus de Ballore (1907). Davison contributed important historical studies on great earthquakes. Finally, Gutenberg and Richter (1954) published their *Seismicity of the Earth* which is still the authoritative reference on the subject.

Montessus de Ballore gave considerable importance to the relationship between earthquakes and recent geologic structures. His conclusions in this respect still stand. In general, the pattern of world seismicity largely follows the pattern of Cenozoic orogenic belts.

Gutenberg and Richter (1954) classified earthquake regions into seven broad divisions (Table 13.1).

The percentages of world seismicity are based on our energy computations for 1904—1952. Each of the seven divisions above was furthermore subdivided by Gutenberg and Richter (1954), into a total of 51 separate earthquake regions. This regional subdivision was adhered to in this book. It may be used as an initial basis for quantitative work, as the maps show.

TABLE 13.1

Classification of earthquakes (from Gutenberg and Richter, 1954)

Division	% of world seismicity
A. Circum-Pacific Belt	75.6
B. Alpide—Asiatic Belt	22.1
C. Ocean ridges	1.8
D. Continental rifts	0.2
E. Marginal areas	0.2
F. Regions of old seismicity	0.0
G. Stable masses	0.0

REGIONAL DISTRIBUTION

Table 13.2 gives the Gutenberg–Richter (1954) regions, with the major divisions to which they belong. The yearly average energy totals correspond to the period 1904–1952.

During the period of record including the years 1904–1952 the mean annual value of seismic activity has been $2429.34 \cdot 10^{21}$ ergs. This amount represents about the energy of a single shock of magnitude 8.6.

The minimum yearly total occurred in 1930 ($215.13 \cdot 10^{21}$ ergs, or the energy of a shock of magnitude 8.0), and the maximum was registered in 1906 ($12,090.13 \cdot 10^{21}$ ergs, or the energy of a shock of magnitude 9.1). Shocks of magnitude less than 6.5 were not fully represented in these totals; the error corresponding to such omissions was estimated by Gutenberg at less than 4%, which is well within the error of magnitude determinations.

SEISMICITY MAPS

The contour maps presented in this book were obtained by adding the energies of earthquakes which occurred under each square degree of the earth's surface during the period 1904–1952. A list of shocks for this period of time was published by Gutenberg and Richter (1954); no other list as extensive or as homogeneous has been available since that time.

Most seismicity maps show earthquakes as dots or other symbols of varying size, denoting their Richter magnitude. Since the energy of an earthquake is an exponential function of the magnitude, the size of the dots is no trivial matter. Ultimately it becomes desirable to look at the energy release directly, though the details of epicentral location may be lost in the process.

To emphasize the generalized character of these maps, we have not attempted to separate earthquakes by focal depth. The prevailing depths are given in kilometers wherever feasible; when no focal depth is given, the epicenters are presumably shallow or normal. The computation of energies was made through the Richter formula:

$$\log E = 1.5M + 11.4 \tag{13.1}$$

which was preferred for the reason that the magnitudes were also given by the same authority. Revised magnitudes by Richter were used wherever available.

Smoothing of the data prior to contouring was made over a 5° by 5° window, using a curve which gave a weight of 0.5 to the epicentral square degree and weighted the others in proportion to the inverse square of their distance to the epicenter. A special study of the minimum magnitude to be included showed that shocks of magnitude 6.5 and greater had been reasonably well catalogued over the entire world since about 1932. For the period prior to 1930 (and particularly for 1904–1918), earthquakes of magnitude 6.5 may be missing for the more remote regions, although Gutenberg and Richter made an effort to include all such shocks in their list. If the magnitude threshold is lowered to 6.0, the number of missed events becomes considerable.

The result of contouring the energy release for magnitudes of 6.5 and above for the period 1904–1952 may be appreciated in the first chart (Map 1). The contours in this and successive maps are numbered in units of 10^{15} ergs per square kilometer per year.

Map 3 shows the seismic regions of the world in conjunction with population density. This affords an appreciation of problems of earthquake risk. Map 2 gives a survey of the world's main tectonic structures. It is essential to understand that these contour maps must be used with the text and other illustrative material for best results. As an example, Fig.13.1 shows a map of earthquake epicenters for the years 1961–1971 plotted in the conventional manner. A comparison with Maps 1 and 2 brings out similarities as well as important differences. Thus, no epicenters in the eastern United States or northwestern Europe would be inferred from the contour maps. No earthquakes of magnitude 6.5 have occurred in these regions during the present century. Yet smaller earthquakes can and do cause important damage when they occur in the immediate vicinity of population centers (such as Long Beach, California, 1933; Agadir, Morocco, 1960; Skopje, Yugoslavia, 1963, and so on).

In the following, the earthquake regions of the world will be discussed following a plan by Gutenberg and Richter (1954; Map 3). The number of regions was arbitrarily set at 51 on the basis of information available in 1949, when *Seismicity of the Earth* was first

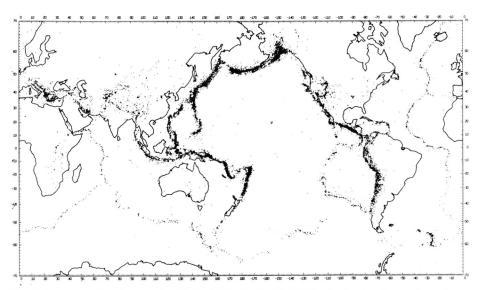

Fig.13.1 A map of epicenters for 1961–1971 (depths 0–100 km), showing the outline of major tectonic plates. (Courtesy of NOAA.)

TABLE 13.2

Major divisions of earthquake regions
(According to Gutenberg and Richter, 1954)

Region	Division		E ($\times$ 10^{21} ergs/year)
1	A	Aleutian Arc	107.71
2	A	Alaska–British Columbia	8.90
3	A	California	21.40
4	A	Baja California	1.64
5	A	Mexico	75.33
6	A	Central America	28.99
7	A	Caribbean Arc	21.38
8	A	South America	358.71
9	A	Patagonia	7.02
10	A	Southern Antilles	20.78
11	A	New Zealand	31.16
12	A	Tonga–Kermadec–Samoa	139.76
13	A	Fiji Is.	0.78
14	A	New Hebrides	99.16
15	A	Solomon–Bismarck Is.	57.79
16	A	New Guinea	53.35
17	A	Caroline Is.	10.45
18	A	Marianas Is.	95.05
19	A	Japan to Kamchatka	335.92
20	A	S. Japan–Ryukyu Is.	101.84
21	A	Formosa	38.79
22	A	Philippines	79.32
23	A	Celebes–Moluccas Is.	117.19
24	A	Sunda Arc	100.99
25	B	Burma arc	10.60
26	B	Himalayan arc	135.81
27	B	China	59.16
28	B	Baikal active zone	155.16
29	B	Iran	18.04
30	B	Asia Minor, Levant, Balkans	26.95
31	B	Western Mediterranean	22.25
32	C	Mid-Atlantic Ridge	5.66
33	C	Indian Ocean	29.47
34	D, E, F	Eastern North America	0.68
35	E	Brazilian Shield	0
36	E, F	Europe	0.02
37	D	East African Rifts	1.39
38	D, E	Australia	2.29
39	C	Central Pacific Ocean	0.24
40	C	Arctic Ridge	0.64
41	E, F	Northeast Asia	0.40
42	E	East Siberian Sea to Baffin Bay	0.76
43	C	South Pacific	1.89
44	C	Galapagos Rise	0.12
45	C	Indian–Antarctic Rise	0.86
46	A	Kurile–Japan deep shocks	10.07
47	B	Baluchistan	2.15
48	B	Pamir–Balkash	33.30
49	C	Eurasian Shield	0.06
50	C	Antarctica	0.01
51	B	Romania	0.80

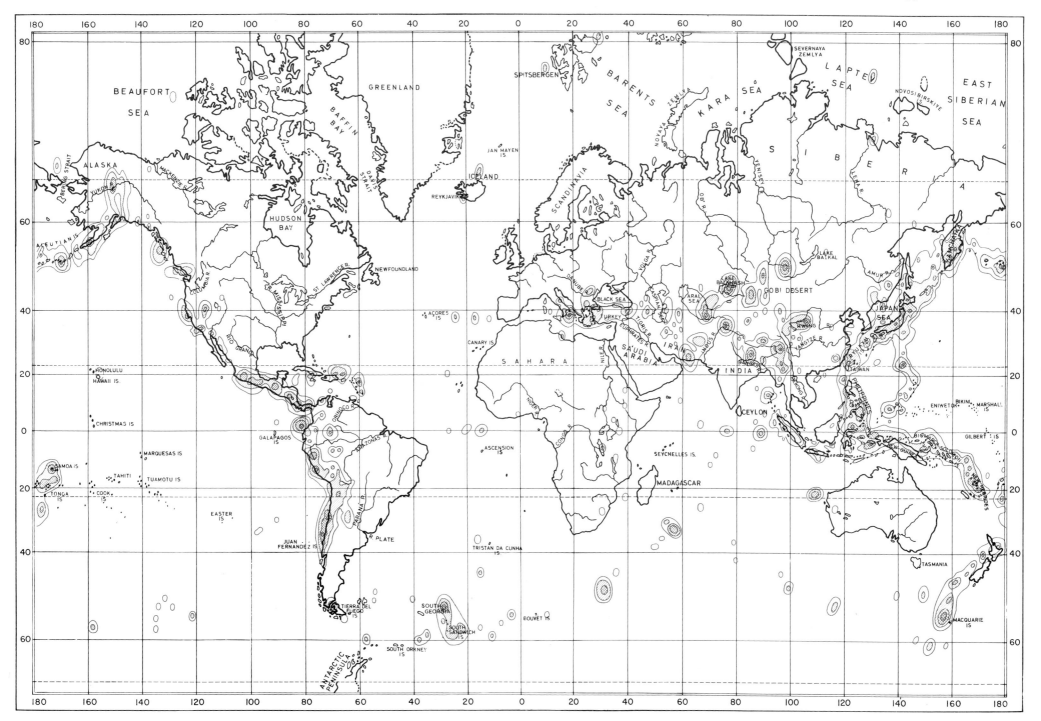

Map.1. World seismicity map. (Seismicity contours are numbered in units of 10^{15} ergs km^{-2} year^{-1}.)

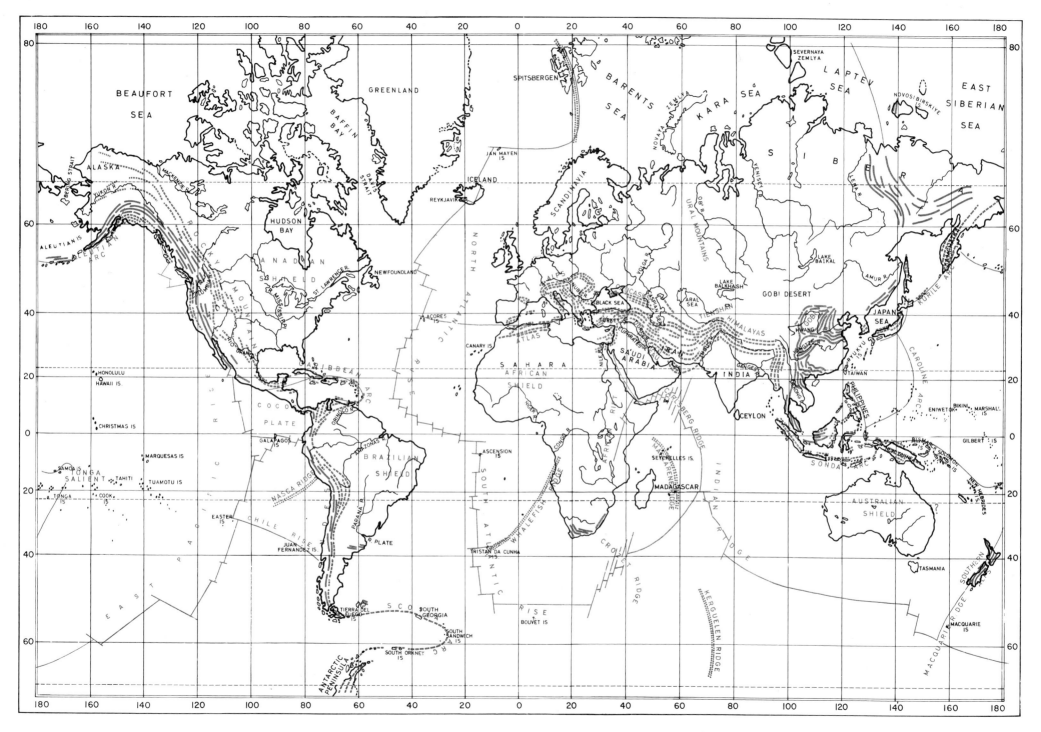

Map.2. World tectonic map.

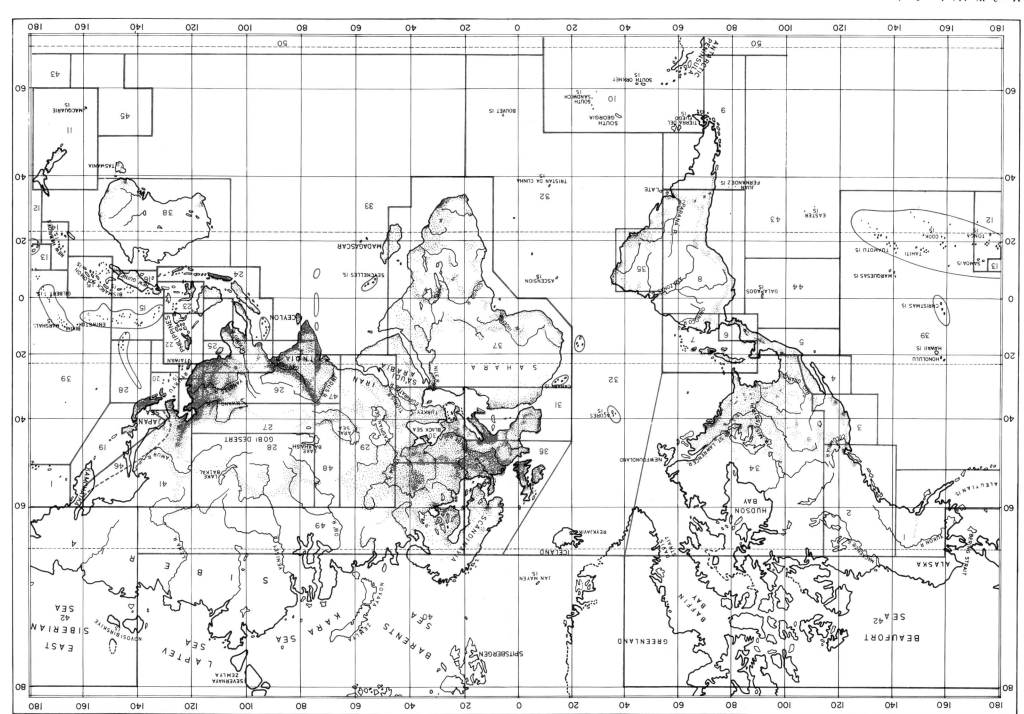

Map 3. World index of regions.

published. Large active regions (such as Region 8) were left as units; others were subdivided in greater detail, perhaps due to better coverage by stations or more favorable location with reference to the Pasadena seismic network. This regionalization has proven exceedingly useful because of its grasp of the basic tectonic units. Only minor revisions have been suggested, to facilitate its use in computer applications. The seismicity figures given in this book are based on the original regionalization by Gutenberg and Richter. Percentages of world seismicity are based on the period 1904–1952.

CHAPTER 14

Circum-Pacific Belt

INTRODUCTION

During the period 1904–1952 more than 75% of the world's earthquake energy release has taken place in a long narrow belt surrounding the Pacific Ocean. This structure is extremely large, since the Pacific Ocean occupies nearly an entire hemisphere; it is also exceedingly complex, being a sequence of arcs, loops, branches and parallel zones of activity. These include the world's most intensely seismic areas; features such as deep-focus earthquakes, island arcs and oceanic trenches are found almost exclusively in the Circum-Pacific Belt.

Actually the so-called "subduction" tectonic structure is neither typical nor exclusive of the Pacific Ocean. Island arcs and deep-focus earthquakes may be found in the Mediterranean. On the other hand, large parts of the Circum-Pacific Belt, including its North American section, lack the attributes of "Pacific" tectonics. Instead of broad generalizations, it would seem preferable to analyze each region on its own terms.

One feature which deserves recognition because of its importance in Pacific Ocean structures is the oceanic trench (Fig.14.1). A trench is a deep, wide furrow which runs roughly parallel to the structural lines in the region. In all cases the presence of oceanic trenches indicates tectonic instability extending into the mantle of the earth (gravity anomalies, volcanism, intermediate earthquakes). These features are displaced from the center of the trench, away from the Pacific Ocean. The trench itself, probably the oldest part of the structure, is the seat of normal-depth earthquakes.

Many geophysicists have remarked on the structural regularities associated with oceanic trenches. Vening Meinesz (1964) attributed them to down-buckling of the earth's crust, due to the presumed convergence of two convection cells in the mantle; Benioff (1955) assumed great faults dipping away from the Pacific Ocean down to depths of 600 km or more. It is usually (but not invariably) true that the earthquake foci become progressively deeper with distance from the trench. However, the intermediate and deep-focus earthquakes appear to cluster around certain disturbed regions of the mantle and do not always follow a single dipping surface. Some epicenters in South America generate earthquakes at all depths between the surface and 200 km or more.

NORTH AMERICA

The North American continent is geologically organized around the nucleus of the

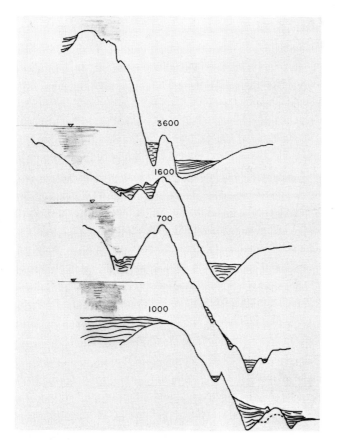

Fig.14.1. Four profiles of the Middle America Trench, lined up to show evolution of landward ridge (depth in meters) and accretion of the continental shelf from the coast of Jalisco (top) to Panama (bottom). (Redrawn after Ross and Shor, 1965.)

Canadian Shield, a large Precambrian peneplain. Around this stable mass are several geologic provinces patterned largely in a succession of broad belts (Fig.14.2).

The most active of these belts is associated with the Circum-Pacific orogeny. It borders the Pacific Ocean from the tip of the Aleutian Island chain to Mexico and beyond. The seismicity in this belt is not evenly distributed, and several successive regions separated by conspicuous gaps can be recognized.

The Rocky Mountains form a slightly older orogeny, and their seismic activity is currently much lower. Other structural divisions will be mentioned under each individual region.

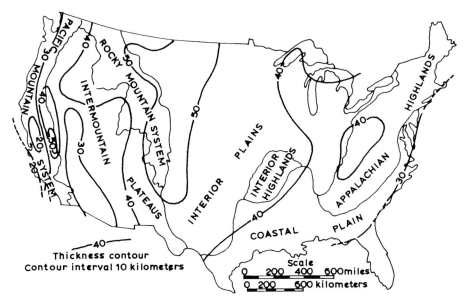

Fig.14.2. Geologic provinces and crustal thickness in km for the United States. (From Healy, 1967.)

Alaska (Region 1: Maps 4 and 5; Table 14.1)

Extension and Seismicity

The first region of Gutenberg and Richter (1954) comprises the State of Alaska with the exception of its northern part, a zone of low seismicity included in the Arctic (Region

TABLE 14.1

Earthquakes of the Aleutian Arc (Region 1)

Date	Epicenter	M	Comments
1901 Dec. 13	Andreanof Islands	7.8	
1902 Jan. 1	Unimak Island	7.8	
1903 Jun. 2	Alaska Peninsula	8.3	depth 100 km
1904 Aug. 27	Alaska Range	8.3	
1905 Feb. 14	Andreanof Islands	7.9	
1906 Aug. 17	Rat Islands	8.3	
1907 Sep. 2	Near Islands	7¾	
1929 Mar. 7	Fox Islands	8.6	
1940 Jul. 14	Rat Islands	7¾	depth 80 km
1964 Mar. 27	Prince William Sound	8.4	130 dead
1965 Feb. 4	Rat Islands	7.9	
1965 Mar. 30	Amchitka Is.	7.5	

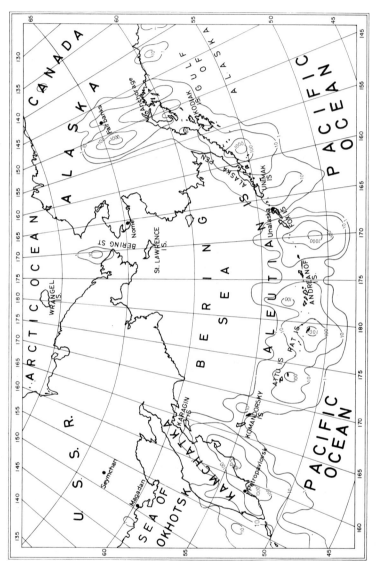

Map 4. Seismicity of the Aleutian Arc: Region 1. (Seismicity contours are numbered in 10^{15} ergs km^{-2} $year^{-1}$.)

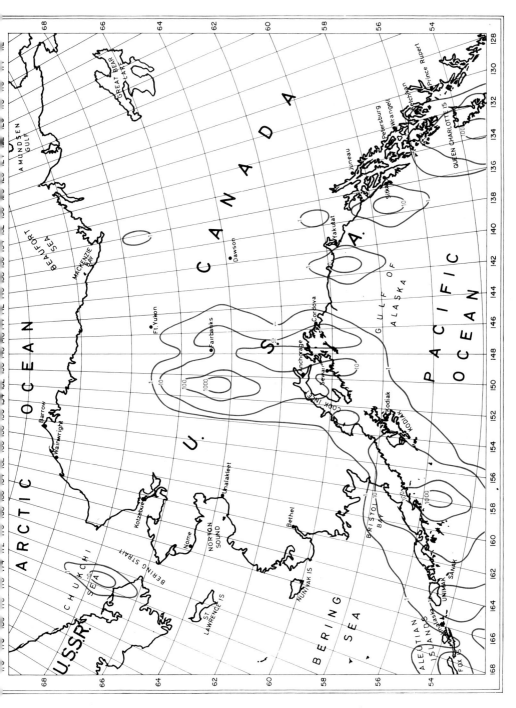

Map 5. Seismicity map of Alaska–Canada: Regions 1–2. (Seismicity contours are numbered in 10^{15} ergs km^{-2} $year^{-1}$.)

42). It is one of the world's major seismic regions and it accounts for 4.4% of the world's activity. The pattern of seismicity follows the arc of the Aleutian Islands and its prolongation into the mainland. The geometric pattern of earthquake distribution is shaped like a perfect arc.

Closer investigation shows that the structure is divided into segments which may have incurred displacements normally to the arc. The major tectonic mechanism is assumed to be large-scale thrusting southward from the Bering Sea over the Pacific plate.

On the Alaskan mainland there are major tectonic features, such as the Denali Fault and the Alaska Range, which parallel the Gulf of Alaska in a broad sweeping curve. Yet the pattern of seismic activity follows the trend of the Aleutian Arc toward the north rather than the structural trends to the south.

Seismic geography

The Aleutian chain begins off the coast of Kamchatka (Region 19). It meets the Kamchatka active zone at nearly right angles. Its islands are the visible summits of a great submarine ridge.

Flanking this ridge to the south is the Aleutian Trench, 50–100 miles wide and up to 8 km deep. The chain contains about 50 active volcanoes.

Most shallow earthquakes occur between the trench and the island arc; shocks at intermediate depth are located along the principal axis of the arc (volcanic axis). Deep-focus earthquakes are inexistent.

The westernmost link in the Aleutian chain is the Komandorsky (Commander) group, administratively a part of Kamchatka (U.S.S.R.). Bering Island is the largest in the group. Seismic activity is moderate and exclusively shallow. No well-developed trench appears in the Commander Island sector. The Olyutorskiy Ridge, a submarine prolongation of the Siberian coast of the Bering Sea, crosses the arc between the Commander and Near Island groups.

In the Near Islands (U.S.A.) the largest island is Attu. Its seismicity is much higher than that of the adjoining Commander Islands but slightly lower than in the center of the arc. Intermediate shocks occur rarely.

The Rat Islands, with Kiska and Amchitka as the principal ones, generate many large shallow and intermediate shocks. The Aleutian Trench widens and deepens considerably in this area. The larger earthquakes are notable for their extensive aftershock sequences. Any major shock between the Rat and Fox Islands groups may activate the entire central chain for many months.

The numerous Andreanof Islands stretch from Amchitka Pass (180°) to Amukta Pass (172°W). Adak and Atka are close to the geographical center of the Aleutian chain. The earthquake of March 9, 1957 (magnitude 8.3) generated a damaging tsunami in the Pacific.

The Fox Island group consists chiefly of three larger islands: Umnak, Unalaska and Unimak. The Unimak earthquake of April 1, 1946 had a magnitude of only 7.4 but caused a very large and severely damaging tsunami in Hawaii.

The Aleutian Arc is one of the world's most prolific sources of tsunamis. An interesting shock of magnitude 8.3 in the Rat Islands region occurred just half an hour before the destructive Valparaiso, Chile earthquake of August 16, 1906. Some of the minor sea-level oscillations observed in Chile after that earthquake were possibly due to this shock.

The Aleutian Ridge emerges to the east at the Alaska Peninsula. Shallow earthquakes scatter off the south shore of the peninsula over a broad area, including Kodiak Island, Prince William Sound, the Kenai Peninsula and Cook Inlet. This is the region activated by the Alaskan earthquakes of 1964. The Aleutian Trench diverges toward the south and terminates in the Gulf of Alaska.

The great earthquake of March 28, 1964 (magnitude 8.4) had its epicenter in Prince William Sound. It caused vertical displacements of several feet along a wide coastal area. The tsunami was locally destructive along the coast of the Kenai Peninsula, Kodiak Island, southern Alaska, and ports of western Canada and the U.S. The damage was particularly severe at Seward and Anchorage.

The Alaska mainland is moderately seismic along the prolongation of the Aleutian Arc northward up to the Yukon River. Earthquakes are shallow and tend to cluster about the intersections of the arc with major tectonic trends, such as the great Denali Fault, which runs through the Alaska Range. The Brooks Range and the rest of northern and western Alaska are practically inactive. There are a few minor shocks across the Bering Straits.

Eastern Alaska is quite low in seismicity. There is a seismic gap which separates the Aleutian Arc structure from the panhandle coastal region.

Alaskan panhandle to Washington State (Region 2: Maps 5 and 6, Table 14.2)

Extension and seismicity

This region includes a long coastal belt of fjords and islands, geographically similar to southern Chile. Its seismicity is among the lowest in the Circum-Pacific Belt (0.4% of the

TABLE 14.2

Earthquakes of Alaska and Canada (Region 2)

Date	Epicenter	M	Comments
1872 Dec. 14	Puget Sound	unknown	transcurrent
1899 Sep. 3	Yakutat Bay	8.3	transcurrent
1899 Sep. 9	Yakutat Bay	8.5	accumulated displacements up to 47 ft.
1949 Apr. 13	Puget Sound	7.1	damage in Seattle area
1949 Aug. 22	Queen Charlotte Is.	8.1	
1958 Jul. 10	Lituya Bay	8.0	transcurrent: 21 ft.
1965 Apr. 29	Puget Sound	6.5	some damage in Seattle area

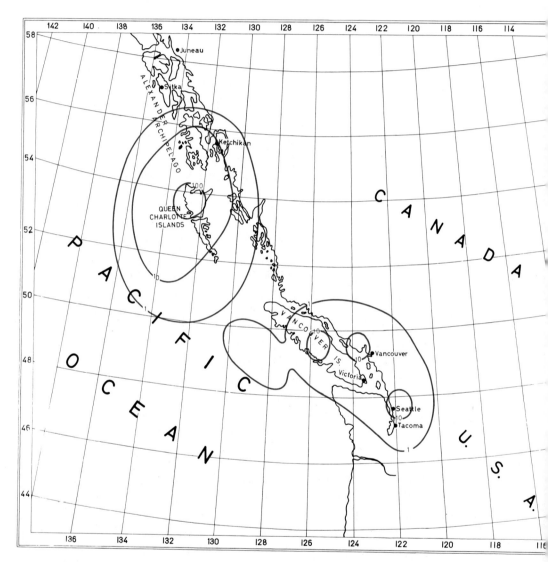

Map 6. Seismicity of British Columbia: Region 2. (Seismicity contours are numbered in 10^{15} ergs km^{-2} year^{-1}.)

world total); however, as in southern Chile, it is found that the proportion of large shocks is higher than average.

The epicenters are distributed along major fault zones which run roughly parallel to the coastal trend. A region of minor seismicity occurs in Yukon Territory, along the border of the Northwest Territories and along the Mackenzie and Stikine Ranges. This minor zone extends northward into the Arctic Ocean (Region 42). Some minor seismicity is also associated with the eastern slopes of the Canadian Rockies (Alberta Province).

The area is typically a coast of subsidence; it has been conjectured that earthquakes in this region are connected with vertical block tectonics. Gutenberg and Richter (1954) point out that no intermediate or deep-focus activity exists. Though transcursion may occur, "the drowned topography indicates vertical displacement." Volcanism is practically absent.

Seismic geography

The similarities between this region and southern Chile do not extend to its boundaries to the north. Southern Chile is the direct prolongation of an active region. In Alaska, on the other hand, we have a definite gap of low seismicity between the abutment of the Aleutian Arc and the southern region.

The Alaska panhandle owes its high seismicity to the Fairweather fault zone, which runs southwest of the St. Elias Mountains. Major earthquakes occurred at Yakutat Bay (September 3 and 10, 1899; magnitudes 8.3 and 8.5) and Lituya Bay (July 10, 1958; magnitude 8.0). Gutenberg and Richter (1954) emphasize the very large horizontal displacements (up to 47 ft.) associated with the Yakutat Bay earthquakes. The more recent Lituya Bay earthquake showed equally dramatic horizontal displacements (up to 21 ft.). The seismic activity is concentrated offshore, west of Sitka, as one approaches the Canadian border.

The Queen Charlotte Islands (British Columbia, Canada) form the center of an important active region. Major earthquakes occur to the West of the main island. The epicenters follow the trend of the islands to a considerable distance to the south, down to the latitude of Seattle.

Vancouver Island and Puget Sound have a complex seismicity, most of it to the south of the 50th Parallel. Earthquakes are infrequent but tend to be damaging, particularly in the low-lying areas associated with deep sedimented basins. One active area trends NNE along the western margin of Puget Sound into British Columbia east of Vancouver; another zone follows the Strait of Georgia.

The seismicity of the State of Washington (U.S.A.) is almost entirely connected with the Puget Sound structure, presumably a tectonic trough. These earthquakes are widely felt throughout western Washington and British Columbia; they may reach depths of almost 100 km.

California, Nevada and Oregon (Region 3: Map 7; Table 14.3), *and Baja California* (Region 4: Map 8; Table 14.3)

Extension and seismicity

This is a moderately seismic region of exclusively shallow-focus activity. Its seismic energy release amounts to 1% of the world's total; this is relatively low when compared to regions of equal or lesser size, such as the Philippines (3.2%), southern Mexico—Guatemala (3.1%), Taiwan (1.6%), or New Zealand (1.2%).

TABLE 14.3

Earthquakes of western U.S.A.—Mexico (Regions 3 and 4)

Date	Epicenter	M	Comments
1716 Feb. 6	Baja California		
1838 Jan.	San Francisco		
1857 Jan. 9	Fort Tejón	about 8	
1868 Oct. 21	Hayward		
1872 Mar. 26	Lone Pine	about 7½	
1906 Apr. 18	San Francisco	8.3	destructive in northern California, 700 dead
1915 Oct. 2	Pleasant Valley, Nevada	7.6	
1925 Jan. 29	Sta. Barbara	6.3	damage
1927 Nov. 4	Sta. Barbara	7.5	offshore epicenter
1932 Dec. 21	Cedar Mtn, Nevada	7.3	
1933 Mar. 10	Long Beach	6.3	damage
1934 Dec. 30, 31	Baja California	7.0, 7.1	
1936 Jul. 15	Milton, Ore.	5.7	minor damage
1940 May. 18	El Centro	7.1	damage in Imperial Valley
1952 Jul. 21	Kern Country	7.7	extensive damage, 11 dead
1954 Jul., Dec.	Fallon—Dixie Valley, Nev.	7.0	
1954 Dec. 21	Eureka	6.6	damage
1956 Feb. 9—Mar. 1	San Miguel Swarm, Baja California	6.8	
1957 Mar. 22	San Francisco	5.3	damage
1971 Feb. 9	San Fernando	6.6	damage in Los Angeles area

Much of the seismic activity occurs on land and in the vicinity of populated areas. The seismic hazard is associated largely (but by no means exclusively) with the San Andreas Rift and related structures.

The San Andreas Rift is a feature of rather unique character, both because of its great length and of its rate of right-hand lateral motion of 2—7 cm/year. If this rate is extrapolated backwards into the Tertiary past one infers displacements of the order of hundreds of miles. Indeed, from geologic evidence it is assumed that the accumulated lateral motion since Early Miocene time totals more than 260 km in southern California; dis-

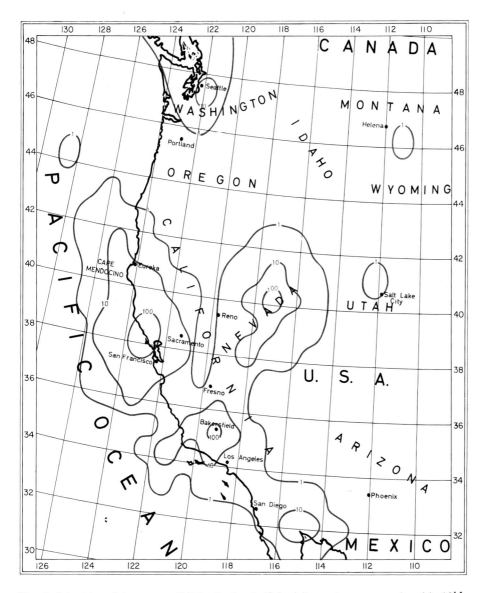

Map 7. Seismicity of the western U.S.A.: Region 3. (Seismicity contours are numbered in 10^{15} ergs km^{-2} year^{-1}.)

placements in central California were found to be of greater magnitude. These conclusions rest on geologic correlations involving considerable uncertainty but are now generally accepted by most California geologists.

These are rather large movements, when compared to what is observed in other
regions; yet the seismicity of the San Andreas Rift is relatively low. Presumably the
earth's crust opposes less resistance to horizontal distortion than it does to vertical shifts,
so that much of the total motion may take place by continuous slippage (fault creep). A
considerable part of the seismic activity in the San Andreas Rift is localized near geometric bends or intersections with other tectonic structures. Some of the major regional
structures which may be brought into a genetic relationship with California seismicity
are: the East Pacific Rise, which appears to cause the opening of the Gulf of California;
and the Murray and Mendocino fracture zones, two large oceanic scarps which intersect
the continent somewhere along the 35th and 40th parallels (Fig.14.3). Menard has suggested that the San Andreas Rift might actually be the continuation of the East Pacific
Rise in the continent. Most authors postulate a mechanism of right-lateral shear involving
displacement of the ocean floor in a northwesterly direction.

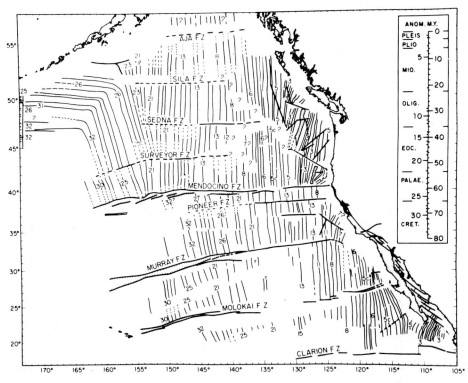

Fig.14.3. Tectonics of the ocean floor off Western North America. The age of numbered magnetic
anomalies is shown in the inset. (From Atwater, 1970.)

The San Andreas Rift slices through the North American continent from the Gulf of California to the San Francisco Peninsula; then it follows the coastline of northern California and terminates at Cape Mendocino where it intersects the Mendocino Escarpment. Its continuation offshore is complex; but the oceanic area to the northwest of Cape Mendocino is highly seismic. The section between Cape Mendocino and the San Francisco Bay is relatively inactive. The fault follows a straight line across the Coast Ranges, parallel to the San Joaquin Valley. Where the valley ends it swerves broadly to the east and then back on course. This wide inflection lies roughly on the inland prolongation of the Murray fracture zone; it is highly seismic. Finally, its southern end follows a series of broad depressions (Salton Sea, Imperial Valley, Gulf of California) which show strong earthquake activity.

Seismic geography

A plot of epicenters in California and western Nevada shows the distribution of minor seismicity. Earthquakes are widely scattered around the Great Valley; but the scarcity of epicenters under the valley itself is no guarantee of safety, since towns in the valley have been repeatedly damaged by large shocks in the Coast Ranges or across the Sierra Nevada.

The major shocks tend to occur along the San Andreas Rift and the Owens Valley Rift, a structure which runs parallel to the eastern scarp of the Sierra Nevada. The Owens Valley earthquakes and the earthquakes of western Nevada have shown predominant vertical displacements. The Garlock Fault is a major left-handed lateral fault which connects the San Andreas and Owens Valley systems, giving rise to a Y-shaped seismicity pattern. The earthquakes on the eastern flank of the Sierra are presumably connected with the continuing uplift of the Sierra block and downfaulting of the Owens Valley floor (Fig.14.4).

A number of parallel faults in the San Andreas system have individual names and a recognized seismicity pattern of their own. These include the San Jacinto, Hayward, Nacimiento, Inglewood, San Gabriel, Calaveras, Elsinore, and several other faults. The White Wolf Fault was activated in the 1952 Kern Country earthquake, the first major shock that did not occur on one of the major recognized faults. The tectonics of this earthquake were closely related to a structural complex which marks the intersection between the San Andreas and Garlock fault systems. The 1857 Fort Tejon earthquake, believed the largest in the western United States, occurred in the same structural region but was clearly on the San Andreas Fault.

The seismic activity along the eastern scarp of the Sierra Nevada seems to continue northward into the State of Nevada. Actually the earthquakes of Nevada are not directly related to the California fault systems. They occur chiefly on a series of parallel structures trending north—south, which are characteristic of the Basin and Range Province. The most active region includes western Nevada from the latitude of the Mendocino Fracture Zone to the region of Death Valley. The region is of recent settlement and still sparsely populated, but the evidence of fresh fault scarps is a good indication of its high activity.

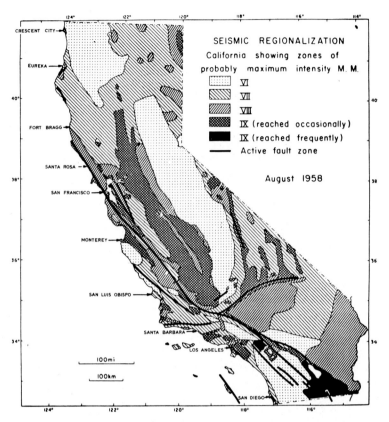

Fig.14.4. Seismic regionalization of California. (After Richter, 1959.)

North of the 40th Parallel is a region of low seismic activity which includes the State of Oregon. A shock in the northeast corner of the State of July 15, 1936 caused minor damage. Large shocks in California, Washington and the Mendocino offshore region may be felt in Oregon. Small local shocks occur in the Cascade Range and along the Washington border.

Eastern and central North America (Region 34; Table 14.4)

Extension and seismicity
This is an extensive region of low seismicity. Its core is the Canadian Shield, one of the large stable continental shields of the world. The shield itself is practically free from earthquakes. No major internal rift zones are known, besides the St. Lawrence Rift.

By order of importance and extension the two main zones of seismicity are (1) the Rocky Mountain zone, from Alberta through Montana, Idaho, Wyoming, Utah, Arizona,

TABLE 14.4

Earthquakes of eastern and central North America (Region 34)

Date	Epicenter	M	Comments
1638 Jan. 2	New England		
1663 Feb. 5	Trois Rivieres, Quebec		largest in eastern Canada
1727 Nov. 8	Newburg, Mass.		
1737 Dec. 17	New York State		
1811 Dec. 16	New Madrid, Mo.	about 8	largest U.S. earthquakes
1812 Jan. 23, Feb. 7	New Madrid, Mo.	about 8	
1852 Nov. 1	Yuma, Ariz.		
1869 Oct. 22	New Brunswick to New England		
1875 Dec. 22	Chesterfield County, Va.		
1882 Nov. 7	Denver, Colorado		
1884 Nov. 10	Ogden, Utah		
1886 Aug. 31	Charleston, South Carolina		
1887 May 3	Bavispe, Sonora		damage in northern Mexico
1895 Oct. 31	Charleston, Mo.		
1897 May 31	Giles County, Va.		
1897 Nov. 24	Dillon, Montana		
1900 Nov. 23	Central Utah		
1901 Nov. 17	Salt Lake, Utah		
1903 Nov. 11	Idaho		
1906 Jul. 16	Socorro, New Mexico		
1912 Aug. 18	Williams, Arizona		
1925 Jan. 27	Lombard, Montana	6.7	
1925 Mar. 1	Tadoussac, Quebec	7.0	
1929 Nov. 18	Grand Banks, off New-Foundland	7.2	
1931 Aug. 16	West Texas	6.4	
1934 Mar. 12	Kosmo, Utah	6.6	
1935 Oct. 18, 31	Helena, Montana	6.3, 6.0	
1935 Nov. 1	Timiskaming, Quebec	6 ¼	
1940 Dec. 20	New Hampshire		minor damage
1944 Jul. 12	Challis, Idaho	6.1	
1947 Nov. 23	Cameron, Montana	6¼	
1959 Aug. 17	Hebgen Lake, Montana	7.1	

Colorado, New Mexico, into Sonora; (2) the St. Lawrence–Findlay structure, reaching from the mouth of the St. Lawrence River into the Mississippi Valley.

Seismic geography

The Rocky Mountains represent an earlier phase, now relatively quiescent, of the Pacific orogeny. Earthquakes follow largely the backbone of the Rockies and of the Colorado Plateau. The largest and most damaging of these earthquakes was undoubtly the Sonora earthquake of 1887. Most shocks in the area are widely felt.

The St. Lawrence–Findlay active zone extends from the Atlantic Ocean through southern Ontario and along the U.S.–Canadian border, following the Findlay arch across northwestern Ohio, and the central Mississippi Valley between Missouri, Illinois, Arkansas, and Tennessee.

The largest earthquakes in this region occurred on December 16, 1811, January 23, and February 7, 1812, in the region of New Madrid, Missouri. All three probably exceeded magnitude 8 and were, singly or jointly, the largest U.S. earthquakes in historic tir⌐ (excluding Alaska). They were felt from the Canadian border to the Gulf of Mexico, and from Boston to Kansas.

The seismicity in the Appalachian Fold area is minor, as befits a mountain chain of pre-Cretaceous age.

Some rare earthquakes fall outside broad regions. The most important one was the Charleston, South Carolina, earthquake of August 31, 1886 which was fairly severe and widely felt throughout the eastern United States.

CENTRAL AND INSULAR AMERICA

Between $10°$ and $25°N$ the American continent narrows down to a mountainous land bridge, and a great island arc develops to the east. A deep oceanic trench parallels the Pacific coast, and intense volcanism appears inland. The tectonic structure is quite different from that of North or South America. The region is bounded to the north by the Mexican desert, of low seismicity; the southern limit in the Darien region of eastern Panama is also a seismicity gap.

Mexico to Guatemala (Region 5: Map 8; Table 14.5)

Extension and seismicity

The region comprising central to southern Mexico and Guatemala is among the major seismic regions of the world (3.1% of the total world energy release). Large shallow-focus earthquakes are frequent near the coasts of the States of Jalisco, Colima, Michoacán, Guerrero, Oaxaca, Chiapas, and in southern Guatemala; they tend to occur between the Middle American Trench and the Coast Ranges, particularly the Sierra Madre del Sur. Important transverse structures may be related to the Trans-Mexican Volcanic Belt and the abutment of the Antilles Arc in the Atlantic (Fig.14.5).

Seismic geography

In Mexico the seismicity appears to be distributed in a sequence of belts. North of Cape Corrientes the seismicity follows the trend of the southern Rockies into Sonora, western Chihuahua, western Durango, Sinaloa, western Zacatecas, and Nayarit. This is a region of minor seismicity, which we discussed partly in connection with the Rocky Mountains of North America. The important seismic structure of the Gulf of California belongs to Region 4.

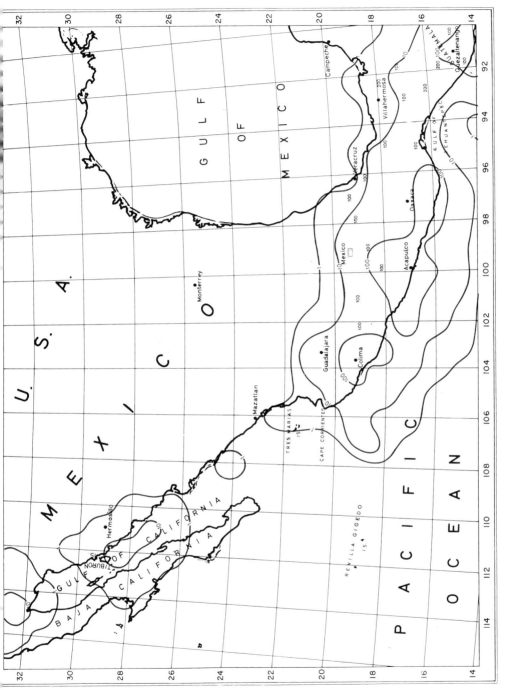

Map 8. Seismicity of Mexico: Regions 4–5. Seismicity contours are numbered in 10^{15} ergs km^{-2} year^{-1}.)

TABLE 14.5

Earthquakes of Mexico–Guatemala (Region 5)

Date	Epicenter	M	Comments
1538	Mexico		
1542 Mar. 17	Mexico		
1568 Dec. 27	Cocula, Jalisco		
1573	Colima		
1575	Puebla		
1582	Mexico		
1586	Guatemala		
1603	Oaxaca		
1604 March	Oaxaca		
1608 Jan. 8	Oaxaca		
1611 Aug. 25	Mexico		very large
1619 Jan. 13	Oaxaca		
1622 May 6	Zacatecas		
1626	Puebla		
1655 Nov. 25	Oaxaca		
1662 Jun. 7	Oaxaca		
1667 Jul. 30	Puebla		
1697 Feb. 25	Acapulco, Guerrero		
1701 Dec. 21	Oaxaca		destructive
1711 Aug. 16	Mexico, Colima, Guadalajara		several dead
1727 Mar. 10	Oaxaca		
1739 Jul. 14	Colima		
1749	Mexico		
1750	Mexico		
1754 Sep. 1	Acapulco, Guerrero		tsunami
1773 Jul. 29	Guatemala		100 dead; capital city moved to present site
1784 Mar. 28	Acapulco		tsunami (12 ft), several dead
1801 Oct. 5	Oaxaca		7 dead
1806 Mar. 25	Jalisco		many dead
1818 May 31	Mexico, Colima		
1820 May 9	Acapulco		tsunami
1830 Apr. 1	Guatemala		
1838	Veracruz		tsunami
1845 Apr. 7	Acapulco	about 7	tsunami
1852 May 17	Amatitlan, Guatemala		
1854 Apr. 15	Guatemala		
1858 Jun. 19	Michoacán	about 7	
1862 Dec. 19	Antigua, Guatemala		
1864 Oct. 3	Puebla		
1870 May 11	Oaxaca	about 7	
1872 Mar. 27	Oaxaca		
1874 Sep. 18	Guatemala		
1875 Feb. 11	Zapopan, Jalisco	7.5	
1882 Jul. 19	Puebla		
1897 Jun. 5	Oaxaca	7	

TABLE 14.5 (continued)

Date	Epicenter	M	Comments
1899 Jan. 29	Oaxaca	8.9	
1900 Jan. 19	Jalisco		
1902 Jan. 16	Guerrero	7	
1902 Apr. 19	Quetzaltenango, Guatemala	8.3	many dead
1902 Sep. 23	Chiapas	7.8	
1903 Jan. 14	Oaxaca	8.3	
1907 Apr. 15	Acapulco	8.3	
1908 Mar. 26	Guerrero	7.5	
1909 Jul. 31	Guerrero	7¾, 7	
1909 Sep. 5	Guerrero	6.6	
1909 Oct. 31	Guerrero	7	
1910 May 31	Guerrero	6.5	
1911 Feb. 3	Oaxaca	7.25	
1911 Jun. 7	Jalisco	8	45 dead, damage in Mexico City
1911 Aug. 27	Oaxaca	6.7	
1911 Dec. 16	off Guerrero	7	
1912 Nov. 14	Acambay, Jal.	7	
1918 Jan. 3	Guatemala		destructive in Guatemala City; several dead
1919 Apr. 17	Guatemala	7.0	
1920 Jan. 3	Oxochoacán, Puebla		
1920 Apr. 19	Jalapa, Veracruz	about 6	
1928 Feb. 9	Oaxaca	7.7	
1928 Mar. 21	Oaxaca	7.5	
1928 Apr.16	Oaxaca	7.7	
1928 Jun. 17	Oaxaca	7.9	
1931 Jan. 15	Oaxaca	7.9	
1932 Jun. 18	Jalisco	7.9	tsunami
1932 Jun. 22	Colima	7.9	tsunami
1936 Dec. 14	Tuxtla Gutiérrez Chiapas		
1941 Apr. 15	Guerrero	7.0	
1942 Aug. 6	Guatemala	7.9	
1943 Feb. 20	Paricutín, Mich.		volcanic eruption
1943 Feb. 22	Guerrero	7.5	damaging in Mexico City
1948 Dec. 4	Islas Marias	7¼	
1954 Feb. 5	Chiapas	6¼	
1956 Nov. 9	Tehuantepec		
1957 Jul. 28	Guerrero	7½	several dead, damage in Mexico City
1959 May 24	Oaxaca	6.8	
1959 Aug. 26	Veracruz	6.5	
1962 May 11	Acapulco	6.7	
1962 May 19	Acapulco	6.5	
1962 Nov. 30	Guerrero	5.5	local damage
1964 Jul. 6	Guerrero	6.5	
1965 Dec. 9	off Guerrero	6.8	
1967 Mar. 11	Veracruz	5.5	damage
1968 Aug. 2	Oaxaca	6.5	damage
1968 Sep. 25	Chiapas	6	
1970 Apr. 29	Chiapas	6.3	
1973 Jan. 30	Michoacán–Colima	7.7	56 dead
1973 Aug. 28	Puebla-Veracruz	7.1	100 km depth; 600 dead

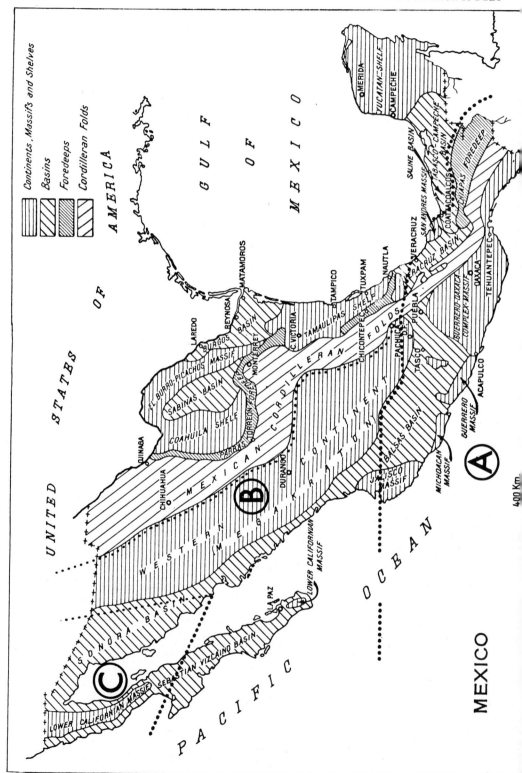

The first typically Central American structure is the Anahuac Range (volcanic belt), a transverse mountainous structure which cuts across Mexico from Cape Corrientes to Veracruz. Epicenters follow the Rivera fracture zone inland, through Jalisco, Colima, Michoacán, Mexico State, the Federal District, Morelos, Tlaxcala, Puebla, and Veracruz. Volcanism is very active. Volcanic centers and related tectonic depressions, such as the Valley of Mexico, are associated with shallow seismicity.

In the *southern Sierra Madre* the seismicity is of the Pacific type. Epicenters of normal depth are between the Acapulco Trench and the coastal ranges of Michoacán, Guerrero, and Oaxaca. The Sierra Madre structure extends for about 1,000 km parellel to the coast and is deeply faulted and intruded. Major offshore earthquakes tend to activate the whole region. Intermediate-depth epicenters are located underneath the Sierra complex, and in the Chiapas–Tehuantepec area.

The southern region including *Chiapas and Guatemala* is separated from the preceding by the transverse graben of Tehuantepec, a low isthmus with some seismic activity. The southern region is transitional and partakes both of the transverse range structure and of the coastal volcanism typical to El Salvador and Nicaragua. The Caribbean arc structure appears to penetrate inland, in a transverse rift structure from the Gulf of Honduras into Guatemala, with some evidence of left-lateral movement.

Coastal shocks tend to be deeper than normal; inland epicenters in Chiapas and Guatemala reach depths of 250 km. Shallow earthquakes in Guatemala follow the volcanic axis. Collapse earthquakes occur occasionally in the limestone caverns of Yucatán and Tabasco. Practically all destructive shocks in Guatemala had shallow depths and were located inland, near the volcanoes. Earthquake swarms occur frequently in this region.

Central America (Region 6: Map 9; Table 14.6)

Extension and seismicity

This region accounts for 1.2% of the world's seismicity and includes El Salvador, Honduras, Nicaragua, Costa Rica, Panama, and part of the Panama–Galapagos Ridge.

Through Costa Rica volcanism is high. Shallow earthquakes occur between the Middle American Trench and the coast. Intermediate earthquakes fall closer to the coast or inland. In western Panama the structural trends become transverse to the isthmus and the earthquake epicenters follow a southward direction out to sea. Eastern Panama has no active volcanoes and little earthquake activity. This is the transition zone between the Central American and Andean regions.

Fig.14.5. A tectonic map of Mexico, showing a possible regionalization into three regions. *A* = Southern Mexico subduction zone; *B* = Sierra Madre Occidental; *C* = Gulf of California region; *D* = Mexican Cordillera and East Coast.

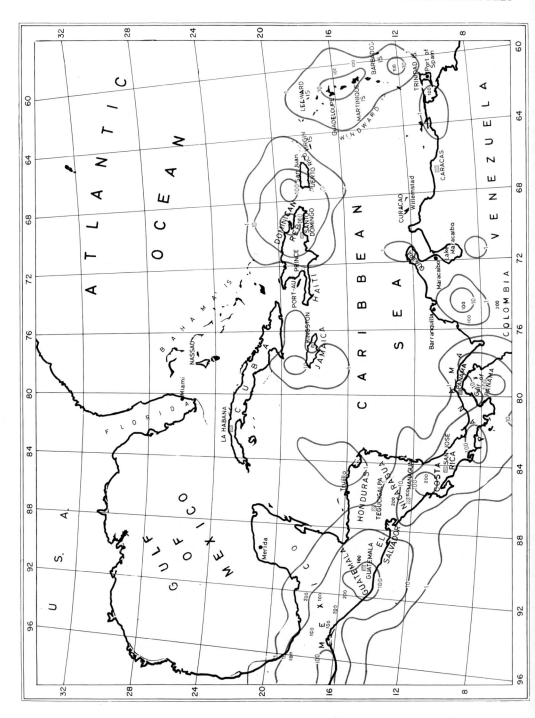

TABLE 14.6

Earthquakes of Central America (Region 6)

Date	Epicenter	M	Comments
1707	San Salvador		
1719	San Salvador		
1765 April	San Salvador		
1774 July	San Salvador		
1798 Feb. 2	San Salvador		
1806	San Salvador		
1820 Oct. 19	San Pedro Sula, Honduras		
1822 May 7	Cartago, Costa Rica		
1841 Sep. 2	central Costa Rica		
1847 Jul. 31	Nicaragua		
1851 Mar. 18	Costa Rica		
1856 Aug. 4	Honduras		
1857 Dec.	El Salvador		
1859 Dec. 8	El Salvador		
1860 Dec.3	El Salvador		
1873 Mar. 4	El Salvador		
1878 Oct. 2	Jucuapa, El Salvador		
1879 Dec. 31	San Salvador		eruption of Volc. Ilopango
1882 Sep. 7	off Panama		
1883 Dec. 30	Costa Rica		
1898 Apr. 29	Nicaragua	7.9	
1904 Jan. 20	Gulf of Panama	7.9	
1904 Dec. 20	Costa Rica, Panama	8.3	
1917 Jun. 7	San Salvador		
1919 Apr. 28	San Salvador		
1951 May 6	Jucuapa, El Salvador	6.5	400 dead
1965 May 3	San Salvador	6.2	120 dead
1972 Dec. 23	Managua	6.5	about 10.000 dead

Seismic geography

In El Salvador most epicenters occur between the oceanic trench and the coast. Frequent intermediate shocks are found along the coastline.

The volcanic axis, crossing into El Salvador from southern Guatemala, becomes a tectonic trough ("Median Trough") which includes the Gulf of Fonseca and the great lakes of Nicaragua. Many destructive shallow earthquakes in this region have happened along the southwestern margin of the Median Trough. Volcanism is extremely active, there are 30 recognized active volcanoes, and the distinction between volcanic and tectonic activity is frequently unclear. Persistent swarms of small to medium shallow earthquakes are characteristic of this region; these swarms are not necessarily associated with volcanic activity.

On the Atlantic side we find some minor activity in northern and western Honduras. These earthquakes may indicate a connection with the Cayman Trough structure, a part of the Caribbean Arc.

In Costa Rica the Middle American Trench becomes shallower and gradually dies out. The structure becomes transverse to the coast, but some intermediate shocks still occur. In the Azuero Peninsula (Panama) the shallow epicenters follow a southern trend into the Pacific Ocean. The oceanic structure here includes several parallel ridges running north–south. The north–south line between the Gulfs of Montijo and Mosquitos marks a seismic boundary between Central and South America.

Caribbean Arc and Venezuela (Region 7: Map 9; Table 14.7)

Extension and seismicity

The Caribbean region (0.9% of world seismicity) is an oval-shaped sea containing three separate basins: The Yucatan Basin to the west, the Colombia Basin to the south-west, and the Venezuela Basin to the southeast. The main arc branches off Central America in northern Honduras and follows the Cayman Trench between Jamaica and southern Cuba, across the Windward Passage.

The remainder of the Arc trends along the Antilles (Dominican Republic, Puerto Rico, Virgin Islands, Antigua, Guadeloupe, Martinique, Barbados, Grenada, Trinidad) and curves westward through northern Venezuela. A branch follows the trough of Grenada and Bonaire parallel to the South American coast.

Seismic Geography

From Cuba to Yucatán there extends a northern, largely inactive branch of the Antilles Arc. This branch merges with the main arc in the Sierra Maestra of southern Cuba.

The other branch to the west of this junction is only slightly more active. It follows the southern edge of the Cayman Trough, but the epicenters scatter at both ends of the trough, into Honduras, and north and south of Jamaica into southern Cuba.

The Antilles from the Dominican Republic through the Leeward Islands, have the highest level of seismicity in the arc. Many shocks occur in the Mona Passage between Puerto Rico and the Dominican Republic, and along the Puerto Rico Trench to the Virgin Islands. Here the structure of the arc becomes complicated; the trends change to north–south.

The Lesser Antilles, a set of volcanic islands directly fronting on the Atlantic Ocean, are associated with shallow and intermediate activity.

The structure again changes direction in Trinidad and volcanism disappears. The inner section of the arc (Margarita, Bonaire, Curaçao, Aruba) has a moderate seismicity. The outer structure (northern Venezuela, Mérida Range, northern Colombia) is active, with destructive earthquakes in the areas of Cumaná and Mérida.

TABLE 14.7

Earthquakes of the Caribbean Arc and Venezuela (Region 7)

Date	Epicenter	M	Comments
1530 Sept. 1	Cumaná, Venezuela		tsunami
1580	Santiago, Cuba		
1610 Feb. 2	Mérida, Colombia		
1624 Oct.	Santiago, Cuba		
1641 Jun. 11	Caracas, Venezuela		
1644 Jan. 16	Pamplona, Colombia		
1675 Feb. 11	Santiago, Cuba		
1690 Apr.	Antigua, Barbados		
1692 Jun. 7	Jamaica		
1751 Nov. 21	Haiti		
1766 Jun. 11	Cuba, Jamaica		
1766 Oct. 21	Cumaná, Venezuela		
1770 Jun. 3	Haiti		
1788 Oct. 12	St. Lucía		
1794 Sep. 10	Cumaná, Venezuela		
1797 Dec. 14	Cumaná, Venezuela		
1812 Mar. 26	Caracas, Venezuela		destructive
1831 Aug. 11	Barbados		
1842 May 7	northern Haiti		
1842 Feb. 8	Guadeloupe		
1852 Aug. 20	Santiago, Cuba		
1853 Jul. 15	Cumaná, Venezuela		
1869 Mar. 6	Mérida, Colombia		
1871 Aug. 21	St. Thomas		
1874 Sep. 26	Antigua		
1875 May 18	Cúcuta, Colombia		
1878 Apr. 12	Cuá, Venezuela		
1887 Sep. 23	off N. Haiti		
1894 Apr. 28	Mérida, Venezuela		
1899 Jun. 14	off Jamaica	7.8	
1900 Jun. 21	Cayman Islands	7.9	
1900 Oct. 29	Caracas, Venezuela		
1907 Jan. 14	Kingston, Jamaica		1,000 dead
1923 Dec. 22	Boyaca, Colombia	6.9	tsunami
1932 Mar. 14	Mérida, Colombia	6¾	
1943 Jul. 29	Mona Passage	7.9	
1946 Aug. 4	N. Santo Domingo	8.1	
1950 Jul. 8	Cúcuta, Colombia		
1950 Aug. 3	El Tocuyo, Venezuela		
1954 Dec. 4	Port of Spain, Trinidad		1 dead, $500.000 damage
1967 Jul. 29	Caracas, Venezuela	6.5	250 dead, $100 million damage

SOUTH AMERICA (Region 8, 9, 10 and 35: Maps 10 and 11)

Extension and seismicity

The South American continent has a complex tectonic structure, broadly related to the uplift of the Andes on the emplacement of an Old Paleozoic mountain range. The core of the continent is the stable Brazilian Shield (Region 35), of Precambrian age. Active areas are developed along the Pacific Ocean between two arcs fronting to the east: the Caribbean Arc (Region 7) and the Scotia Arc (Region 10). Between the Scotia Arc and the southern end of the Andean "geosyncline" is the Patagonian area (Region 9), of minor seismicity.

The Andean structure is the result of several superposed orogenies, chiefly in the Jurassic, Late Cretaceous, and Cenozoic through the present time. If this entire structure is regarded as a single region, as Gutenberg and Richter (1954) have done (Region 8), it tops the list of seismic regions with 14.8% of the world's total energy release. Lack of knowledge of the details of Andean tectonics still forces us to treat this complex region as a whole.

Patagonia (Region 9) accounts for 0.3% of the world's activity. The northern boundary of this region should be moved south to the 47th Parallel; otherwise it includes much of the aftershock area of the great Valdivia earthquakes of 1575, 1837, and 1960. It seems more natural to draw the line between the Patagonian and Andean regions at the jucture of the Chile Rise with the continent.

The Scotia Arc (Region 10) is a well-developed arc structure similar to the Caribbean Arc. Its seismicity is equal to the Caribbean: about 0.9% of the world's seismicity.

The massive Brazilian Shield (Region 35) is relatively free of rifts or marginal active zones. The area of low seismic activity includes the adjacent parts of the Atlantic Ocean between the coast and the Mid-Atlantic Rise. An earthquake in the Upper Orinoco—Rio Negro region was reported by Humboldt in 1798.

Northern Andes (Table 14.8)

Seismic geography

In Colombia and Ecuador the Andes are divided into three branches of different geologic structure. Seismicity associated with the eastern Andes of Colombia and Venezuela has been discussed under Region 7 (Caribbean Arc).

The eastern Andes represent a trough containing up to 8,000 m of sediments, which became positive after the Eocene orogeny. It contains important transcurrent structures like the Boconó Fault.

Most earthquakes occur in a belt which follows the Pacific coast from the Panama—Colombia border to the mouth of the Guayas River. Intermediate earthquakes occur under the volcanic axis of the western and central Andes. Deep-focus earthquakes down to

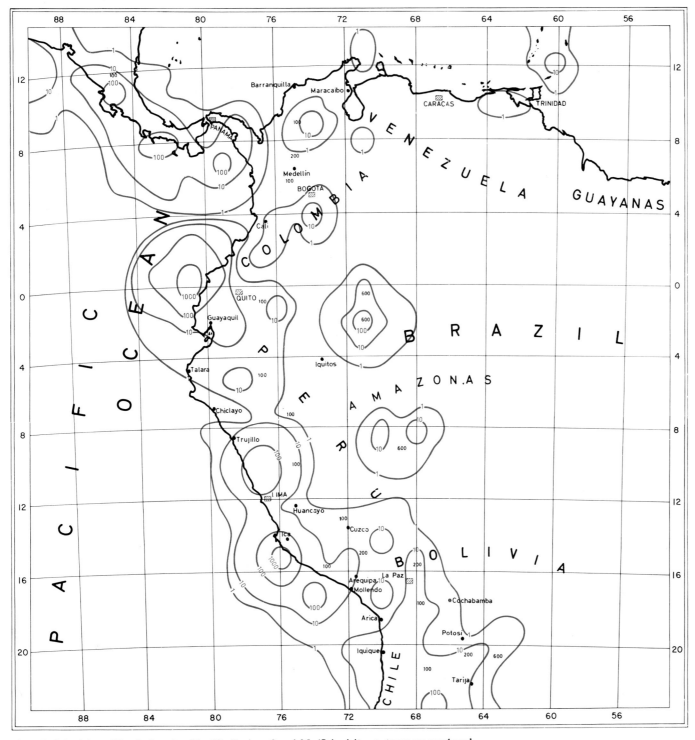

Map 10. Seismicity of South America (North): Regions 8 and 35. (Seismicity contours are numbered in 10^{15} ergs km^{-2} year^{-1}.)

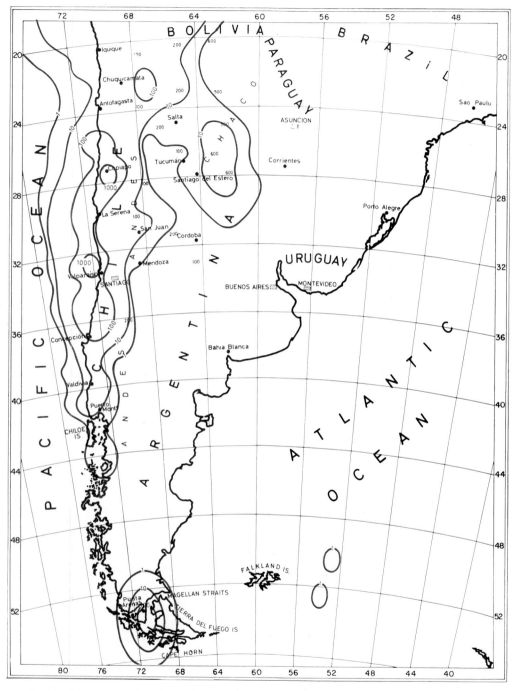

Map 11. Seismicity of South America (South): Regions 8–9–10. (Seismicity contours are numbered in 10^{15} ergs km^{-2} year^{-1}.)

TABLE 14.8

Earthquakes of the Andes region (Region 8)

Date	Epicenter	M	Comments
1570 Febr. 8	Concepción, Chile	about 8	tsunami
1575 Dec. 16	Valdivia, Chile	about 8½	tsunami
1582 Jan. 16	Arequipa, Peru		
1587 Aug. 30	Quito, Ecuador		
1604 Nov. 24	Arica, Chile–Peru	about 8½	tsunami
1619 Feb. 16	Trujillo, Peru		
1644 Jan. 16	Pamplona, Colombia		Region 7
1647 May 13	Santiago, Chile	about 8½	1,000 dead
1650 Mar. 31	Cuzco, Peru		
1657 Mar. 15	Concepcíon, Chile	about 8	tsunami
1658 Feb. 14	Trujillo, Peru		
1687 Oct. 21	Callao, Peru		tsunami
1698 Jun. 19	Ambato, Ecuador		
1725 Jan. 8	Ancash, Peru		
1730 Jul. 8	Valparaiso, Chile	about 8½	tsunami
1735 Feb. 2	Popayán, Colombia		
1742 Mar. 23	Taitao, Chile		
1743 Oct. 18	Bogotá, Colombia		
1751 May. 25	Concepción, Chile	about 8½	tsunami
1755 Apr. 26	Quito, Ecuador		
1757 Feb. 22	Latacunga, Ecuador		
1766 Jul. 9	Cali, Colombia		
1782 May 22	Santa Rita, Argentina		
1784 May 13	Moquegua, Peru		
1785 Jul. 12	Bogotá, Colombia		
1796 Mar. 30	Copiapó, Chile		
1797 Feb. 4	Ambato, Ecuador		
1805 Jun. 16	Honda, Colombia		
1807 Jul. 16	Magdalena Valley, Colombia		
1819 Apr. 3–4–11	Copiapó, Chile	about 8	tsunami
1821 Jul. 10	Arequipa, Peru		
1822 Nov. 19	Valparaiso, Chile	about 8	72 dead
1826 Jun. 17	Bogotá, Colombia		
1827 Nov, 16	Popayán, Colombia		
1828 Mar. 30	Callao, Peru		
1834 Jan. 20	Pasto, Colombia		
1835 Feb. 20	Concepción, Chile	about 8½	tsunami
1837 Nov. 7	Valdivia, Chile	about 8	tsunami
1844 Oct. 18	Salta, Argentina		
1847 Oct. 8	Illapel, Chile		
1849 Apr. 9	San Luis, Argentina		
1851 Apr. 2	Casablanca, Chile		
1859 Mar. 22	Quito, Ecuador		
1861 Mar. 21	Mendoza, Argentina		18,000 dead
1861 Apr. 13	Ayacucho, Peru		

TABLE 14.8 (continued)

Date	Epicenter	M	Comments
1868 Aug. 13	Arica, Chile—Peru	about 8½	tsunami
1868 Aug. 16	Ibarra, Ecuador		
1871 Feb. 23	San Antonio, Bolivia		
1871 Oct. 23	Oran, Argentina		
1873 Jul. 7	La Ligua, Chile		
1875 May 18	Cúcuta, Colombia		Region 7
1877 May 9	Iquique, Chile	about 8	tsunami
1885 Mar. 30	Mendoza, Argentina		
1885 May 25	Popayán, Colombia		
1887 Aug. 2	Cuenca, Ecuador		
1901 Jan. 7	Guayaquil, Ecuador		
1906 Jan. 31	off north Ecuador	8.9	
1906 Aug. 17	Valparaiso, Chile	8.6	
1908 Dec. 12	off central Peru	8.2	
1914 Jan. 30	San Luis Argentina	8.2	
1917 Aug. 31	Tolima, Colombia	7.2	
1922 Oct. 11	Arequipa, Peru	7.2	
1922 Nov. 11	Vallenar, Chile	8.4	tsunami
1928 Dec. 1	Talca, Chile	8.3	
1935 Aug. 7	Pasto, Colombia	7.5	
1939 Jan. 25	Chillán, Chile	8.3	30,000 dead
1940 May 24	off central Peru	8.4	
1942 May 14	off Ecuador	8.3	
1942 Aug. 24	Nasca, Peru	8.6	
1943 Apr. 6	Illapel, Chile	8.3	11 dead
1944 Jan. 15	San Juan, Argentina		5,000 dead
1946 Nov. 10	Ancash, Peru	7.8	1,500 dead
1947 Jul. 14	Pasto, Colombia		
1949 Aug. 5	Ambato, Ecuador	6.8	6,000 dead
1958 Jan. 19	Colombia—Ecuador	7.8	
1960 May 21–22	Southern Chile	8.5	
1965 Mar. 28	La Ligua, Chile	7.3	
1966 Oct. 17	off central Peru	7.6	
1966 Dec. 28	Taltal, Chile	7.5	
1967 Feb. 9	Neiva, Colombia		
1967 Jul. 29	Santander, Colombia		
1970 May 31	Ancash, Peru	7.8	40,000 dead
1971 Jul. 8	La Ligua, Chile	7.5	

depths of the order of 650 km occur under the western Amazon region (Brazil—Peru—Colombia border).

Shallow activity occurs inland; it appears to be associated chiefly with the tectonic graben of the Cauca Valley, and with the eastern Andes. Major destructive earthquakes have happened in this part of Colombia. Farther south, where the main trend of the Andes changes to the southeast (southern Ecuador) there is a region of important shallow earthquakes.

Central Andes (Table 14.8)

Seismic geography

In the Peruvian Andes two parallel ranges may be distinguished. Between the eastern and western Andes are the remains of old Paleozoic ranges forming the Puna Block. This block broadens toward the south until it occupies a gigantic area in the Bolivian Altiplano. The coast is marked by two well-developed oceanic trenches: the Peru Trench and the Chile Trench, separated by the Nasca Ridge.

The northern coast of Peru is a zone of shallow to intermediate seismic activity extending inland from the Tumbes Peninsula to the Marañón Valley. The structure of this region is little known in spite of extensive oil exploration. The Andes break up into isolated ridges with varying orientation.

South of Trujillo the seismicity is sporadic, with isolated coastal shocks plus a high intermediate activity under the Peruvian highlands (Puna). Deep-focus earthquakes with depths in the 500–600 km range occur under the southwestern Amazon Basin and particularly near the junction between the Brazil, Peru, and Bolivia borders.

By far the major part of Peruvian seismicity is concentrated along the coast of southern Peru, between the trench and the volcanic chain. In the Arequipa area the seismic activity is both shallow and intermediate; earthquakes are frequently destructive. Individual epicenters in this area have been shown to generate shocks at depths ranging from shallow to 200 km.

The Bolivian Altiplano, a Paleozoic high plateau (mean elevation about 4 km) is a stable block. It is geologically related to the Puna Block to the north and south; it forms a separate geographic unit without drainage to either ocean. Large intermediate earthquakes occur under the entire Puna Block and some deep epicenters occur toward the Paraguay border. Shallow shocks are rare.

Southern Andes (Table 14.8)

Seismic geography

There is a discontinuity in the Andean structure at the entrant corner of the coast between Peru and Chile. Here the trend of the Andes becomes southward and follows the Chilean border with Bolivia and Argentina. It is probably the longest continuous seismic zone in the world. The following subdivisions may be distinguished:

(a) In northern Chile (north of Antofagasta) the offshore activity is intermittent and produces extremely large shocks, which generate destructive tsunamis. Intermediate shocks around 120 km depth occur between the Coast Ranges and the volcanic axis, and shocks near 220 km depth exist under the Puna Block straddling the Argentina–Chile border.

(b) From Taltal to La Serena we find a gap in the volcanic chain. Both the Puna Block and the Central Valley disappear. This is a transition zone, with shallow shocks both along the Trench and inland.

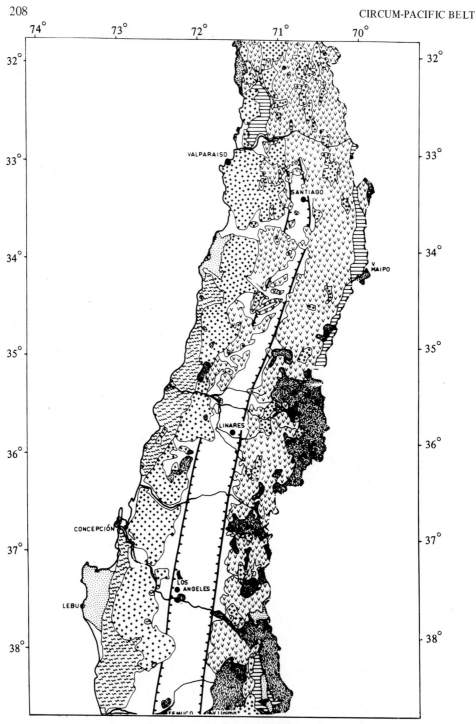

Fig.14.6. Structural setting of central Chile, showing the Central Valley as a tectonic graben bordered on the west by the Coast Range batholith. The Paleozoic metamorphic basement is found along the coast south of latitude 34°. (From Zeil, 1964.)

(c) In central Chile (Ovalle to Chillán) the Andes reach their maximum elevation (Mt. Aconcagua, 7,500 m); but the Chile Trench begins to decrease in depth. This region features a well-developed Coast Range and Central Valley (Fig.14.6); volcanism reappears and becomes increasingly active toward the south. Shallow earthquakes occur along the Coast Range Fault, a long structure which shows evidence of vertical displacement and is responsible for relatively rare but very large earthquakes; important shallow epicenters are also found offshore (Valparaiso) and throughout the Andean Massif. Intermediate shocks may reach depths of the order of 100 km.

(d) Southern Chile (Concepción to Taitao) marks the terminal region of the Andean geosyncline. The Andes fall off in height; below Puerto Montt the Central Valley becomes a submerged channel between the mainland and the offshore islands. The minor seismicity is low, but large earthquakes occur which are severely damaging. These are frequently coupled with large tsunamis. The Chile Trench becomes shallow and filled with sediments at the juncture of the Chile Rise with the coast. At this point the trend of the seismicity bends westward and follows the Chile Rise to Easter Island.

(e) Western Argentina is an important region of deep earthquakes, under the provinces of Salta and Santiago del Estero. Some intermediate-depth activity persists as far south as the end of the Andean geosyncline (Rio Negro Basin).

An important source of shallow activity of western Argentina is found in the "Sierras Pampinas", a series of north–south ranges which arose from blockfaulting of the old Paleozoic plateau. They form the southern end of the Puna Block. Earthquakes on the eastern flank of the Andes are less frequent than in the corresponding latitudes of the western flank; but they can be quite destructive. The region includes the Argentina provinces of Mendoza, San Juan, San Luis, La Rioja, and parts of Córdoba and Cajamarca.

A complete list of historic earthquakes for Region 8 is difficult to compile, as the records are rather inhomogeneous. Table 14.8 attempts to include the more important seismic events only.

Patagonia (Region 9)

Seismic geography

The southern tip of South America contains the Patagonian Andes, a low range forming the abutment of the Scotia Arc. It corresponds to a different geosyncline than the main Andes to the north.

The Patagonian Andes constitute a chain of low relief. Their western flank is occupied by a granodioritic batholith, and by extensive metamorphic schist complexes. Volcanism is relatively low. The juncture with the main Andean chain is a structurally complex transition zone between 40–42°S latitude. Tectonic evidence shows that the coastal active zone follows the Chile Trench down to latitude 47°S, where it continues along the

Chile Rise toward Easter Island. Hence the 47th Parallel may be regarded as the Northern boundary of the Patagonian region.

Historic earthquakes are rare, unless one includes the coastal activity north of the Chile Rise. The western branch of the Straits of Magellan follows an active fault, which has generated a few damaging earthquakes: February 2, 1879; December 17, 1949 (magnitude 7¾, epicenter near Lake Fagnano), and June 14, 1970 (magnitude 6.5).

Scotia Arc (Region 10; Table 14.9)

Seismic geography

The Scotia Arc (or Southern Antilles) is composed of several island groups of varying seismicity. The South Sandwich group, at the front of the arc, accounts for most of the earthquakes, and practically all of the volcanism. Shallow shocks occur between the South Sandwich Trench and the islands; intermediate earthquakes fall inside the arc. No deep shocks are known.

The ocean bottom topography indicates a closed basin structure. The rim is marked by the emerging island groups (South Georgia, South Orkneys, Shag Rocks), and by the islands off the West Antarctic Peninsula (South Shetlands). The Scotia Sea is open to the Pacific Ocean; the threshold between Cape Horn and Antarctica is very broad and free of islands. Seismic activity is small along both flanks of the arc, and insignificant along the West Antarctic Peninsula. Deception Island in the South Shetlands group is a large ruptured caldera accessible to navigation; it has volcanic activity, with several recent eruptions.

Among recent earthquakes of large magnitude most are in the South Sandwich area (Table 14.9).

TABLE 14.9

Earthquakes of the Scotia Arc (Region 10)

Date	Epicenter	M	Comments
1910 Nov. 15	South Sandwich	7.4	
1921 Sep. 13	South Sandwich	7.2	
1929 Jun. 27	South Sandwich	8.3	
1933 Aug. 28	South Sandwich	7.4	
1936 Jan. 14	South Sandwich	7.2	
1943 Mar. 9	South Sandwich	7.3	
1943 Mar. 25	South Sandwich	7.3	
1943 Nov. 2	South Sandwich	7.2	
1961 Sep. 1	South Sandwich	7.5	
1961 Sep. 5	South Sandwich	7.7	
1964 May 26	South Sandwich	7.3	
1970 Jun. 15	Falkland area	7.0	unusual epicenter

SOUTH PACIFIC OCEAN

This extensive and little explored area is bordered by segments of the Circum-Pacific Belt. Seismic areas are distributed along the boundaries between the Melanesian Basin and the Coral Sea, and around the Fiji—Tonga Salient through New Zealand and the Macquarie Islands.

Off the South American coast the East Pacific Ocean is divided into two relatively shallow basins: the Chile Basin and the Peru Basin. They are separated by the East Pacific Rise and by two shorter ridges irradiating from Easter Island: the Sala-y-Gómez Rise with the Nasca Ridge, and the Chile Rise to the south.

The East Pacific Rise follows a broad meridian sweep from the Macquarie Islands to Easter Island. It continues northward to the vicinity of the Galapagos Islands, where it intersects with other shallow ridges (Cocos Ridge, Carnegie Ridge). The Albatros Rise, off the Central American coast, is the continuation of the East Pacific Rise to the north.

Most of the South Pacific activity occurs in the islands between New Guinea and New Zealand: Kermadec and Tonga groups, Samoa, Fiji, New Caledonia and the New Hebrides, the Solomon Islands, and the Bismarck Archipelago. New Zealand appears to be a transitional segment. The East Pacific Rise and its branches generate only shallow earthquakes.

The South Pacific Basin proper is practically free of earthquakes.

New Zealand (Region 11: Map 12; Table 14.10)

Extension and seismicity

New Zealand, together with the rather dissimilar Macquarie Island area, form a complex seismic region which accounts for 1.2% of the world's total activity.

The tectonics and seismicity of New Zealand are better known than those of other areas of the South Pacific. Most authors distinguish a main seismic region (which includes most of the inhabited areas of New Zealand), and the Fiordland region comprising the South Island to the south of the latitude of Christchurch.

The highest activity occurs in Fiordland, and in the region of the Macquarie Islands about 1,000 km to the southwest. The seismicity pattern follows the curve of the East Pacific Rise. Only shallow shocks are known from the Rise itself, including the Macquarie Islands. However, intermediate shocks are frequent in New Zealand.

The South Island is traversed by the Alpine Fault, a long rift which has been compared to the San Andreas Rift in California. It shows right-lateral displacement; but, unlike the San Andreas Fault, it does not represent a locus of concentrated seismic risk for the region.

The seismicity of the North Island appears to merge with the Kermadec region to the north. However, the Northland Peninsula has only nominal seismic activity. In the South Island the seismicity dies out near 42°S and reappears in Fiordland (southwest coast), by

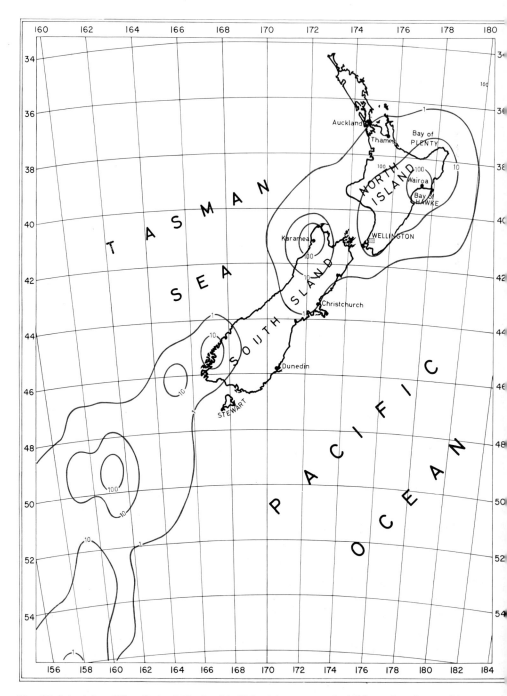

Map 12. Seismicity of New Zealand: Region 11. (Seismicity contours in 10^{15} ergs km^{-2} year^{-1}.)

TABLE 14.10

Earthquakes of New Zealand (Region 11)

Date	Epicenter	M	Comments
1460±	Wellington	8	
1826	Fiordland	7½–8	
1843 Jul. 8	Wanganui	7½	
1848 Oct. 19	Awatere	7–7½	
1855 Jan. 23	S.W. Wairarapa	8	vertical faulting
1888 Sep. 1	North Canterbury	7	transcurrent faulting
1897 Dec. 8	Wanganui Bight	7	
1901 Nov. 16	Cheviot	7	
1904 Aug. 9	Off Cape Turnagain	7½	
1914 Oct. 7	E. Bay of Plenty	7–7½	
1921 Jun. 29	Hawkes Bay	7	depth 80 km
1929 Mar. 9	Arthur's Pass	7½	
1929 Jun. 17	Buller (Murchison)	7¾	vertical faulting
1931 Feb. 3	Hawkes Bay	7¾	
1932 Sep. 16	Wairoa	7¼	
1934 Mar. 5	Pahiatua	7½	
1942 Jun. 24	Wairarapa	7.1	
1960 May 24	Fiordland	7.0	
1968 May 23	Inangahua	7.0	

far the most active region of New Zealand. There is relatively minor activity in the Canterbury Plain and in Otago Province. Volcanism is important particularly in the North Island, and is associated with shallow earthquake swarms. Deep-focus shocks down to depths of 600 km occur under the North Island.

Tonga, Kermadec, Fiji, and Samoa (Regions 12 and 13: Map 13)

Extension and seismicity

This entire region is sometimes referred to as the "Tonga Salient", as it resembles a corner jutting into the Pacific Basin. It is a region of intense subduction, comparable in seismicity to the southern Andes but with a higher proportion of deep-focus shocks. The magnitude distribution is also different, with a larger number of small earthquakes as compared to South America. The total seismicity amounts to 5.8% of the world's earthquake activity.

The core of the salient is a shallow stable block which emerges in the Fiji Islands. The active zone faces east, along a sequence of deep oceanic trenches from New Zealand to Samoa. There the seismicity bends rather sharply to the west and gradually diminishes in intensity.

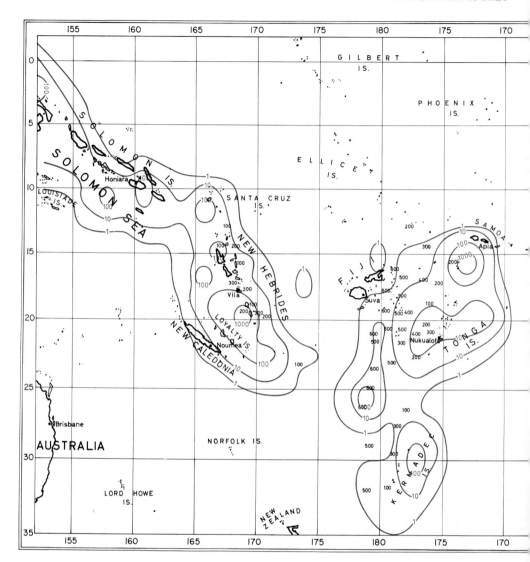

Map 13. Seismicity of Fiji–Tonga–Samoa–New Hebrides: Regions 12–13–14. (Seismicity contours are numbered in 10^{15} ergs km^{-2} year^{-1}.)

Seismic geography

Shallow earthquake activity is grouped by the island pattern: the Kermadec area (25–35°S), the Tonga area (17–25°S) and the Samoa area (north of 17°S). There appears to be a sequence of flat, rectilinear island arcs. Intermediate earthquakes occur chiefly under the islands themselves, while deep-focus shocks scatter over a wide region to the west, chiefly between the Tonga and Fiji Archipelagoes. Volcanism is fairly active.

The oceanic trench stops short of Samoa and the arc apparently has no well-defined abutment or flank zone there. Instead, the shallow activity gradually diminshes toward the west. There is some continuity across the Fiji block; a number of small shallow shocks occur around the Fiji Islands. Most of the considerable seismic activity in the Fiji region takes place at depths of 500–600 km and is clearly related to the Tonga subduction zone.

TABLE 14.11

Earthquakes of Tonga, Kermadec, Fiji and Samoa (Regions 12 and 13)

Date	Epicenter	M	Observations
1902 Feb. 9	Tonga	7.8	
1909 Feb. 22	Tonga	7.5	$h = 550$ km
1910 Aug. 21	Tonga	7.3	$h = 600$ km
1913 Jun. 26	Tonga	7.6	
1915 Feb. 25	Tonga	7.3	$h = 600$ km
1917 May 1	Kermadec	8.6	
1917 Jun. 26	Tonga	8.7	
1917 Nov. 16	Kermadec	7.5	aftershock of May 1
1919 Jan. 1	Tonga	7.8	$h = 180$ km
1919 Apr. 30	Tonga	8.4	
1924 May 4	Tonga	7.3	$h = 560$ km
1932 May 26	Kermadec	7.8	$h = 600$ km
1934 Oct. 10	Tonga	7.3	$h = 540$ km
1937 Apr. 16	Tonga	7.8	$h = 400$ km
1943 Sep. 14	Kermadec	7.6	two earthquakes
1944 May 25	Tonga	7.2	$h = 640$ km
1948 Jan. 27	Tonga	7.2	$h = 630$ km
1948 Sep. 8	Tonga	7.9	
1949 Aug. 6	Tonga	7.5	$h = 70$ km
1950 Dec. 14	Tonga	7.7	$h = 200$ km
1956 Jan. 10	Tonga	7.7	
1956 May 23	Fiji	7.2	$h = 450$ km
1956 Dec. 27	Tonga	7.0	$h = 300$ km
1957 Apr. 14	Samoa	7.6	
1957 Jul. 14	Tonga	7.1	$h = 200$ km
1957 Sep. 28	Fiji	7.3	$h = 650$ km
1959 Sep. 14	Kermadec	7.8	
1959 Sep. 15	Kermadec	7.0	aftershock
1960 Nov. 24	Tonga	7.0	$h = 23$ km
1961 Mar. 7	Kermadec	7.3	$h = 43$ km

New Hebrides and Santa Cruz Islands (Region 14: Map 13; Table 14.12)

Extension and seismicity

The *New Hebrides* structure may be considered a Pacific-type island arc molded around the Fiji nucleus. A branch of the East Pacific Rise runs parallel to this structure but is largely inactive, except for occasional shocks in the New Caledonia area. The island of New Caledonia appears to be geologically unrelated to the New Hebrides across the ocean trench.

TABLE 14.12

Earthquakes of New Hebrides and Santa Cruz Islands (Region 14)

Date	Epicenter	M	Comments
1875 Mar. 28	Loyalty Islands		tsunami
1894 Oct. 15	Ainbrim		
1900 Jul. 29	Santa Cruz Islands	8.1	
1901 Aug. 9	S. New Hebrides	8.4	
1903 May 13	Mallicolo Is.	7.9	
1920 Sep. 20	S. New Hebrides	8.3	
1934 Jul. 18	Santa Cruz Islands	8.1	
1950 Dec. 2	S. New Hebrides	8.1	
1961 Jul. 23	Vaté Island	7.5	
1964 Jul. 5	Espiritu Santo Is.	7.5	
1965 Aug. 11	Mallicolo Is.	7.5	

Region 14 also includes the highly active Santa Cruz Islands to the north. The total activity of the region reaches 4.1% of world seismicity.

Seismic geography

The apparently anomalous position of the New Hebrides arc, facing away from the Pacific Ocean, actually agrees with the general structure of the region. The East Pacific Rise runs between it and the Australian continental mass. Farther on, the Rise seems to intersect the island arc chain and to die out north of the Solomon Islands.

Both the New Hebrides—Santa Cruz and the Solomon Islands arcs are increasingly narrow; intermediate shocks tend to occur practically under the same line as the shallow earthquakes. Thus, a reversal from concave to convex structure appears to occur gradually. Deep shocks are infrequent. The structural relation with the Samoa—Tonga region is still unclear. There may be a shallow connection trending northeast between the Fiji and Tonga Islands.

This area is among the least well-studied seismic zones, due to the scarcity of local stations. Most shallow shocks appear to occur between the island arcs and the New

Hebrides Trench. Volcanism is very active. Major shallow earthquakes generate tsunamis and can be destructive over a wide area.

Solomon and Bismarck Archipelagoes (Region 15: Map 14; Table 14.13)

Extension and seismicity

The Solomon group is a double row of elongated islands trending northwest; it includes San Cristobal, Guadalcanal, Malaita, Santa Isabel, New Georgia, Choiseul, Bougainville, and others. Between Bougainville and the west coast of New Guinea are the two islands of New Britain and New Ireland, largest of the Bismarck group. They form a small arc open to the west and enclosing the Bismarck Sea. The entire region accounts for 2.2% of the world's seismic activity.

TABLE 14.13

Earthquakes of the Solomon and Bismarck Archipelagoes (Region 15)

Date	Epicenter	M
1906 Sep. 14	New Britain	8.4
1916 Jan. 1	New Ireland	7.9
1919 May 6	N. Bougainville	8.1
1939 Jan. 30	Bougainville	7.9
1939 Apr. 30	off Guadalcanal	8.1
1945 Dec. 28	New Britain	7.8
1964 Nov. 17	New Britain	7.6

Seismic geography

The region is among the most seismic in the world, though the proportion of very large shocks is not as great as in the New Hebrides. The structure is largely unknown. The ocean-bottom topography is complicated by the juncture with the branch of an oceanic rise coming from the Loyalty Islands. A deep trench occurs south of the Solomon Islands. The seismicity is largely shallow to intermediate; deep earthquakes are rare and volcanism is moderate.

The Bismarck Archipelago is a small arc fronting on its own oceanic trench: the Bougainville Trough. It resembles the curved arcs typical of Indonesia. Most of the shallow seismicity in this region takes place near the fork or juncture between the Solomon Ridge and the Bismarck Arc (Bougainville, New Ireland, Gazelle Peninsula). Intermediate epicenters fall along the same general axis as the shallow seismicity.

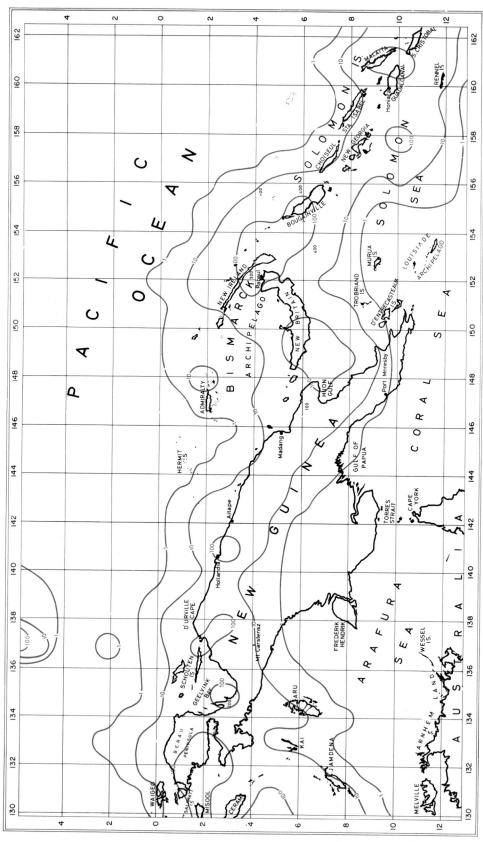

Map 14. Seismicity of New Guinea–Solomon Islands: Regions 15–16. (Seismicity contours are numbered in 10^{15} ergs km^{-1} year^{-1}.)

New Guinea (Region 16: Map 14; Table 14.14)

Seismic geography

The New Guinea region (2.2% of world seismicity) is usually divided into an eastern sector attached to the Bismarck Arc, and a western region (Irian Barat) related to the Indonesian arcs.

The Bismarck Sea is elliptical in shape and includes the Admiralty, Hermit, and Ninigo Islands, of relatively low seismicity. On the southern shores are the volcanic islands of Long, Karkar etc., off the coast of New Guinea. These coastal islands may be a continuation of the Bismarck Arc; the activity is high along the island axis and into the New Guinea coast, where the epicentral depths increase down to about 150 km. The trend of activity in New Guinea follows the entire length of the central mountain range even beyond its branch point with the Bismarck structure. Thus, the Owen Stanley Range of eastern Papua is also highly seismic.

TABLE 14.14

Earthquakes of New Guinea (Region 16)

Date	Epicenter	M
1900 Oct. 7	central New Guinea	7.8
1902 Jan. 24	Trobriand Is.	7.8
1914 May 26	north-central New Guinea	7.9
1916 Jan. 13	Geelvink Bay	8.1
1926 Oct. 26	Orange Range	7.9
1935 Sep. 20	north-central New Guinea	7.9
1943 Nov. 6	Aru Islands	7.6

The activity is strongest in central and northern New Guinea; it diminishes rapidly toward the west. Epicenters follow the Nassau Range and continue offshore under the Arafura Sea, where they merge with the seismicity of the Banda Arc. This is a region of shallow activity. There are larger shocks mostly along the northern shore and on the Berau Peninsula, by way of the Banggai Archipelago and the islands of Obi and Misol. North of this geanticline is the island of Halmahera, an important branch point of regional tectonics. South of the same structure is the Banda Arc, which eventually leads into the Alpide structures of Southeast Asia.

WESTERN PACIFIC OCEAN

Looking at a map of epicenters of the Pacific Ocean one is struck by the extremely high seismicity of the western Pacific border islands. These epicenters occur in a continuous belt, shaped like a bow, with its two extremes in Kamchatka and the Mariana Islands and its midpoint in central Japan.

This important structure is fairly symmetrical. Deep and intermediate earthquakes occur chiefly near the center and decrease in frequency toward both ends. Most of the largest shocks are found in the Japanese segment; in general the northern branch is more active than its southern counterpart.

Behind the active arcs are the Sea of Okhotsk and the Philippine Sea, two large oceanic basins. The Philippine Sea is completely surrounded by seismic activity, since its western border is formed by the East Asian insular belt (southern Japan, Ryukyu, Taiwan, Philippines, and Indonesia). This particular active belt appears to terminate in the Island of Kyushu.

It may be assumed that the western Pacific structure should be continuous with the rest of the Circum-Pacific Belt. In the north it is joined with the Aleutian Arc, and in the south it is connected to western New Guinea or to Halmahera. In both cases there are gaps of low seismicity or sudden changes in geographical trend; this is reflected in the shape of the island arcs and of the oceanic trenches.

Micronesia (Regions 17 and 18: Map 15; Table 14.15)

Extension and seismicity

From the western tip of New Guinea to the north we find a chain of islands, the largest of which is Palau in the Caroline Archipelago. Here the trend of the islands curves toward the east. The Caroline Islands are scattered over a wide portion of the Pacific Ocean, occupying roughly the same longitude range as New Guinea but centering some $10°$ to the north. The seismicity amounts to 0.4% of the world total.

East of the islands is the Philippine Sea, a large, deep oceanic basin. Its boundary with the Pacific Ocean is occupied by island chains: the Caroline Islands, Mariana Islands, Volcano Islands, Bonin Islands, and Nampo Islands off the Japan Coast. These are sections of a single arc structure. The seismicity in the Mariana, Volcano, and Bonin Archipelagoes totals 3.9% of the world's seismicity, only slightly less than that of the New Hebrides region.

TABLE 14.15

Earthquakes of Micronesia (Regions 17, 18)

Date	Epicenter	M
1849 Jan. 25	Mariana Islands	
1862 Jul. 1	Guam	
1902 Sep. 22	Central Marianas	8.1
1911 Aug. 16	Palau Island	8.1
1953 Nov. 25	Nampo Island	8.0

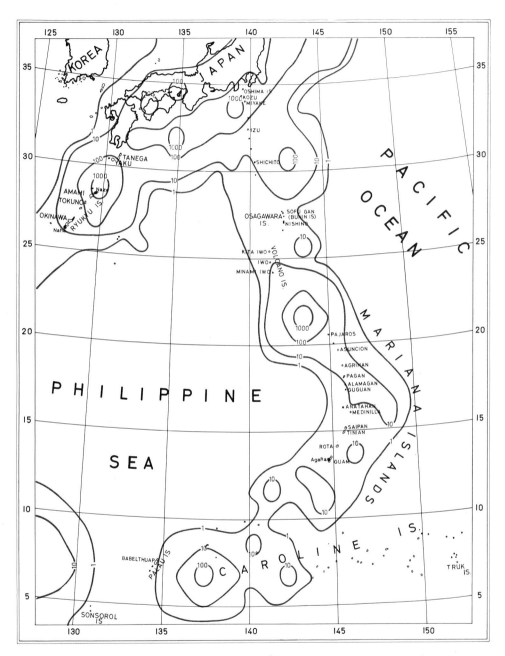

Map 15. Seismicity of Micronesia: Regions 17–18. (Seismicity contours are numbered in 10^{15} ergs km^{-2} $year^{-1}$.)

Seismic geography

The southern end of the Caroline active region is open; there is a gap in earthquake activity between New Guinea and Palau Island.

In the Carolines most of the activity may be traced along the oceanic trenches east of Palau and Yap. A number of earthquakes scatter eastward as well. Only shallow shocks are known from this region.

The Mariana Islands (formerly known as Ladrones Islands) border on an important oceanic trench, which reaches maximum depth near the south end of the island chain (Guam Island). Shallow earthquakes occur between the trench and the islands; intermediate and deep earthquakes are displaced toward the west, in the pattern common to all Pacific arcs. Deep-focus activity is proportionately greater in the northern continuation of the Mariana Arc (Volcano, or Kazan, Islands) and increases toward Japan (Ogasawara, Bonin, Nampo, Shichitu, and Izu Islands). The active seismic trend continues into northern Honshu. Volcanism increases toward the north. Large shallow shocks are relatively infrequent; they tend to be associated with tsunamis.

Northern Japan, Kurile Islands, and Kamchatka (Regions 19 and 46: Maps 16 and 17; Tables 14.16 and 14.17)

Extension and seismicity

Gutenberg and Richter (1954) divided Japan into two different seismic regions. They assumed that the boundary was near the Fossa Magna, a volcanic rift which crosses central Honshu in a transverse direction. This rift marks a change in trend of the West Pacific structure.

Northern Japan was included by Gutenberg and Richter (1954) into a single region with Kamchatka and the Kurile Islands, thereby becoming the most active seismic area in the world. It accounts for 13.8% of the world's seismicity. The deep-focus earthquakes under the Sea of Okhotsk were considered as Region 46, but we do not follow this distinction. The density of seismic activity is probably the highest in the world, both as to frequency and number of large shocks.

Seismic geography

Northern Honshu and Hokkaido form an arcuate pattern, with the Japan Trench to the east. An extremely active shallow seismic zone follows the western slope of the trench. Intermediate shocks occur between the coast and the well-developed volcanic alignment. The distribution of intermediate and deep shocks is interesting. At every depth level the trend curves around toward the Mariana Arc. No deep-focus activity is present in Southern Japan or in the Ryukyu Arc to the south.

The great shallow earthquakes off the coast of northern Honshu tend to cause destructive tsunamis. Near the Fossa Magna is a major coastal source of normal activity, which was responsible for the great Sagami Bay (Tokyo) earthquake of 1923. Important active

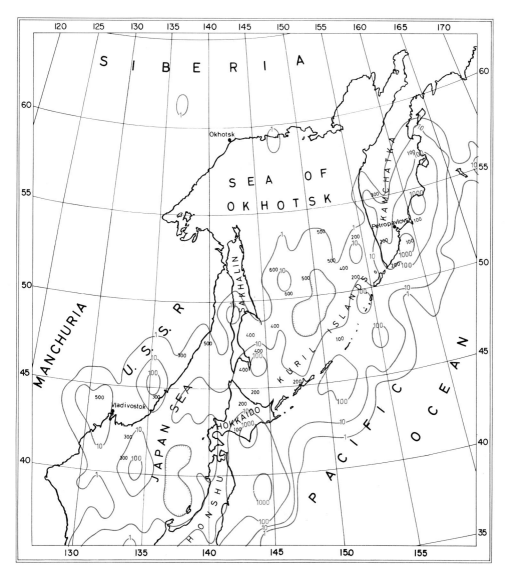

Map 16. Seismicity of Hokkaido–Kuriles–Kamchatka: Regions 19 and 46. (Seismicity contours numbered in 10^{15} ergs km^{-2} year^{-1}.)

TABLE 14.16

Earthquakes of Japan (Regions 19, 20)

Date	Epicenter	M	Comments
684 Nov. 29	Nankaido	8.4	
745 Jun. 5	Mino	7.9	
818 Aug. 10	Tokyo	7.9	
869 Jul. 13	Osju	8.6	
887 Aug. 26	Mino	8.6	
1293 May 27	Kamakura	7.1	
1361 Aug. 3	Kinai	8.4	
1498 Sep. 20	Totomi	8.6	tsunami
1596 Sep. 4	Kyushu	6.9	
1605 Jan. 31	Shikoku	7.9	tsunami
1611 Dec. 2	Sendai	8.1	tsunami
1614 Nov. 26	Central Japan	7.7	tsunami
1677 Apr. 13	Tsugaru	8.1	
1703 Dec. 31	Tokyo	8.2	5,233 dead
1707 Oct. 28	Shikoku	8.4	4,900 dead; tsunami
1751 May 20	Echigo	6.6	2,000 dead
1843 Apr. 25	Yedo	8.4	tsunami
1847 May 8	Zenkoji	7.4	12,000 dead
1854 Dec. 23, 24	Simoda	8.4, 8.4	3,000 dead; tsunami
1855 Nov. 11	Sagami	6.9	6,757 dead
1891 Oct. 28	Mino—Owari	8.4	7,273 dead
1896 Jun. 15	N. Japan	7.6	27,122 dead; tsunami
1923 Sep. 1	Tokyo	8.3	99,331 dead
1927 Mar. 7	Tango	8.0	3,017 dead
1933 Mar. 2	N. Honshu	8.9	2,986 dead; tsunami
1943 Sep. 10	Tottori	7.2	1,190 dead
1944 Dec. 7	Tonankai	8.3	998 dead; tsunami
1945 Jan. 12	Mikawa	7.1	1,901 dead (aftershock of 1944 Dec. 7)
1946 Dec. 20	Nankaido	8.5	1,330 dead; tsunami
1948 Jun. 28	Fukui	7.3	5,386 dead
1952 Mar. 4	S.E. Hokkaido	8.6	600 dead
1964 Jun. 16	Niigata	7.5	25 dead; tsunami
1968 May 16	Tokachi-Oki	7.8	48 dead; tsunami

faults run parallel to the Fossa Magna to the west, in the provinces of Echizen, Mino, Owari, and Mikawa. Motion on these transverse faults is left lateral. In spite of the much higher offshore activity in the Pacific Ocean or the Philippine Sea, historical records show that the most frequent damage is to be expected from epicenters on land. These epi-centers occur throughout Japan, but particularly in the transverse zone from Ise Bay to Wakasa Bay, and along the coast of the Sea of Japan. Geologically, these shallow earth-quakes are attributed to block faulting in an older mountain complex; their genetic relationship with global tectonics and volcanism is still unclear.

TABLE 14.17

Earthquakes of the Kamchatka–Kuril region (Region 19)

Date	Epicenter	M	Comments
1737 Oct. 6	Kamchatka		
1899 Nov. 23	Kamchatka	7.9	
1901 Apr. 5	Kuril Is.	7.9	
1904 Jun. 25	Kamchatka	8.3	aftershocks of $M = 8.1$ and 7.9
1915 May 1	Kuril Is.	8.1	
1917 Jan. 30	Kamchatka	8.1	
1918 Sep. 7	Kuril Is.	8.3	
1923 Feb. 3	Kamchatka	8.4	
1952 Nov. 4	Kamchatka	8.4	
1958 Nov. 6	Kuril Is.	8.7	
1959 May 4	Kamchatka	8.3	
1963 Oct. 13	Kuril Is.	8.3	

The total length of the Japan–Kamchatka Arc is about the same as of the Aleutian Arc. The overall seismicity of Hokkaido is moderate. There are intermediate earthquakes under the volcanic zone.

The Kuril Islands, an archipelago with arcuate structure, bars the entrance to the Sea of Okhotsk. The seismicity is intense; it is probably highest near the center of the arc (Urup Island) where the Kuril Trench is deepest. Intermediate and deep-focus earthquakes occur under the Sea of Okhotsk and Sakhalin, but the deep-focus activity is lower than in the Honshu-Volcano Island segment (Fig.14.7).

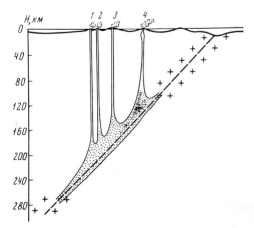

Fig.14.7. Intermediate seismicity and volcanism of the Kurile Islands. (After an interpretation by Markhinin and Stratula, 1971.)

The Kamchatka Peninsula forms the direct continuation of the Kuril Arc. Large shallow earthquakes occur off the coast of Kamchatka through the latitude of the Komandorsky Islands. North of this point there is hardly any activity. Intermediate earthquakes originate under the volcanic chains of the Peninsula. Important tsunamis may be generated by the major shallow shocks.

The seismic history of the Japanese region is extremely long and eventful. Earthquakes of magnitude 8 or over have occurred every 3 or 4 years (on the average) during the present century. In Table 14.16 we list only the more disastrous shocks, omitting many important earthquakes of lesser consequence. The magnitudes of the older shocks are given according to Kawasumi (1951).

CHAPTER 15

East Asian Insular Belt and Eurasia

INTRODUCTION

In southern Honshu begins a major branch of seismic activity, which follows the Ryukyu Islands to Indonesia passing through Taiwan and the Philippines. This structure is intermediate in position between the Pacific and Asian domains; seismically speaking it provides a link between the Circum-Pacific and Alpide systems.

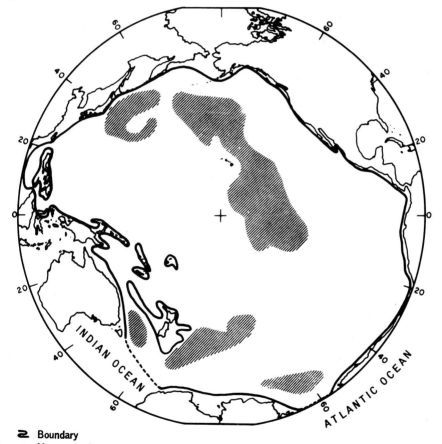

⇌ Boundary
⫻ Most normal regions

Fig.15.1. The Pacific Ocean basin and the boundary of "continental" structure – also called the Andesite line. (From Menard, 1964.)

The Philippine Sea, the South China Sea, and other ocean basins inside these arcs are historically different from the Pacific basin proper. They are free of seamounts and manifestations of ancient volcanism. The East Asian insular belt is entirely within the so-called "Andesite Line", which forms the geologic boundary of the Pacific Ocean proper (Fig.15.1). On the other hand, these island arcs do not differ fundamentally from Pacific arcs in terms of seismicity and crustal structure. There is the characteristic sequence of deep oceanic trench, outer island arc, inner volcanic axis and stable interior. The shallow shocks occur along the zone of negative gravity anomalies, between the trench and the island arc. Intermediate shocks are found under the volcanic axis, and deep earthquakes scatter under the interior of the arc. The arc abutments in Kyushu, Taiwan, and Sumatra are predominantly regions of block faulting, where deep-focus earthquakes are absent. North of Sumatra the seismicity decays markedly in the Nicobar and Andaman Islands, and in the Ranges of Burma.

The East Asian insular belt begins at the Ryukyu Arc which has. its northern abutment in the Japanese island of Kyushu. Its southern abutment is in Taiwan, a transition region of shallow seismicity. From here the belt follows a southerly direction into Luzon Island in the Philippines.

EAST ASIAN INSULAR BELT

Kyushu and Ryukyu Islands (Region 20; Map 17)

Seismicity and seismic geography

This region participates in the high seismicity level of Region 19 to the north. It accounts for 4.2% of the earth's seismicity.

Southern Honshu to the southwest of the Fossa Magna is a zone of block tectonics. Earthquakes have surface expressions, frequently in the form of left-lateral faults striking transversely to the island. A major longitudinal tectonic trend begins to develop to the west; this is associated with a large thrust fault called the Median Tectonic Line, which was active until the Tertiary age in a southerly direction. The Median Tectonic Line continues into Shikoku and Kyushu and disappears under the East China Sea. Mesozoic mountain ranges associated with the Median structure are similar to the Chinling Range and its continuation across east China. They may represent an intermediate orogeny between the Altaid and the.Alpide.

In Kyushu the trend of the active arc intersects the Median Tectonic Line. Volcanism reappears and follows a southwesterly direction (Ryukyu Islands). The main islands are not volcanic; volcanoes appear on a row of smaller islands along the inside of the arc (Tokara Islands). This pattern is characteristic of island arcs in the East Asian insular belt.

Shallow earthquakes occur along the oceanic trenches and the main islands. Intermediate shocks are found under the volcanic axis, particularly near both ends of the arc (Kyushu, and Sakishina group). No deep-focus earthquakes are known.

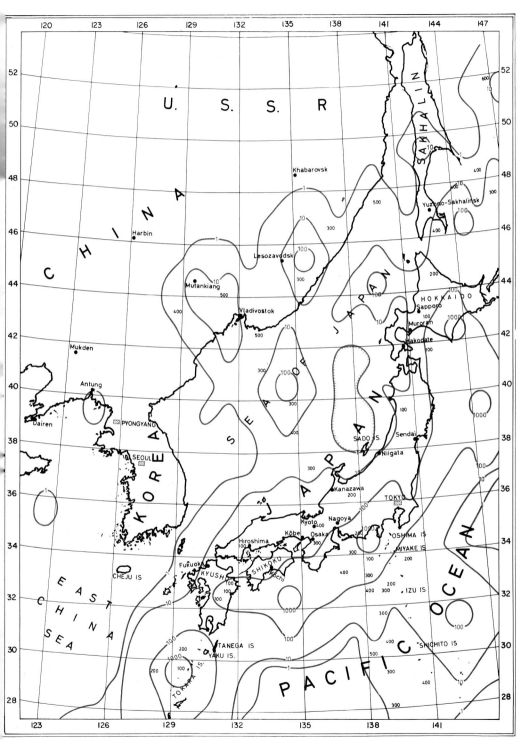

Map 17. Seismicity of Japan: Regions 19–20. (Seismicity contours are numbered in 10^{15} ergs km^{-2} year^{-1}.)

Major earthquakes of Kyushu were listed with the Japanese earthquakes (p.224). Recent large earthquakes in the Ryukyu Islands region include: June 24, 1901 (magnitude 7.9); August 24, 1904 (Tokara Islands, 7.9); April 12, 1910 (Senkaku Islands, 8.3); June 15, 1911 (Tokara Islands, 8.7); June 16, 1938 (Tokuno Island, 7.4); September 26, 1947 (Sakishima Island, 7.4); March 11, 1958 (Sekibi Island, 7.5); April 26, 1959 (off northeast Taiwan, 7.7).

Taiwan (Region 21: Table 15.1)

Seismicity and seismic geography

Taiwan is a large island forming the southern abutment of the Ryukyu Arc. It is a region of block tectonics totaling about 1.6% of the world's seismicity. Taiwan has no volcanic activity and no deep-focus earthquakes.

TABLE 15.1

Earthquakes of Taiwan (Region 21)

Date	Epicenter	M	Comments
1655 Jan. 21	Tainan		
1686 May 12	central Taiwan		
1720 Nov. 1	Tainan		large aftershock on Jan. 5, 1721
1776 Dec.	Kagi		
1792 Jul. 20	Kagi		
1815 Jul.	Garan		
1832 Nov.	Garan		
1840 Nov.	Unrin		
1848	Unrin		
1862 Jun. 6	Kagi		
1867 Dec. 18	Kilung		
1906 Mar. 16	Kagi	7.1	1,258 dead
1935 Apr. 20	Shinchiku	7.0	
1951 Oct. 21, 22 and Nov. 24	E. Coast of Taiwan	7.3, 7.1, 7.3	100 dead
1959 Aug. 15	S. Taiwan		16 dead
1966 Mar. 12	N.E. Taiwan	7.5	several dead

Most shocks occur on a fault system striking NNE–SSW parallel to the east coast of the island. Some fall on land and some offshore; since this area is rugged and moderately populated they rarely cause much damage. The better-known damaging earthquakes have their epicenter under the Western plains. They are frequently accompanied by surface faulting. Right-hand lateral displacements were observed in the 1906 and 1935 earthquakes, but the main fault system is associated with left lateral motion.

Philippines (Region 22: Map 18; Table 15.2)

Extension and seismicity

The Philippines Archipelago is a large and complex region, which accounts for over 3.2% of the world's seismic activity. It consists of several arcs with associated rifts and areas of block tectonics.

TABLE 15.2

Earthquakes of the Philippines (Region 22)

Date	Epicenter	M	Comments
1599 June 21	Manila		
1619 Nov. 20	N. Luzon		
1645 Nov. 30	Manila		several hundred dead
1658 Aug. 20	Manila		
1675 Mar.	Mindoro		
1743 Jan. 12	Tayabas, Luzon		
1787 May 13	Panay		
1796 Nov. 5	Manila		
1824 Oct. 26	Manila		
1830 Jan. 18	Luzon		
1852 Sep. 16	SW. Luzon		
1863 Jun. 3	Manila		300 dead
1869 Aug. 16	S. Masbate		
1871 Dec. 8	S. Mindanao		
1876 Jul. 26	N. Mindanao		
1878 Sep. 16	Mindanao		
1879 Jul. 1	Surigao, Mindanao		
1880 Jul. 18	Luzon		
1889 May 26	Batangas, Luzon		
1892 Mar. 16	Luzon		
1897 Sep. 20, 21	Basilan, W. Mindanao	8.6, 8.7	tsunami
1897 Oct. 18, 20	Samar	8.1, 7.9	
1901 Dec. 14	Batangas, Luzon	7.8	
1903 Dec. 28	off E. Mindanao	7.8	
1907 Apr. 18	S. Luzon	7.2	
1911 Jul. 12	N. Mindanao	7.7	
1918 Aug. 15	off S. Mindanao	8.3	
1924 Apr. 14	off SE. Mindanao	8.3	
1934 Feb. 14	off N. Luzon	7.9	
1937 Aug. 20	central Luzon	7.5	
1942 Apr. 8	N. Mindoro	7.9	
1943 May 25	off Mindanao	8.1	
1948 Jan. 24	S. Panay	8.3	20 dead
1949 Dec. 29	NW. Luzon	7.2	
1952 Mar. 19	off N. Mindanao	7.9	
1955 Mar. 31	Lanao, Mindanao	7.6	400 dead
1968 Aug. 1	Casiguran, Luzon	7.3	270 dead
1970 Apr. 7	Luzon		

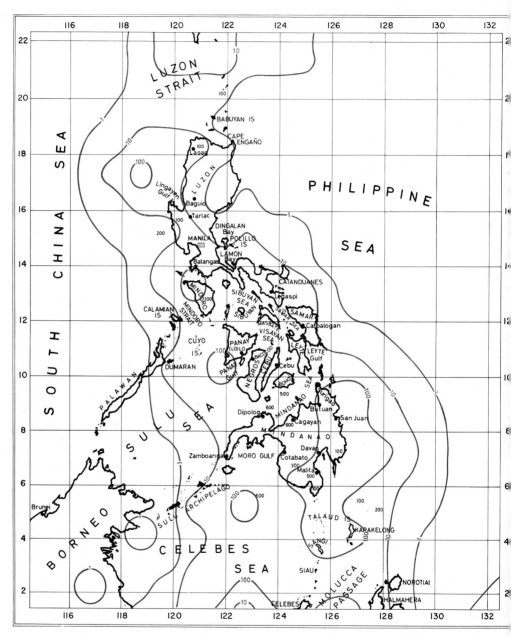

Map 18. Seismicity of the Philippines. Region 22. (Seismicity contours are numbered in 10^{15} ergs km^{-2} year^{-1}.)

On the Pacific side there is a long trench, which includes Mindanao Deep (10,497 m), among the deepest in the world. The tectonic trend of the islands is approximately S-shaped, with the Luzon Arc fronting on the South China Sea, and the Mindanao Arc on the Philippine Sea. Two interior arcs join these structures with the massive older nucleus of Borneo.

The axis of the archipelago is an active left-lateral fault zone called the Philippine Rift. The surface expression of this rift is outstanding and it appears to be associated with the more destructive shallow earthquakes on Mindanao and Luzon. Other large shallow earthquakes occur off the east coast of Mindanao, between the island and the oceanic trench.

Seismic geography

Volcanism reappears to the south of Taiwan in Batan Island, but the ridge between Taiwan and Luzon shows little activity. There are shallow earthquakes in western Luzon and off the west coast. Intermediate earthquakes occur inland. Volcanism is most active in central and southern Luzon. The more destructive shocks are along the Philippine Rift, particularly in Luzon, Mindoro, Masbate, and Mindanao; they may be associated with surface faulting. The Rift crosses the narrowest part of Luzon into the Sibuyan Sea, through the islands of Masbate and Leyte and into eastern Mindanao. Earthquakes in the interior seas (Sibuyan Sea, Visayan Sea, Mindanao Sea) are not frequent. The activity concentrates along the western margin of the Mindanao Trench; intermediate earthquakes occur under eastern Mindanao, and deep shocks under the volcanic axis (western Mindanao, Mindanao Sea). Large shallow shocks off the Gulf of Davao and between Mindanao and Talaud Island may cause destructive tsunamis.

The Palawan Ridge and Sulu Ridge join the Philippine region with Borneo. These structures have a low level of activity. About Mindanao the epicenters scatter considerably; both shallow and deep shocks occur throughout Mindanao and the eastern Celebes Sea.

Molucca Sea (Region 23: Map 19; Table 15.3)

Seismicity and seismic geography

The star-shaped outlines of the islands of Celebes and Halmahera reflect some of the structural features of this region. The area is about the same as in neighboring New Guinea but the activity is twice as high (4.8% of the world total).

Gutenberg and Richter (1954) assumed tectonic continuity between the Caroline Islands (Palau Island) and Halmahera. Actually the ridge between these points is intersected by the Philippine Trench, a fact which explains the lack of seismicity along this ridge.

The Mindanao Arc curves through the Talaud and Sangihe Islands into northern Celebes. The Halmahera Arc confronts this structure across the Molucca Straits, an oceanic channel which contains a belt of large negative gravity anomalies. Both the

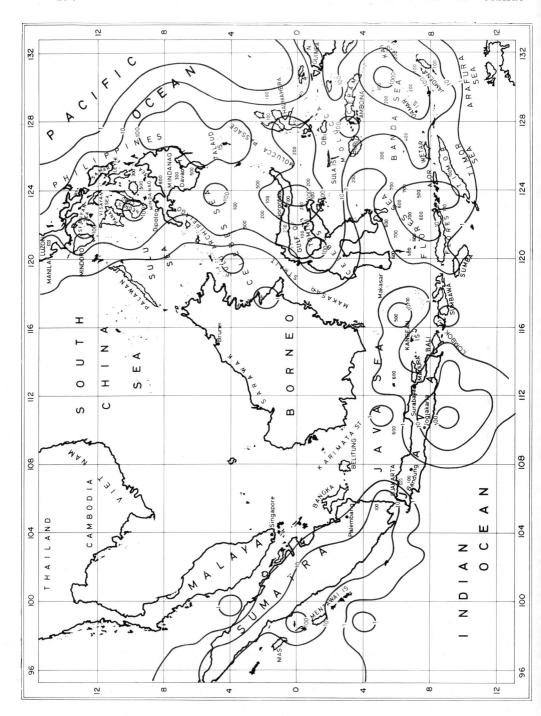

TABLE 15.3

Earthquakes of Celebes–Moluccas Islands (Region 23)

Date	Epicenter	M	Comments
1845 Feb. 12	Menado, Celebes		
1865 Nov. 25	Kema, Celebes		
1905 Jan. 22	N. Celebes	8.4	depth 90 km
1913 Mar. 14	Talaud Is.	8.3	
1932 May 14	Molucca Straits	8.3	
1938 May 19	Dongala, Celebes	7.9	8 dead, tsunami
1939 Dec. 21	N. Celebes	8.6	depth 150 km

Celebes and Halmahera arcs are volcanic. Most of the shallow seismicity occurs in the Molucca Straits. Large intermediate earthquakes take place in northern Celebes and Halmahera. Deep-focus earthquakes are confined to the Celebes Sea.

The connection between Halmahera and northern New Guinea is a tectonic problem area. Negative gravity anomalies in the Molucca Straits terminate at the Sula geanticline, an east–west trending structure which joins New Guinea to central Celebes. This geanticline marks a definite low in seismicity. Perhaps the Molucca Straits are a transition region between Philippine tectonics and the great arc structure of the Banda Sea.

Occasional shallow shocks in the Macassar Straits area were attributed by Gutenberg and Richter (1954) to a marginal fracture zone of the Borneo stable area.

Banda and Sunda Arcs (Region 24: Map 19; Table 15.4)

Extension and seismicity

The Banda Arc is on the emplacement of an S-shaped geosyncline. It was folded during the Laramide orogeny and possesses clear Pacific-type features. The Sunda Arc appears to branch off this structure in the region north of Timor; it trends west and later northwest toward continental Asia. It has all the characteristics of a Pacific Arc. Sumatra is a region of block tectonics and contains a long right-lateral fault zone. The Sumatra structure continues into the Nicobar–Andaman Ridge which connects with the tectonics of Burma. The total seismicity of the Banda–Sunda structure is about the same as for the Moluccas: 4.2% of the world's total seismicity.

Seismic geography

The Banda Arc abuts in the relatively inactive region of central Celebes. It consists of the islands of Buru and Ceram, Kai, Tanimbar, Babar, Timor, and intervening smaller islands, forming the outer belt of a strongly curved arc. The volcanic axis follows an inner belt of small islands, including Banda and the Damar group. Between the two belts is the Weber Deep, which is well within the axis of negative gravity anomalies.

TABLE 15.4

Earthquakes of the Banda and Sunda Arcs (Region 24)

Date	Epicenter	M	Comments
1828 Dec. 29	S. Celebes		tsunami
1843 Jan. 6	Tapanuli, Sumatra		tsunami
1847 Oct. 31	Nicobar Is.		
1847 Nov. 16	Java–Sumatra		
1849 May 28	Amboina		
1852 Nov. 26	Banda Is.		tsunami
1852 Dec. 20	W. Java		
1861 Feb. 16	off central Sumatra		tsunami
1867 Jun. 9	central Java		
1871 May 25	Malacca Straits		
1873 Aug. 9	Tapanuli, Sumatra		
1875 Dec. 13	N. Java		
1881 Dec. 31	Andaman Is.		tsunami
1883 Aug. 27	Krakatau, Sunda Straits		volcanic explosion; tsunami, 3,600 dead
1883 Nov. 25	Amboina		
1885 Apr. 30	Amboina		
1892 May 17	Tapanuli, Sumatra		
1893 Jun. 12	S. Sumatra		
1896 Apr. 18	Timor		
1899 Sep. 29	Ceram	7.8	
1903 Feb. 27	off W. Java	8.1	
1935 Dec. 28	off W. Sumatra	8.1	
1938 Feb. 1	Banda Sea	8.6	
1948 Mar. 1	W. Ceram	7.9	
1950 Nov. 2	Ceram	8.1	
1958 Oct. 20	S. Java	6.5	7 dead

The front of the arc looks toward New Guinea and the Arafura Sea. There is a belt of shallow shocks from southern New Guinea into the arc, by way of the Aru Islands group.

Both the Banda and Sunda Arcs are noted for their intense volcanism, and for the high proportion of intermediate and deep-focus earthquakes. Large shallow shocks occur chiefly along the northern section of the Banda Arc (Ceram), while the juncture with the Sunda Arc is most active at depths of 500–700 km, with epicenters in the west Banda Sea. However, shallow earthquakes occur throughout the region, including the coast of southern Celebes (Fig.15.2).

The Sunda Arc is a very long structure including Lomblen, Flores, Sumba, Sumbawa, Lombok, Bali, Java, Sumatra, the Nicobar and Andaman Islands and many lesser islands. The Java Trench faces the Indian Ocean along the center of the arc. Shallow earthquakes occur between the trench and the southern coasts; this is the axis of negative gravity anomalies discovered by Vening Meinesz in 1923. Intermediate shocks occur largely along

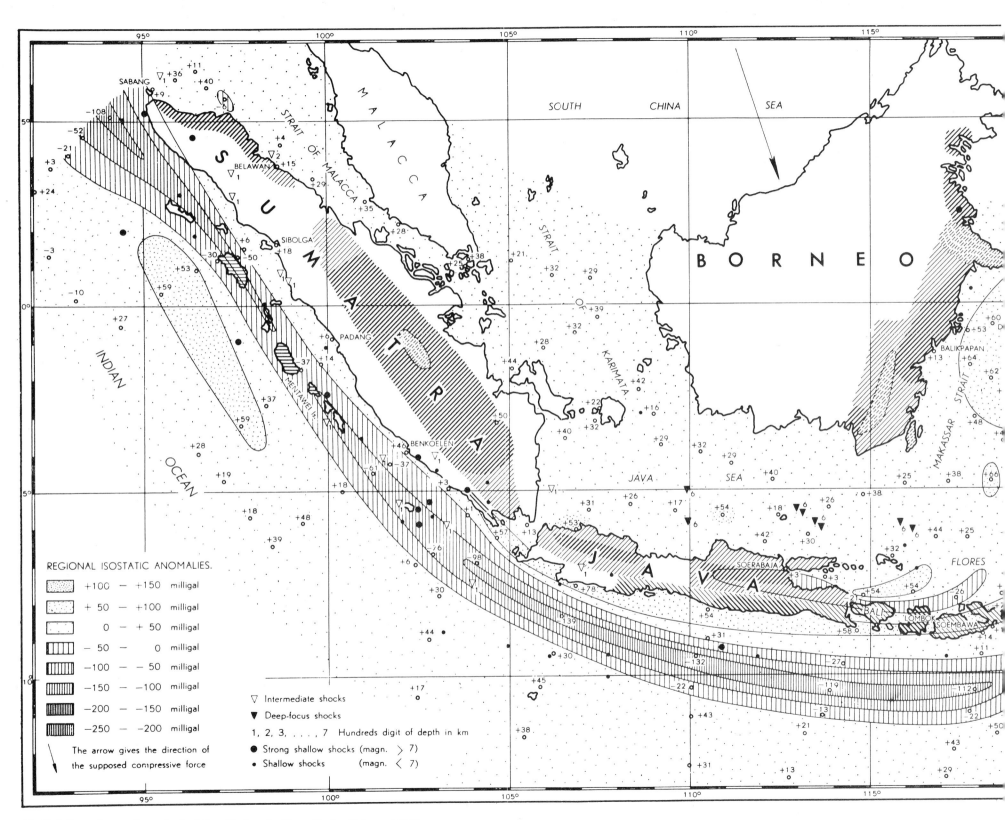

Fig.15.2. Tectonics, gravity, and seismicity of Indonesia. (From Vening Meinesz, 1964.)

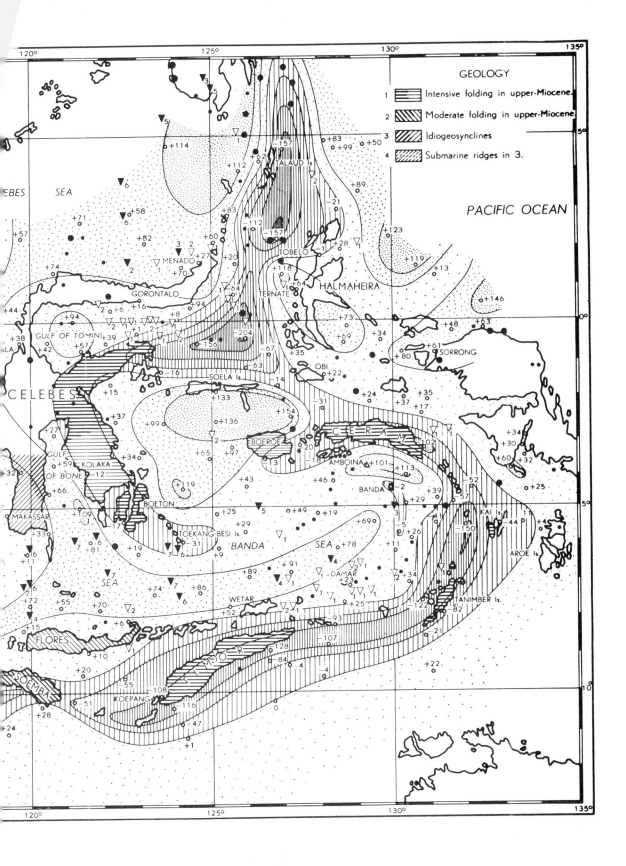

the volcanic axis, and deep-focus earthquakes are scattered over the Flores and Java Seas.

Some of the largest shallow earthquakes in this region occur on the Indian Ocean coast of Sumatra. Deep earthquakes are less frequent toward northwest Sumatra; they disappear completely in the Andaman Sea. No deep shocks are known anywhere to the west of Sumatra (with two recent exceptions in the western Mediterranean).

Shallow earthquakes in Sumatra are associated with right-hand lateral faulting in the lengthwise direction of the island. They have caused extensive damage in historical time. Offshore shocks may generate tsunamis in the Indian Ocean. Occasional shallow shocks also occur in the Malacca Straits. Shocks in the older mountain ranges of the Malay Peninsula are rare. The Andaman and Nicobar Islands bridge the gap between Sumatra and the Burmese mainland. Their seismicity is low, but occasional large shocks are known to occur.

EURASIAN DOMAIN

Consideration of the boundaries and structure of the Eurasian domain leads to problems of geologic history which are still largely unsolved. E. Suess was the first to suggest a structural model of Eurasia based on the idea of a stable mass in the north and a continuous border of mountain ranges to the south. The Arabian and Indian Peninsulas were recognized as remnants of the ancient continent of Gondwana (also including the cores of Africa and South America), which became appendages of the central Asian continental mass.

The basic conception of Eurasia by Suess is still largely valid. Looking at a map of Eurasia (Fig.15.3), one finds that all mountain ranges seem to come together in a single knot in the Pamir region. Actually, there is a close juxtaposition of two mountain systems of very different structure and age. The southernmost chain belongs to the Alpide system including the Himalaya and the ranges of Baluchistan, the Zagros, the Caucasus, and the mountains of Anatolia and the Alps. This mountain system was formed during the Tertiary age, as was the Circum-Pacific (Laramide) system.

On the other hand, the interior mountains of Asia represent a sequence of older chains, that Suess compared to ripples spreading out concentrically from the Altai region at the edge of the Siberian shield. These mountains were collectively designated "Altaids" by Suess, a term which we may retain for purposes of seismotectonic description. The Altaid System occupies an enormous area of Central Asia. Its northernmost ranges border the stable shield: Kipet-Dagh, Hindu Kush, Tian Shan, Altai, Yablonovy, Stanovoi, and Jugjur. All these ranges are seismically active. Between them and the Alpide Belt are a sequence of parallel ranges and high plateaus, including Tibet, Mongolia, and western China. The older plateaus are inactive but the ranges which surround them show seismic activity.

The geologic structure varies considerably, both within the Alpide and the Altaid systems. Alpide ranges are often associated with large-scale concentric folding and

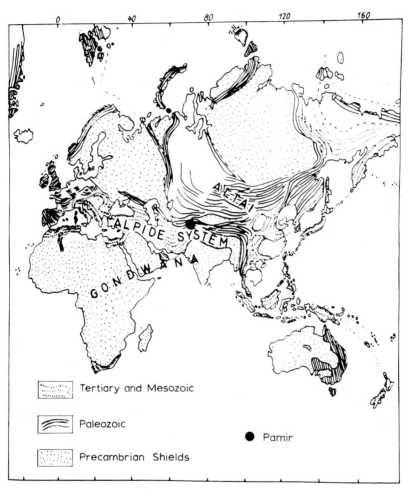

Fig.15.3. Structural setting of Eurasia, showing the Alpide–Himalayan and Altai systems and the intermediate-depth Pamir focus.

thrusting. Volcanism is rare. Intermediate earthquakes occur in a few isolated areas, but deep-focus shocks are practically absent. The Altaids, on the other hand, are mostly Paleozoic ranges (like the Appalachians). They are well-worn mountain blocks, in which metamorphism is intensive and widespread. These mountains extend as far east as the backbone of the East Asian island belt, where they include the mountainous cores of Borneo, western Celebes, etc. In Central and Western Europe they are represented by the Variscan and Armorican Ranges, such as the Bohemian Massif, the Harz, the Vosges, the Black Forest, the Central Plateau of France, the English Pennine, the hills of Britanny, and others. All these structures are now of very low seismicity, and only the larger uplifts of Central Asia remain highly active.

Where the Alpide and Altaid systems overlap or run closely along each other, it is sometimes difficult to distinguish between each component. The island arcs of Southeast Asia might be considered an extension of the Alpide system through Burma and the Andaman Islands into Sumatra; on the other hand, the Altaid ranges of Thailand and Yunnan are also continuous with Sumatra and Borneo across the Malay Peninsula.

Further complications result from the presence of certain structures which belong to neither type. In southern Honshu and Kyushu one finds active Mesozoic ranges, corresponding to an intermediate orogeny between the Altaid and the Alpine. These ranges continue into the Asian mainland; they are found in the hills of Taiwan and Korea, and in the Chinling Range as well as the mountains of Yunnan and Ssuchuan (Szechwan).

China (Regions 25, 26, 27, 41: Map 20; Table 15.5)

Seismicity and seismic geography

This vast region is famous for its destructive earthquakes. The seismic activity in terms of energy is 2.2% of the world total, an amount comparable to New Guinea. Yet the total number of earthquakes is small; Montessus de Ballore believed that China and the whole of Central Asia were non-seismic.

TABLE 15.5

Earthquakes of China (Regions 25, 26, 27, 41)

Date	Epicenter	M	Comments
7 Nov. 10	Shensi		
46 Oct. 23	Honan		
119 Mar. 11	Honan		
600 Dec. 13	Kansu		
756 Nov. 27	Kansu		
788 Feb. 13	Shensi, central China		
793 May 27	Shensi		
814 Apr. 1	Yunnan		
849 Oct. 20	Hopeh, Shansi		
867 Mar. 9	Shansi		
975 Nov. 3	S. Shantung		
1038 Jan. 24	central Shansi		2,200 dead
1102 Jan. 15	Shansi		
1125 Aug. 30	Ala Shan, N. Kansu		
1290 Sep. 27	Jehol		100,000 dead
1303 Sep. 17	Shansi		
1305 May 3	Shansi		
1334 Sep. 14	Peking		
1336 Jan. 12	Anhwei, Hupeh, Yangtse River		
1337 Sep. 9	Hopeh, incl. Peking		
1352 Apr. 18	Chinling Range, Shensi		
1477 May 22	N. Kansu		

TABLE 15.5 (continued)

Date	Epicenter	M	Comments
1481 Mar. 18	Kiangsu–Anhwei border		
1484 Feb. 7	N. of Peking		
1501 Jan. 29	Shensi–Shansi, N. of Yellow River		
1502 Oct. 27	W. Shantung, Yellow River Valley		
1505 Oct. 19	Chekian, near Hangchow		
1524 Feb. 11	E. Honan		
1536 Mar. 29	Sikang, Ssuchuan border		
1556 Feb. 2	Shensi, Yellow River Basin		830,000 dead
1561 Aug. 4	Kansu–Ninghsia, Yellow River		
1568 Apr. 11	Shensi		
1568 May 5	Coast of Kiangsu		
1604 Dec. 29	Coast of Fukien		
1605 Jul. 13	Kuangtung, Luichow Peninsula		
1622 Mar. 18	W. Shantung		
1622 Apr. 17	W. Shantung		
1622 Oct. 25	E. Kansu		12,000 casualties
1626 Jun. 28	N. Shansi		
1631 Aug. 14	N. Hunan		
1654 Jul. 21	W. Chinling Range		
1668 Jul. 25	Shantung		major catastrophe
1679 Sep. 2	near Peking		
1695 May 18	S. Shansi		
1709 Oct. 14	NE. Kansu		
1713 Feb. 26	E. Yunnan		
1718 Jun. 19	Chinling Range		
1720 Jul. 12	N. of Peking		
1730 Sep. 30	N. of Peking		
1739 Jan. 3	S. of Ordos Plateau		
1786 Jun. 1	W. Ssuchuan		
1815 Oct. 21	Shensi, Yellow River Basin		
1822 Jun. 18	N. Ssuchuan		
1829 Nov. 18	S. Shantung		
1830 Jun. 12	NE. Honan		
1833 Sep. 6	E. Yunnan		
1846 Aug. 4	Coast of Kiangsu		
1852 Dec. 16	Coast of Kiangsu		
1853 Apr. 14	Coast of Kiangsu		
1870 Apr. 11	Sikang		2,300 dead
1875 Jun. 8	Nanling Range		
1879 Jul. 1	Chinling Range		
1885 Jan. 15	Chinling Range		
1888 Jun. 13	Coast of Hopei		
1920 Dec. 16	NE. Kansu	8.6	180,000 dead
1927 May 22	NE. Tsinghai	8.3	tens of thousand dead
1937 Aug. 1	N. Kiangsi		several dead
1948 May 25	Lihwa, E. Sikang		800 dead
1948 Oct. 8	Nanking, Kiangsu		3 dead
1966 Mar. 8	Singtai, Hopeh	6.8	many victims

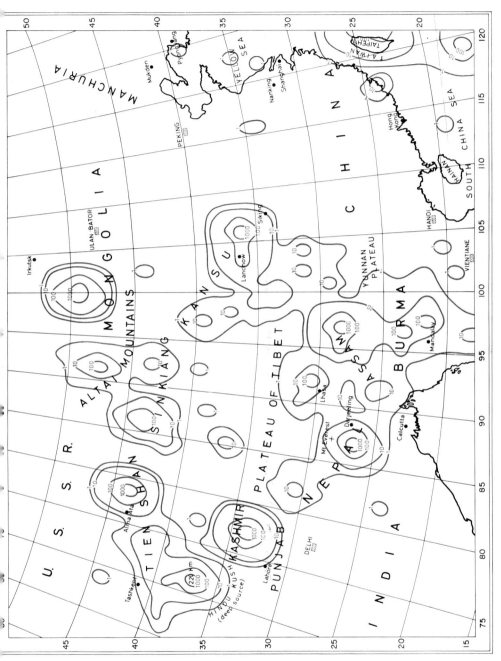

Map 20. Seismicity of China–Central Asia: Regions 26–27–28, 41 and 48. (Seismicity contours are numbered in 10^{15} ergs km^{-2} $year^{-1}$.)

Destructive earthquakes occur along the Lung Tien, a long foothill zone which runs north-northeast from Yunnan to the Yellow River. It features a sequence of parallel rifts trending northwest into upper Sikang. The earthquakes reach their peak of destructiveness in the loess country of Kansu and Shansi. According to chronicles the great 1556 earthquake caused 830,000 deaths in this region. Several thousands of casualties were claimed by a single earthquake in this area as recently as the 1920's.

The trend of seismicity continues into Shensi, Shansi, Hopeh and Honan as far as Shantung Province. An important zone of destructive earthquakes follows the southern border of Inner Mongolia, along the Great Wall, from the Gulf of Chihli into northern Shansi. Many of the major shocks are 50–100 km deep. Isolated destructive earthquakes have occurred along the coast of China, particularly on the coasts of Kiangsu and Kwangtung Provinces. For the earthquakes of Chinese Turkestan (Sinkiang) see also Region 28 (Map 20).

The Kunlun and Astin Tagh Ranges in southeast Ching Hai Province are active. Isolated shocks affecting the Red Basin of Ssuchuan may originate along the northern foothills of Tapa Range.

The Chinling Hills appear to be the Mesozoic continuation of a long Altaid structure which includes the Astin Tagh and Nan Shan Ranges to the west. None of these are highly active, but there have been large earthquakes in the Lanchow area, where the Yellow River crosses the structure.

Pamir–Balkhash Region (Region 48: Map 20; Table 15.6)

Seismicity and seismic geography

The Pamir Mountains have been considered the structural knot where Alpide and Altaid ranges converge. The present region comprises the northern Altaid ranges, including chiefly the Hindu Kush and Tien Shan. This is a relatively small but rather strongly seismic area, accounting for 1.4% of the world's seismicity; not including the eastern Tien Shan (Sinkiang Plateau), which belongs to the Chinese region.

The maximum of shallow seismicity occurs along the southern flank of the Alai Range (northern Pamir, Soviet Tadjikistan), particularly in the region of Garm and Dushanbe (the former Stalinabad). The Tien Shan Range is a northeasterly prolongation of the Alai Range and is less strongly active.

Under the Hindu Kush Range is a well-localized seismic nest of intermediate depth (220 km), which produces some quite large earthquakes. The Hindu Kush nest has a radius of less than 100 km; no other earthquakes of intermediate depth occur in the region.

The Pamir–Balkhash region represents the most active seismic area in the U.S.S.R., with the possible exception of the Kamchatka–Kurile island arc. Earthquakes occur throughout the Tadjik and Kirgiz, and parts of the Uzbek and Kazakh S.S.R. The larger shocks are located in the Alai–Tien Shan mountains and north to west of Lake Issyk-Kul

TABLE 15.6

Earthquakes of the Pamir—Balkhash region (Region 48)

Date	Epicenter	M	Comments
1716	Aksu, Tien Shan		
1832 Jan. 22	Garm—Dushanbe region		
1885 Aug. 3	Byelovodsk, Kirgiz Range		
1887 Jun. 9	Alma Ata; N. of Lake Issyk-Kul		
1889 Jul. 12	Chilyk, Ala Tau Range		
1902 Aug. 22	Kashgar, S. Tien Shan	8.6	
1907 Oct. 21	Karatagh, W. Alai Range	8.1	
1909 Jul. 7	Hindu Kush	8.1	depth 220 km
1911 Jan. 3	Kebin Valley, Ala Tau Range	8.7	
1921 Nov. 15	Hindu Kush	8.1	depth 220 km
1946 Nov. 2	Chatkal Range, west of Lake Issyk-Kul	7.6	
1949 Jul. 10	Khait, Alai Range	7.6	
1965 Mar. 14	Hindu Kush	7.8	depth 220 km
1966 Apr. 25	Tashkent	6	several dead

(Kungei—Ala Tau Range), i.e., roughly in an area bounded to the north by the cities of Samarkand, Tashkent, Frunze, and Alma-Ata. The Lake Balkhash area is weakly active and the Kazakh highlands to the north are stable. Major shocks are usually associated with large-scale surface faulting.

Mongolia—Baikal—Sinkiang area (Region 28: Map 20; Table 15.7)

Seismicity and seismic geography

This region includes a belt-like alignment of Altaid ranges, known for their relatively infrequent but extremely large shallow earthquakes. It borders Mongolia to the north, following the U.S.S.R. border (Tuva autonomous region, Buryat autonomous S.S.R.) around Lake Baikal. North and west of the lake the seismicity is low, following a broad arc along the Stanovoy, Jugjur, and Verkhoyan Ranges into the Arctic Ocean. The region also includes the eastern Tien Shan and Sinkiang Plateau; it accounts for 6.3% of the world's seismicity.

Large shallow shocks occur near the intersection of the borders of China, Mongolia, and the U.S.S.R. Major epicenters appear to be associated with the Mongolian Altai and with the mountain ranges of northwestern Mongolia (Khangai Mountains), of the Caledonian age. They tend to produce surface faulting and lurching on a gigantic scale.

The great earthquakes of Chinese Turkestan (eastern Tien Shan Range, Sinkiang Plateau) may be considered as a continuation of the structural trends of the Pamir—

TABLE 15.7

Earthquakes of the Mongolia–Baikal–Sinkiang area (Region 28)

Date	Epicenter	M	Comments
1814 Sep. 3	Tunka, Irkut Valley		
1828 Mar. 7	SW. Baikal		
1839 Aug. 18	S. Shore of Lake Baikal		
1862 Jan. 12	Kudarin, Lake Baikal		
1869 Nov. 1	Kudarin, Lake Baikal		
1871 Mar. 4	Kudarin, Lake Baikal		
1898 Jun. 19	Novokuznetsk, W. Sayan Range		
1903 Mar. 12	Novokuznetsk, W. Sayan Range		
1905 Jul. 9, 23	Tannu Ola, Mongolia	7.9, 8.4	
1906 Dec. 22	E. Tien Shan, Sinkiang	8.3	
1914 Aug. 4	Lake Lop Nor, Sinkiang	7.3	
1931 Aug. 10	Altai, China–Mongolia border	7.9	
1944 Mar. 9	N. Tien Shan, Sinkiang	7.2	
1950 Apr. 4	Mondin, Irkut Valley	6.8	
1957 Jun. 27	Muya, Yablonovy Range	7.9	
1957 Dec. 4	E. Altai, Mongolia	8.3	20 dead
1959 Aug. 29	S. Shore of Lake Baikal	6.8	

Balkhash region; for geographical reasons they are classed with the Mongolian earthquakes.

The Lake Baikal Rift (southeastern Siberia) has produced a number of historically damaging earthquakes. Most epicenters are located along the southern shore and under the lake itself. They trend eastward from the northern end of Lake Baikal toward the Yablonovy Range.

Burma (Region 25: Map 21; Table 15.8)

Seismicity and seismic geography

Region 25 includes slightly over 0.4% of the world's seismicity. It encompasses Burma, the eastern half of East Pakistan, and parts of south China, as well as other areas of southeast Asia south of the 25th Parallel.

The western ranges of Burma (Arakan Range, Lushai Hills) form a convex arc facing the Gulf of Bengal. Shallow earthquakes occur under these ranges, in continuity with the trend of the Andaman Islands to the south; they may be destructive along the coast of the Gulf of Bengal. An important part of the activity in the area is connected with the

TABLE 15.8

Earthquakes of Burma (Region 25)

Date	Epicenter	M	Comments
1612 Mar. 12	China—Burma border		
1762 Apr. 2	Arakan		tsunami; coastal uplift along 100 miles of Bay of Bengal
1912 May 23	Shan highlands	7.9	
1956 Jul. 16	Mandalay	7.0	30 dead

older Altaid ranges to the east (Pegu Range, Shan Highlands, Sino—Tibetan Range). This activity continues northward into Yunnan.

The intersection with the Himalaya arc occurs just north of the region, in the Indian state of Assam. A number of intermediate shocks have their epicenters in this area and in northern Burma.

The link between Burma and Sumatra is not clearly established on the basis of seismicity, because the activity in the Preparis Channel is low. However, the geologic relationships permit one to infer such a connection.

Himalaya (Region 26: Map 22; Table 15.9)

Seismicity and seismic geography

The Himalayan arc is comparable in length and seismicity to the Tonga—Kermadec Arc; however, the character of earthquake activity is totally different. As defined by Gutenberg and Richter (1954), Region 26 encompasses the Altaid Ranges of central and southern China, including the Sino—Tibetan mountains (e.g., Nyenchen Tanglha Range), but excluding western Punjab and the Pamirs. This area accounts for 5.6% of the world's seismicity.

Most large Indian earthquakes have occurred along the southern front of the Himalaya or under the Assam Hills; they have been destructive in the deeply alluviated Ganges Plain. The area of maximum seismicity marks the eastern abutment of the arc against the ranges trending north—south into Burma and the Chinese provinces of Yunnan and Ssuchuan. In the southwestern structural corner intermediate earthquakes occur; elsewhere the activity is concentrated at normal depth. Since the location of shallow shocks occurs along the belt of negative gravity anomalies a structural parallel with Pacific-type arcs has been suggested. The Ganges Plain would occupy the place of the oceanic trenches of island arcs in this theory.

The seismicity of the Pamirs has been discussed in connection with the Altaid system, although the Hindu Kush intermediate focus ought to be described more properly in connection with the Himalaya arc.

TABLE 15.9

Earthquakes of east and south India, Bangladesh and the Himalaya states (Region 26)

Date	Epicenter	M	Comments
1720 Jul. 5	Delhi		
1737 Oct. 11	Bengal		300,000 dead
1803 Sep. 1	Bengal		
1819 Jun. 16	Kutch and N. Bombay		2,000 dead
1827 Sep.	W. Punjab		1,000 dead
1828 Jun. 6	Kashmir		1,000 dead
1832 Feb. 21	W. Punjab		
1833 Aug. 26	Nepal		
1869 Jan. 10	Khasi Hills, Assam		
1869 Jul. 7	Nepal		
1885 May 30	W. Kashmir		2,000 dead
1897 Jun. 12	Khasi Hills, Assam	8.7	1,500 dead
1905 Apr. 4	Kangra, Himachal Pradesh	8.6	19,000 dead
1934 Jan. 15	N. Bihar	8.4	10,600 dead
1950 Aug. 15	Assam–Sikang border	8.7	1,526 dead
1967 Dec. 11	Koyna, W. Ghats	6.3	180 dead

The Himalaya itself is a contemporary of the Alps, possibly with diminishing activity after Miocene time. Himalayan tectonics have been interpreted as due to compression between the Asian mainland and the Indian Peninsula. This process would also be responsible for molding the Burma arc and the ranges of Baluchistan around the low Precambrian shield of India.

To the north is the plateau of Tibet, a stable high platform; the ranges surrounding it are active. South of the Himalaya is the Ganges Plain, a deep alluvial trough. The Indian shield itself is a peneplain partly covered by Late Cretaceous basalts (Deccan). It is not seismically active, except for rare shocks in the tectonic rift that crosses India from the Gulf of Cambay into Bihar (Vindhya Rift).

A fragment of the old Indian Shield has been squeezed upwards between the opposing thrusts of the Himalaya and Burma arcs. These are the Assam Hills (Khasi Hills, Naga Hills) where some of the most violent Indian earthquakes are centered. The areas subject to maximum destructiveness include the Brahmaputra Valley, northern West Bengal, Bihar, Uttar Pradesh, Himachal Pradesh, Punjab, Kashmir, and adjoining areas of Bangladesh, Nepal, Sikkim, and Bhutan.

Pakistan and West India (Region 47: Maps 22 and 23; Table 15.10)

Seismicity and seismic geography

Like Burma, this is a region of low seismicity. During the 1904–1952 period it

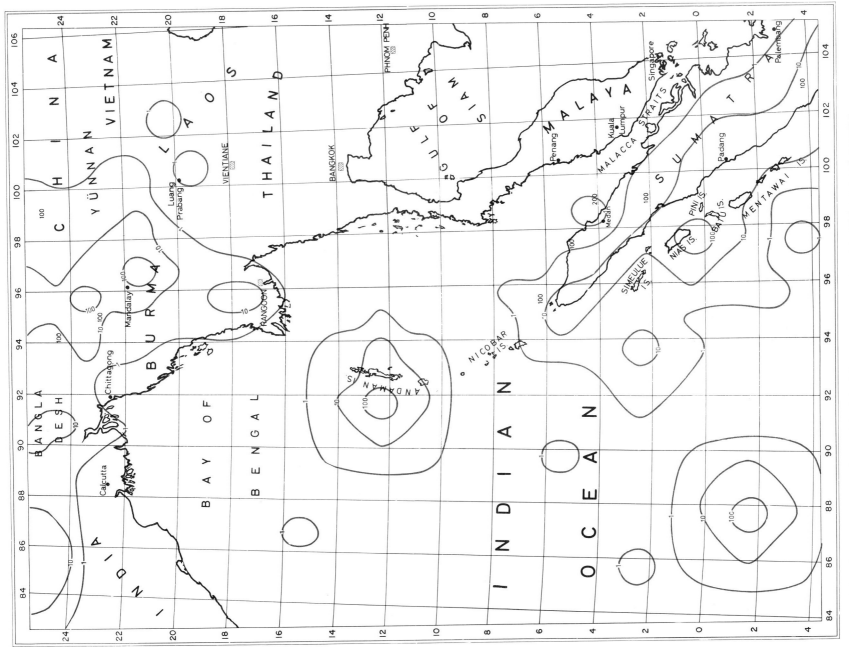

Map 21. Seismicity of Burma– Laos: Region 25. (Seismicity contours are numbered in 10^{15} ergs km^{-2} year^{-1}.)

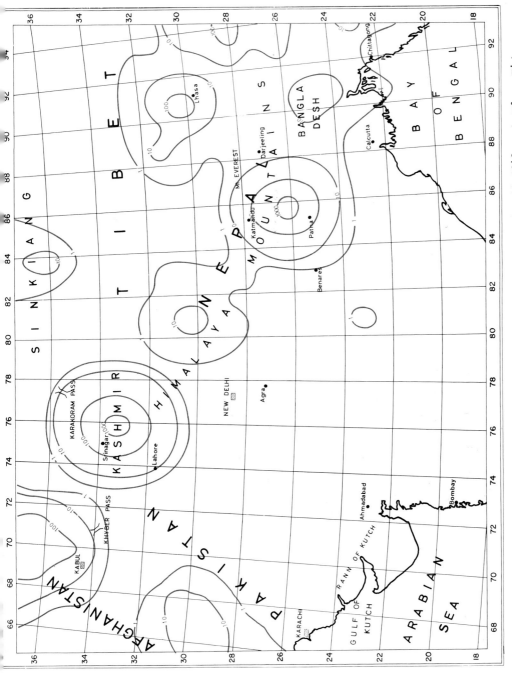

Map 22. Seismicity of North India–Himalaya: Regions 26 and 47. (Seismicity contours are numbered in 10^{15} ergs km^{-2} year^{-1}.)

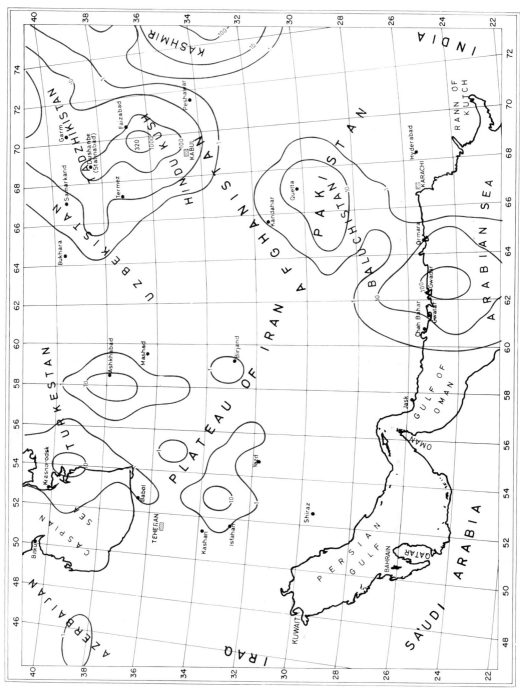

Map 22. Seismicity of Afghanistan, Pakistan, Iran. 45, 46, 123, 59 +, 444

TABLE 15.10

Earthquakes of Pakistan and west India (Region 47)

Date	Epicenter	M	Comments
1505 Jul. 6	Kabul		
1668 May	Karachi		
1819 Jun. 16	Kutch		2,000 dead; felt through northern India
1852 Jan. 24	Murree Hills, Indus		
1874 Oct. 18	Kabul		
1892 Dec. 20	Chaman and Nushki		Afghan–Pakistani border
1931 Aug. 24, 27	Quetta	7.0, 7.4	
1935 May 30	Quetta	7.5	30,000 dead
1945 Nov. 27	off Karachi coast	8.3	4,000 dead
1947 Aug. 5	coast of Pakistan	7.3	
1955 Feb. 18	Quetta		many casualties
1956 Jun. 9	central Afghanistan	7.6	350 dead
1956 Jul. 21	Anjar, Kutch	6.5	many dead

accounted for only 0.1% of the world's seismicity. It includes Pakistan, eastern Afghanistan, and the Indus Valley and the Rann of Kutch.

Most of the larger shallow earthquakes occur between the Sulaiman Range and the Afghan border. This structure forms a broad arc fronting towards the Indian peninsula; observed faulting has been left-lateral along the trend of the arc. Other active ranges branch into Afghanistan from the Hindu Kush region.

Highly destructive earthquakes occur in North Pakistan and along both margins of the Indus Valley, particularly in the Rann of Kutch. Some intermediate shocks are recorded near the Pakistan–Afghanistan border, in the region of Quetta.

Iran–Caspian Sea (Region 29: Map 24; Table 15.11)

Seismicity and seismic geography

This large region comprises all of Iran, western Afghanistan, Azerbaijan, Soviet Turkmenia, and parts of the Uzbek and Kazakh S.S.R. including the Ural region up to the 60th Parallel. Its share of world seismicity is 0.7%.

Large earthquakes in this region are not frequent. However, there is a long record of disasters caused by shallow shocks in the magnitude range 6.5–7.5, around the borders of the plateau of Iran and on the ranges that stretch from Afganistan to the Caucasus. (Fig.15.4). The Alpide Belt can be divided into two main branches, tied together in the active Khurasan Range of eastern Iran. The southern belt follows the Baluchistan Ranges of Pakistan along the coast of the Gulf of Oman and trends northwest through the Zagros Mountains into Turkey. A few intermediate shocks occur along this belt, in the Oman region (Chagai Hills).

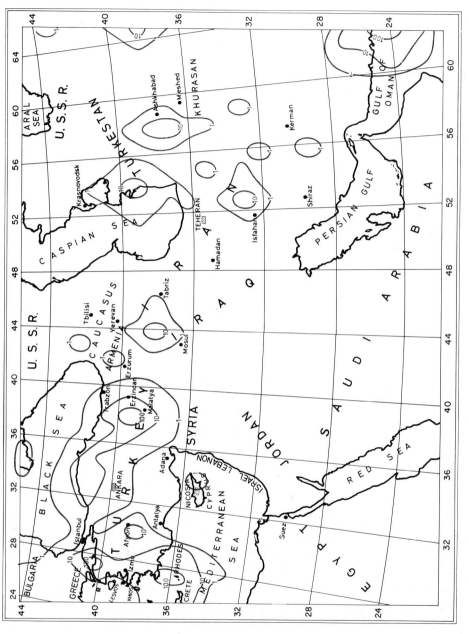

Map 24. Seismicity of Iran–Turkey–Asia Minor: Regions 29–30 and 51. (Seismicity contours are

TABLE 15.11

Earthquakes of Iran–Caspian Sea (Region 29)

Date	Epicenter	M	Comments
1549	Qain, Khurasan		3,000 dead
1611 Dec. 9	Zuhrabad, NE. Iran		
1619 Nov. 27	Zuhrabad		
1641 Feb. 5	Tabriz; Kurdistan		30,000 dead
1667 Nov.	Shemakha, Azerbaijan		80,000 dead
1727 Nov. 18	Tabriz		77,000 dead
1755 Jun. 7	Kashan, N. Iran		40,000 dead
1794 Mar. 14	Kazan, Russia		
1824 Jun. 23	Shiraz, Zagros		
1828 Aug. 9	Shemakha, Azerbaijan		
1842 Jan. 2	Baku, Azerbaijan		
1844 May 12	Zagros Range		
1853 Apr. 21	Shiraz, Zagros		12,000 dead
1853 Jul. 11	Isfahan, Zagros		10,000 dead
1856 Jul. 23	Shemakha, Azerbaijan		
1864 Jan. 3	Ardebil, Azerbaijan		
1869 Sep. 2	Shemakha, Azerbaijan		
1872 Jan. 28	Shemakha, Azerbaijan		
1879 Mar. 13	Marand, N. Iran		
1883 May 3	N. Iran		
1884 May 19	Qishm, Persian Gulf		
1895 Jan. 7	Meshed, Kopet Range		
1909 Jan. 23	E. of Isfahan	7.7	
1911 Apr. 18	Buhabad, Plateau of Iran	6.7	
1923 Sep. 22	S. Kush Rud	6.9	
1929 May 1	Germab, Kopet Range	7.1	
1941 Feb. 16	Qain, Khurasan	6.25	600 dead
1946 Nov. 4	Kazandzhik, Kopet	6.75	400 dead
1948 Oct. 5	Ashkhabad, Kopet	7.6	3,000 dead
1956 Oct. 31	Bastak, Laristan	6.75	many dead
1957 Jul. 2	Abegharm, Elburz Range	7.1	1,200 dead
1957 Dec. 13	Kangavar, Panjum Prov.	7.2	2,000 dead
1960 Apr. 24	Lar, Laristan	5.75	450 dead
1961 Jun. 11	Dehkuye, Laristan	6.5	60 dead
1962 Sep. 1	Boyin–Zara, SW. Elburz	7.25	12,400 dead
1968 Aug. 31	Dasht-e-Bayaz, SE. Iran	7.2	10,000 dead
1972 Apr. 10	Ghir, Fars Prov	7.0	17,000 dead

The northern Alpide branch includes the Paropamisus Range of Afghanistan, the Kopet Mountains of Turkestan, the Elburz Range, and the Caucasus. This northern branch has a bifurcation in the Kopet Mountains; one branch crosses under the Caspian Sea and emerges near Baku, while the Elburz branch follows the shore of the Caspian Sea into Armenia and Anatolia.

The Iranian Plateau is relatively stable. Seismicity in the Altaid ranges of the Urals is confined to a few minor shocks.

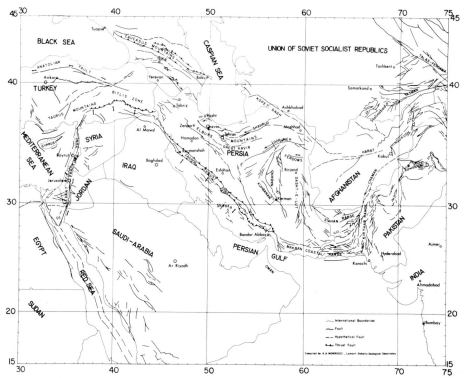

Fig.15.4. Tectonics of Iran, the Caucasus, eastern Anatolia, the Levant fracture zone, and the Red Sea. (After Nowroozi, 1971.)

Asia Minor–Balkans (Regions 30 and 51: Map 24; Table 15.12)

Extension and seismicity

In the classification by Gutenberg and Richter (1954) the area comprised by Turkey, the western Caucasus, the Black Sea, the Aegean Sea, the eastern Mediterranean and adjoining lands is included in Region 30. This vast region corresponds to the Middle East, the eastern Balkans, Greece, and the western Caucasus with Crimea. It contains active regions of arc tectonics, some of which have been studied in detail. The seismicity is 1.1% of the world's total.

The Carpathian arc of Central Romania contains an active focus of intermediate shocks, which had been classed by Gutenberg and Richter (1954) as a separate region (Region 51; less than 0.1% of the world's total activity). Asia Minor is situated between the Mediterranean Sea and the stable masses of Arabia and Africa. It is a region of frequent destructive earthquakes, particularly in Turkey.

The Aegean Sea contains a well-developed island arc, with intermediate earthquakes near the Turkish abutment of the arc (Island of Rhodes). The large intermediate shocks

TABLE 15.12

Earthquakes of Asia Minor–Balkans (Regions 30, 51)

Date	Epicenter	M	Comments
1500? B.C.	Santorini Is., Aegean		largest known volcanic explosion; tsunami, many dead
373 B.C.	Helike, Gulf of Corinth		tsunami
17 A.D.	Asia Minor		
77 or 78	Cyprus		
109 or 110	Antakya, S. Turkey		
342	Antakya, S. Turkey		40,000 dead
375 Jul. 21	Iznik, W. Turkey		
419	Palestine		
427, 411	Istanbul		
471 or 472	Asia Minor		
494	Asia Minor		
518	Hungary		
528 Nov. 29	Antakya, S. Turkey		
543 Sep. 6	Erdek and Kapidag Peninsula		
553 Aug. 15	Istanbul		
565	Antakya		30,000 dead
715	Iznik, W. Turkey		
740 Oct. 26	W. Turkey		tsunami
746 Jan. 18	Syria		
856 Dec.	Corinth, Greece		45,000 dead
859	Antakya and Latakia		
894	Erevan, Armenia		
991 Apr. 5	Damascus, Syria		
989 Oct. 25	Izmit, Istanbul		
995	Capakcur, central Turkey		
1000 Mar. 29	Aegean Sea		felt through E. Mediterranean
1063 Sep. 23	Iznik, Istanbul		
1091	Antakya		
1114 Mar. 12	Samsat–Maras, S. Turkey		
1155	Latakia, S. Turkey		2,000 dead
1168	Erzincan, E. Anatolia		
1170	Kiev, Ukraine		
1183	Syria and Lebanon		20,000 dead
1201	Aegean Sea		100,000 dead
1255	Erzincan, E. Anatolia		
1268	Seyhan Prov., S. Turkey		60,000 dead
1319	E. Turkey		
1384 Aug.	Lesbos, Aegean Sea		500 dead
1402	Syria		
1458	Erzincan, E. Anatolia		
1469	Zante and Cephalonia, Ionian Sea		
1482	Erzincan, E. Anatolia		
1491	Cos, Aegean Sea		

TABLE 15.12 (continued)

Date	Epicenter	M	Comments
1509 Sep. 14	Corum, Istanbul		tsunami
1554	Zante, Ionian Sea		
1584 Jun. 17	Erzincan, E. Anatolia		
1592 May	Zante, Ionian Sea		
1598	Corum and Amasya, W. Anatolia		
1648 Apr. 2	Van, Turkey–Iran border		
1653 Feb. 23	Izmir, W. Turkey		15,000 dead
1666 Nov.	Mosul, N. Iraq		
1679 Jun. 4	Erevan, Armenia		
1688 Jul. 5	Izmir, Aegean coast		15,000 dead
1714 Aug. 28	Cephalonia, Ionian Sea		
1719 May 25	Izmit, Istanbul		
1750 Jun. 7	Corfu, Ionian Sea		2,000 dead
1754 Sep. 14	Izmit, Istanbul		
1759 Oct. 30	Sfat, Jordan Valley		20,000 dead; tsunami
1767 Jul. 11	Cephalonia and Zante		
1770 Jan.	Cephalonia, Ionian Sea		
1780 Oct.	Candia, Crete		
1784 Jul. 23	Erzincan, E. Anatolia		
1786 Feb. 5	Corfu, Ionian Sea		
1788	Vranje, Yugoslavia		
1789	Palu, E. Anatolia		
1791 Nov. 2	Zante, Ionian Sea		
1796 Feb. 26	Latakia, W. Syria		1,500 dead
1802 Nov. 26	Romania		
1810 Feb. 16	Crete		2,000 dead
1821 Jan. 6	Zante and W. Peloponnese		tsunami
1822 Aug. 13	Lower Orontes, Syria		
1825 Jan. 19	Cephalonia		
1827 Jun.	Tokat, central Anatolia		
1829 May 5	Drama, Edirne, Greece–Turkey		
1829 Nov. 26	Kishinev, Moldavia		
1830 Mar. 9	central Caucasus		
1837 Jan. 1	Upper Jordan Valley		
1838 Jan. 23	Carpathian arc		
1840 Jul. 2	Armenia		
1843 Oct. 17	Chalki, Aegean Sea		
1846 Jun. 8	Lesbos, Aegean Sea		
1852 Jul. 24	Erzurum, E. Anatolia		
1853 Aug. 18	Gulf of Euboea, Greece		
1855 Feb. 28	Bursa, W. Anatolia		
1855 Apr. 29	S. Macedonia		
1856 Feb. 22	Samsun, central Anatolia		
1856 Oct. 12	Rhodes, Aegean Sea		
1858 Sep. 20	Delvine, S. Albania		
1859 Jun. 2	Erzurum, E. Anatolia		

TABLE 15.12 (continued)

Date	Epicenter	M	Comments
1861 Dec. 26	Gulf of Corinth		
1862 Nov. 3	Isparta, Central Turkey		
1863 Apr. 22	Rhodes, Aegean Sea		
1869 Dec. 1	Marmaris, S.W. Turkey		
1869 Dec. 26	Tbilisi, Caucasus		
1869 Dec. 28	Corfu, Ionian Sea		
1870 Jun. 24	Rhodes, Aegean Sea		intermediate
1870 Aug. 1	Gulf of Corinth, Greece		
1872 Apr. 3	Lower Orontes, Antakya		1,800 dead
1875 May 3	Isikli, W. Turkey		
1875 May 11	Usak, W. Turkey		
1878 Apr. 19	Izmit, W. Anatolia		
1879 Oct. 28	Transylvania, Hungary		
1880 Jul. 29	Izmir, W. Turkey		
1881 Apr. 3	Chios, Aegean Sea		
1881 Jun. 7	Turkey–Iran border		
1881 Aug. 26	Chios, Aegean Sea		
1883 Oct. 15	Cesme–Urla, W. Turkey		
1885 Mar. 27	Argos, Peloponnese		
1886 Aug. 27	W. Peloponnese		
1890 May 20	Refahye, E. Anatolia		
1891 Apr. 3	Van, Turkey–Iran border		
1893 Jan. 31	Zante, Ionian Sea		
1894 Apr. 27	Locris, Greece		
1894 Jul. 10	Mudurnu, W. Anatolia		many dead
1895 May 13	S. Albania		
1899 Jan. 22	Kiparissia, W. Peloponnese		
1899 Sep. 20	Aydin, W. Turkey		
1903 Aug. 11	off S. Peloponnese	8.3	
1904 Apr. 4	Pirin Mts. Bulgaria	7.5	
1905 Apr. 15	Bursa, W. Anatolia		
1909 Feb. 9	Kelkit, Anatolia	6.75	
1912 Aug. 9	E. Dardanelles	7.7	
1913 Jun. 14	Byela, Bulgaria	6.75	
1914 Oct. 3	Taurus Mts., S. Turkey	7.7	
1916 Jan. 24	Samsun, central Anatolia	7.8	
1922 Aug. 13	Rhodes	6.8	
1926 Mar. 18	off Rhodes	6.9	
1926 Jun. 26	Rhodes	8.3	depth 100 km
1927 Jul. 11	Jordan Valley	6.2	
1927 Sep. 11	Yalta, Crimea	6.5	
1928 Mar. 31	Torbali, Izmir	6.3	
1928 Apr. 14, 18	Rhodope Mts., Bulgaria	6.7, 6.7	
1930 May 6	Turkey–Iran border	7.2	
1931 Mar. 8	Valandovo, Yugoslavia	6.7	

TABLE 15.12 (continued)

Date	Epicenter	M	Comments
1932 Sep. 26	Kassandra Pen., Aegean Sea	6.9	
1933 Apr. 23	Cos Is., Aegean Sea	6.8	
1938 Apr. 19	Kirsehir, central Turkey	6.7	800 dead
1939 Nov. 21	Tercan, central Anatolia	6.0	
1939 Dec. 26	Erzincan, E. Anatolia	8.0	23,000 dead
1940 Nov. 10	Transylvania, Romania	7.4	1,000 dead, depth 150 km
1941 Sep. 10	Van., E. Turkey	6	500 dead
1942 Dec. 20	Erbaa, central Anatolia	7.3	
1943 Jun. 20	Igeyve, W. Anatolia	6.3	
1943 Nov. 26	central Anatolia	7.6	
1944 Feb. 1	Cerkes, Bolu, central Anatolia	7.6	5,000 dead
1944 Oct. 6	Coast of W. Turkey	7.2	
1947 Oct. 6	S. Peloponnese	7.0	
1948 Feb. 9	Carpathos Is., Aegean Sea	7.1	
1948 Jun. 30	Levkas, Is., Ionian Sea		6 dead
1948 Oct. 6	Ashkhabad, Kopet Dagh		
1951 Aug. 13	Cankiri, W. Anatolia	6.8	50 dead
1952 Jan. 3	Hasankale, E. Anatolia	5.5	94 dead
1953 Mar. 18	Yenice, W. Anatolia	7.4	many dead
1953 Aug. 12	Cephalonia, Ionian Sea	7.1	435 dead
1953 Sep. 10	W. Cyprus	6.2	40 dead
1954 Apr. 20	Thessaly, Greece	7.0	25 dead
1955 Sep. 12	off N. Egypt	6.7	20 dead
1956 Jan. 12	Budapest, Hungary	5.8	2 dead
1956 Mar. 16	S. Lebanon	5.5	138 dead
1956 Jul. 9	Santorini Is., Aegean Sea	7.8	48 dead; tsunami
1957 Mar. 8	Thessaly, Greece	7	2 dead
1957 Apr. 25	off Rhodes	7.1	18 dead
1957 May 26	Abant, W. Anatolia	7.1	66 dead
1959 Sep. 1	S. Albania	6.3	
1960 May 26	Albania–Greece border	6.5	90 dead
1962 Jan. 7, 11	Makarska, Yugoslavia	5.8, 6	
1962 Mar. 18	S. Albania	6	15 dead
1963 Jul. 26	Skopje, Yugoslavia	5.8	1,200 dead
1966 Aug. 19	Varto, E. Anatolia	6.8	2,529 dead
1967 Jul. 22	Mudurnu, W. Anatolia	7.1	86 dead

from this epicenter may cause damage over much of the Near East, and have been described since early antiquity. The structure of the Aegean Arc has clear similarities with the island arcs of the Pacific.

The most active section in northern Turkey (Anatolia) is properly described by transcurrent fault tectonics. Here a large fault zone, the Anatolian Rift, may be followed from the Hellespont into Armenia, roughly parallel to the shores of the Black Sea.

Seismic geography

The branches of the Alpide Belt which encompass the Persian Plateau are drawn together into the structural "knot" of Armenia, where the borders of Iran, Turkey and the U.S.S.R. meet. Sequences of mountain ranges trending west from this point are called the Anatolian Ranges. They are crossed by the active Kelkit or Anatolian Rift, a right-lateral fault zone where many large earthquakes take place.

At the Kelkit River the ranges diverge; the southern ranges (Taurides) cross into central and southern Turkey, while the northern Anatolides continue along the Black Sea coast. The Anatolides are more active than the Taurides; in general the activity diminishes somewhat toward the west.

The Aegean Arc abuts in western Turkey and stretches across the Sea of Crete into the Peloponnese. There is also an inner island arc with active volcanism (Cyclades). The arcs front toward the Mediterranean and contain many shallow and intermediate epicenters. Some of the major shocks cause tsunamis in the Aegean Sea and throughout the Mediterranean.

The Alpide structure continues along the Pindhos Mountains and the mountains of Macedonia, into Greece, Albania and Yugoslavia. Another branch follows a broad arc through Bulgaria into Romania where it folds into a tight arcuate structure: the Carpathian arc.

North of the Armenian knot is the Caucasus Range, an Alpide structure that continues a trend from the Kopet Range of Turkestan into Crimea and the Balkans. Part of this structure is submerged under the Caspian and Black Seas and can be inferred from gravity and other data. Its seismicity is low.

A marginal fault zone in the Orontes and Jordan Valleys and the Dead Sea continues into the Gulf of Aqaba where it connects with the Red Sea Rift system. This fault zone has been responsible for rare but destructive earthquakes since Biblical times.

WESTERN EUROPE AND NORTH AFRICA (Regions 31 and 36: Map 25; Table 15.13)

Seismicity and seismic geography

This region accounts for 0.9% of the world's total seismicity. It includes the Alpide zones of Italy, the Alps, Spain, North Africa, and the older active areas in Western Europe.

Most of the activity occurs on the Italian–Sicilian arc that stretches between the Alps and Tunisia. This arc fronts on the southeast with its center in Calabria. An inner volcanic axis includes Vesuvius and Etna as well as the Eolian Islands (Stromboli). Some intermediate and deep earthquakes occur along this axis, rarely reaching a depth of 500 km. Most destructive shocks are quite shallow. They occur with maximum frequency in Calabria, Campania, and Sicily, although damaging earthquakes are known throughout the Apennine chain.

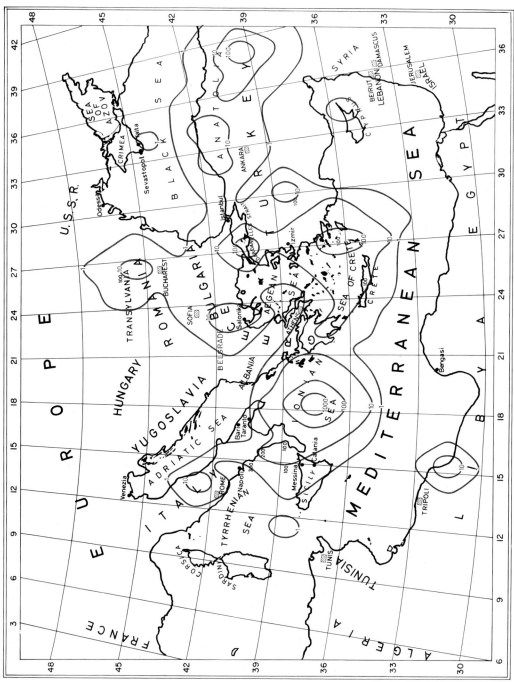

Map 35. Seismicity of M. Kárnik, after Environ. Review 21: 105 (Voitov, A.)

TABLE 15.13

Earthquakes of Western Europe and Africa (Regions 31 and 36)

Date	Epicenter	M	Comments
63	Pompeii, Campania		eruption of Vesuvius
177	Sicily		
258	Rome		
260	Vicenza, N. Italy		
326	Sicily		
365 Jul. 21	Padua, N. Italy		
558 Dec. 25	Ancona, Adriatic coast		
963 Jul. 22	Sicily		
1083 Oct. 18	Catania, Sicily		
1117 Jan. 3	Monte Cassino, N. Campania		
1169 Feb. 4	Catania, Sicily		
1186 Sep.	S. England		
1201 May 4	N. Austria		
1222 Dec. 25	Brescia, N. Italy		
1227	France–Italy border		
1231 Jun. 1	Cassino, Matese Mts., Italy		
1279 Apr. 30	Forli, N. Apennine		
1295 Aug. 8	Chur, Swiss Alps		
1328 Dec. 1	Le Preci, Roman Apennine		
1343 Nov. 24	Malta		
1348 Jan. 25	Villach, Karinthia, S. Austria		
1352 Dec. 25	Rocca d'Elci, Roman Alps		
1356 Oct. 18	Basel, Switzerland		largest shock N. of the Alps
1443 Jun. 5	N. Tatra Mts., Czechoslovakia		
1453 Sep. 28	Firenze, N. Italy		
1456 Dec. 5	Napoli–Brindisi, Campania		30,000 dead
1461 Nov. 27	Aquila, Abruzzi		
1473 May 7	Milano, N. Italy		
1509 Feb. 25	Reggio, Calabria		
1510 Jun. 10	Nördlingen, Swabian Alb Germany		
1511 Mar. 26	Udine, Italy–Yugoslavia border		
1542 Jun. 13	Mugello, N. Italy		
1542 Dec. 10	Siracusa, Sicily		
1551 Jan. 28	Lisbon, Portugal		
1556 Jan. 24	Upper Austria		
1580 Apr. 6	English Channel		
1590 Sep. 15	Bohemia		
1612 Nov. 8	Bielefeld, Teutoburgerwald, Germany		

TABLE 15.13 (continued)

Date	Epicenter	M	Comments
1618 Aug. 25	Jura, Switzerland–France border		
1627 Jul. 30	San Severo, Puglia, Italy		
1638 Mar. 27	Calabria		
1654 Jul. 23	Sora, S. Lazio, Italy		
1659 Nov. 10	Catanzaro, Calabria		
1671 Jun 20	Modena, N. Italy		
1672 Apr. 14	Rimini, Marche, Italy		
1679 Oct. 9	Málaga, S. Spain		
1688 Jun. 5	Benevento, Campania		
1692 Sep. 18	Malines, Belgium		
1693 Jan. 11	Catania, Sicily		
1693 Jun. 11	Malta		
1702 Mar. 14	Campania		
1703 Jan. 14	Aquila, Abruzzi		
1706 Nov. 3	Campobasso, Abruzzi		
1715 May	Algiers		20,000 dead
1741 Apr. 24	Fabriano, Roman Alps		
1743 Feb. 20	Sicily		
1755 Nov. 1	Lisbon, Portugal		60,000 dead
1758 Jan.	Constantine and Tunis		
1763 Jul. 29	Kormend, W. Hungary		
1783–1786	Calabrian earthquakes		60,000 dead
1786 Mar. 9	Patti, Sicily		
1805 Jul. 26	Campanian Apennine		
1810 Mar. 20	Tenerife, Canary Is.		
1825 Mar. 2	Blida, Algeria		
1829 Mar. 21	Murcia, S. Spain		
1847 Sep. 11	Helsinki, Finland		
1855 Jul. 25	Valais, Switzerland		
1867 Jan. 2	Blida, Algeria		
1870 Oct. 5	Cosenza, Calabria		
1873 Jun. 29	Venetian Alps, N. Italy		
1883 Mar. 17	Zuiderzee, Holland		
1883 Jul. 26	Ischia, S. Italy		2,300 dead
1884 Dec. 25	Málaga, Spain		
1885 Dec. 3	Central Atlas, Algeria		
1886 Apr. 22	Colchester, England		
1887 Feb. 23	San Remo, France–Italy border		
1896 Dec. 17	Hereford, England		
1908 Dec. 28	Messina, Sicily	7.5	75,000 dead
1909 Jun. 11	Provence, S. France		40 dead
1911 Nov. 16	Swabian Alb. Germany	6.2	
1915 Jan. 13	Avezzano, Sabine Mts.	7.5	30,000 dead
1915 Jul. 11	Tunis	6.2	
1920 Sep. 7	Reggio, Emilia		1,400 dead
1930 Jul. 23	S. Italy	6.5	

TABLE 15.13 (continued)

Date	Epicenter	M	Comments
1930 Oct. 30	Abruzzi	6	
1935 Apr. 19	Coast of Libya	7.1	
1936 Oct. 18	Venetian Alps		
1941 Nov. 25	off coast of Portugal	8.4	
1941 Dec. 27	Tunis	6.8	
1946 Feb. 12	E. Algeria		264 dead
1954 Mar. 29	off S. Spain	7.0	depth 640 km
1954 Sep. 9	N. Algeria	6.8	1,250 dead
1955 Feb. 19	N. Sicily	5.5	depth 470 km
1956 Apr. 19	Sierra Elvira, Spain		
1957 Feb. 20	Tunisia	5.3	
1960 Feb. 21	Jebel Chukot, Algeria	5.7	
1960 Feb. 29	Agadir, Morocco	5.6	12,000 dead
1962 Aug. 21	Campanian Apennine	6	
1968 Jan. 15	Sicily	5.4	252 dead

Earthquakes in the northern Alps are infrequent. At present the Alpine arc appears to be rather quiescent. This arc curves around northern Italy and continues into the Dinaric Alps of Yugoslavia. Some seismicity is connected with the Variscan and Hercynian Ranges of Western Europe: the Swabian Alb, Britanny and the Channel Islands. The Caledonian and older structures of northern Europe are even less active. The largest known earthquakes in northern and central Europe reach magnitudes 5½ or 6. Some activity is connected with rifts in older structures, such as the upper Rhine Valley.

The southern branch of the Alpide system continues into northern Africa, where it is developed in the Atlas Ranges. Coastal shocks in this area have been destructive in Tunisia and Algeria. Occasional damaging earthquakes occur in the High Atlas of Morocco and in its prolongation in the Canary Islands.

The northern branch of the Alpide system crosses from the Pyrenees into northern Spain and Portugal. Another branch includes southern Spain and northern Morocco. The latter is perhaps the most active area outside of Italy in the region. Its continuation offshore is of considerable importance, as its trend points to a fracture zone between southern Portugal and the Azores. The great 1755 Lisbon earthquake presumably occurred on this structure (see p. 277).

CHAPTER 16

Southern Continental Shields

INTRODUCTION

In the Southern Hemisphere there are four large continental masses: Africa, Antarctica, Australia and South America. All four are essentially shields of Precambrian age, which have remained relatively inactive throughout recent geologic history.

The least active ones among these continental masses are Antarctica and the Brazilian Shield (discussed under South America). Africa and Australia have internal rift zones and zones of weakness which are mildly active.

AFRICA AND ARABIA (Region 37; Table 16.1)

Seismicity and seismic geography

The Atlas Ranges of North Africa have been discussed in connection with the western Mediterranean. The rest of Africa and Arabia is an old peneplain which contains active rift zones responsible for about 0.1% of the world's total seismicity.

TABLE 16.1

Earthquakes of Africa and Arabia (Region 37)

Date	Epicenter	M	Comments
1857 Aug. 14	Capetown, S. Africa		
1862 Jul. 10	Accra, Ghana		
1906 Aug. 25	Central Ethiopia	6.8	
1910 Dec. 13	Lake Tanganyika	7.1	
1912 Jan. 24	Red Sea	6.7	
1912 Jul. 9	N. Uganda	6.7	
1915 May 8	Mozambique Channel	6.8	
1915 Sep. 23	coast of Eritrea	6.7	
1919 Jul. 8	W. Tanzania	6.7	
1928 Jan. 6	Mt. Kenya	7.0	
1932 Dec. 31	coast of Natal	6.7	
1939 Jun. 22	Ghana	6.5	16 dead
1942 Oct. 9	Lake Nyasa	6.7	
1961 Jun. 1	Kara-Kore, Ethiopia	6.7	several dead
1966 Mar. 20	Mt. Ruwenzori, Uganda		100 dead

The East African Rift trends largely north—south, following the great lakes: Albert, Edward, Kivi, Tanganyika and Nyasa. An active branch on the opposite side of Lake Victoria follows the Rift Valley of Kenya, through Lake Rudolf into Ethiopia. This branch intersects the Eritrean coast of the Red Sea. The Red Sea and the Gulf of Aden are recent rift structures with minor seismic activity; the seismicity of the Gulf of Aden continues across the Persian Gulf into the valley of the Indus. The Red Sea structure is less active but its northern end connects into the somewhat more seismic Jordan Rift, which includes the Gulf of Aqaba, the Dead Sea, and the valleys of the Jordan, Litani, and Orontes Rivers.

AUSTRALIA (Region 38; Table 16.2)

The seismicity of Australia is small in terms of world seismicity. However, in spite of the short historical record there is evidence of two zones of earthquake risk: south-western Australia, and the Adelaide seismic zone trending north into the Simpson Desert. Minor seismicity occurs in New South Wales and across Bass Strait into Tasmania; rare shocks occur along the margins of the Precambrian Shield, particularly in northwestern Australia along the coast of the Timor Sea.

TABLE 16.2

Earthquakes of Australia (Region 38)

Date	Epicenter	M	Comments
1897 May 10	S. of Adelaide		
1902 Sep. 19	Warooka, South Australia		
1918 Jun. 6	S.E. Queensland	6	
1939 Mar. 26	Hawker, South Australia	6	
1941 Apr. 29	Meeberrie, west Australia	7	
1954 Feb. 28	Adelaide, South Australia	5.7	
1961 May 21	Robertson, N.S.W.	5.5	
1966 May 3	Mt. Hotham, Victoria	5.7	
1968 Oct. 14	Meckering, west Australia	6.8	extensive thrust faulting
1970 Mar. 10	Meckering, west Australia	5.8	aftershock

ANTARCTICA (Region 50: Map 26)

The establishment of modern seismographic stations in Antarctica has failed to yield much information on the seismicity of that continent. Occasional small shocks in the Antarctic Peninsula have been discussed in connection with the Scotia Arc (Region 10).

The establishment of modern seismographic stations in Antarctica has failed to yield much information on the seismicity of that continent. Occasional small shocks in the Antarctic Peninsula have been discussed in connection with the Scotia Arc (Region 10).

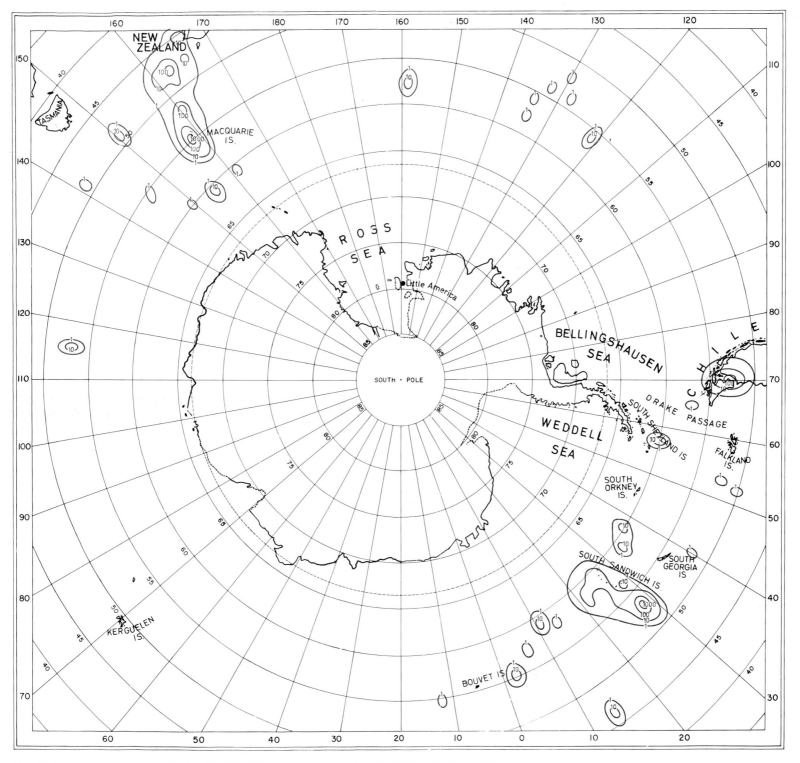

Map 26. Seismicity of Antarctica. Region 50. (Seismicity contours are numbered in 10^{15} ergs km^{-2} year^{-1}.)

CHAPTER 17

Oceanic Rises

INTRODUCTION

Oceanic rises are long mountain chains that occur near the center line of some oceans. They are 1,500—4,000 km wide and reach a height of 1,000—5,000 m above the ocean bottom. Only a few isolated peaks (e.g., Azores, Easter Island) protrude from the water. They are mostly pre-Tertiary in age and are moderately active along much of their total extension. The Mid-Atlantic Ridge has a foundered rift along its crest, indicating that it may be a tensional feature. The East Pacific Rise does not show this rift.

Oceanic rises and continental rifts (e.g., the African Rifts) are connected with active volcanism of basaltic type. The seismicity is entirely shallow; no intermediate or deep-focus earthquakes exist along these features. Most earthquakes occur on the transform faults which offset the rises at right angles.

In the Pacific Ocean there are also large fracture zones which divide the ocean bottom into blocks. These fracture zones may be thousands of kilometers long and may have a throw of several thousands of meters. Some fracture zones, such as the Mendocino and Clarion fractures, show important seismic activity where they intersect a ridge.

Though of considerable importance to the earth scientist, the seismicity of oceanic rises is of no major concern in connection with earthquake hazard.

MID-ATLANTIC AND ARCTIC RIDGE (Regions 32 and 40; Table 17.1)

This region includes the central part of the Atlantic Ocean from latitude 65°N to 50°S (Region 32), and from 65°N through Iceland into the Arctic Ocean (Region 40). Together the two regions account for 0.3% of the world's seismicity.

The Mid-Atlantic Rise occupies rather exactly the center line between the shores of Africa and South America. A notable bend in the Rise occurs between 15°N and the Equator. Here the ridge has been sheared off with lateral offsets of over 100 miles (Romanche fracture zone). This part of the Rise is highly active.

Another region of high activity occurs in the Azores (Açores), a series of emerging volcanic summits of the ridge. Here an active ridge branches off toward Portugal and southern Spain. North of the Azores the activity continues across Iceland, Jan Mayen, and bypassing Spitsbergen on the Greenland side. Under the Arctic Ocean the ridge is slightly less active; it turns east short of the North Pole, under the Laptev Sea, and appears to connect with the Verkhoyan Arc of Siberia.

TABLE 17.1

Earthquakes of the Mid-Atlantic and Arctic Ridge (Regions 32, 40)

Date	Epicenter	M	Comments
1339 May 22	SW. Iceland		
1657 Mar. 16	S. Iceland		
1706 Apr. 20	SW. Iceland		
1725 Apr. 1	S. Iceland		eruption of Mt. Hecla
1755 Nov. 1	Azores–Gibraltar Ridge		60,000 dead (Lisbon)
1757 Jul. 9	Azores		tsunami
1784 Aug. 14	S. Iceland		
1810 Aug 11	Azores		
1838 Jun. 11	off coast of N. Iceland		
1881 Feb.	Azores		
1885 Jan. 25	N. Iceland		
1896 Aug. 26	S. Iceland		
1910 Jan. 22	off N. Iceland	7.2	
1912 May 6	S. Iceland	7.5	
1939 May 8	Azores	7.1	
1958 May	Azores		Fayal eruption
1963 Mar. 28	off N. Iceland	7.0	
1968 Feb. 28	Azores–Gibraltar Ridge	7.6	damage in Portugal

In the South Atlantic the ridge emerges in several small islands (Ascension, Tristan da Cunha, Bouvet Island) and its activity diminishes considerably. It swings around the southern tip of Africa in a wide arc and eventually connects with the Prince Edward Ridge in the Indian Ocean.

Iceland has an ancient written history and many destructive earthquakes are recorded.

INDIAN OCEAN (Region 33; Table 17.2)

The Indian Ocean region is more active than the Mid-Atlantic Ridge (1.25% of world seismicity). However, its coverage by seismographic stations is probably the least adequate of any major area.

The configuration of ridges is relatively complex. A broad north–south ridge (Laccadive–Chagos Rise) extends from the coast of Bombay into the Indian Ocean. This rise contains the Laccadive, Maldive, and Chagos Islands, and continues southwestward toward Mauritius Island. Two major branches occur to the northwest: the Carlsberg Ridge, from the Chagos Islands to the coast of Aden, and the Seychelles Ridge from the islands of the same name to Mauritius Island.

The main rise branches out to the south. One branch follows the Prince Edward Ridge to Bouvet Island where it connects with the Mid-Atlantic Rise. The other branch trends southeast through Amsterdam and St. Paul Islands, and eventually joins the East Pacific

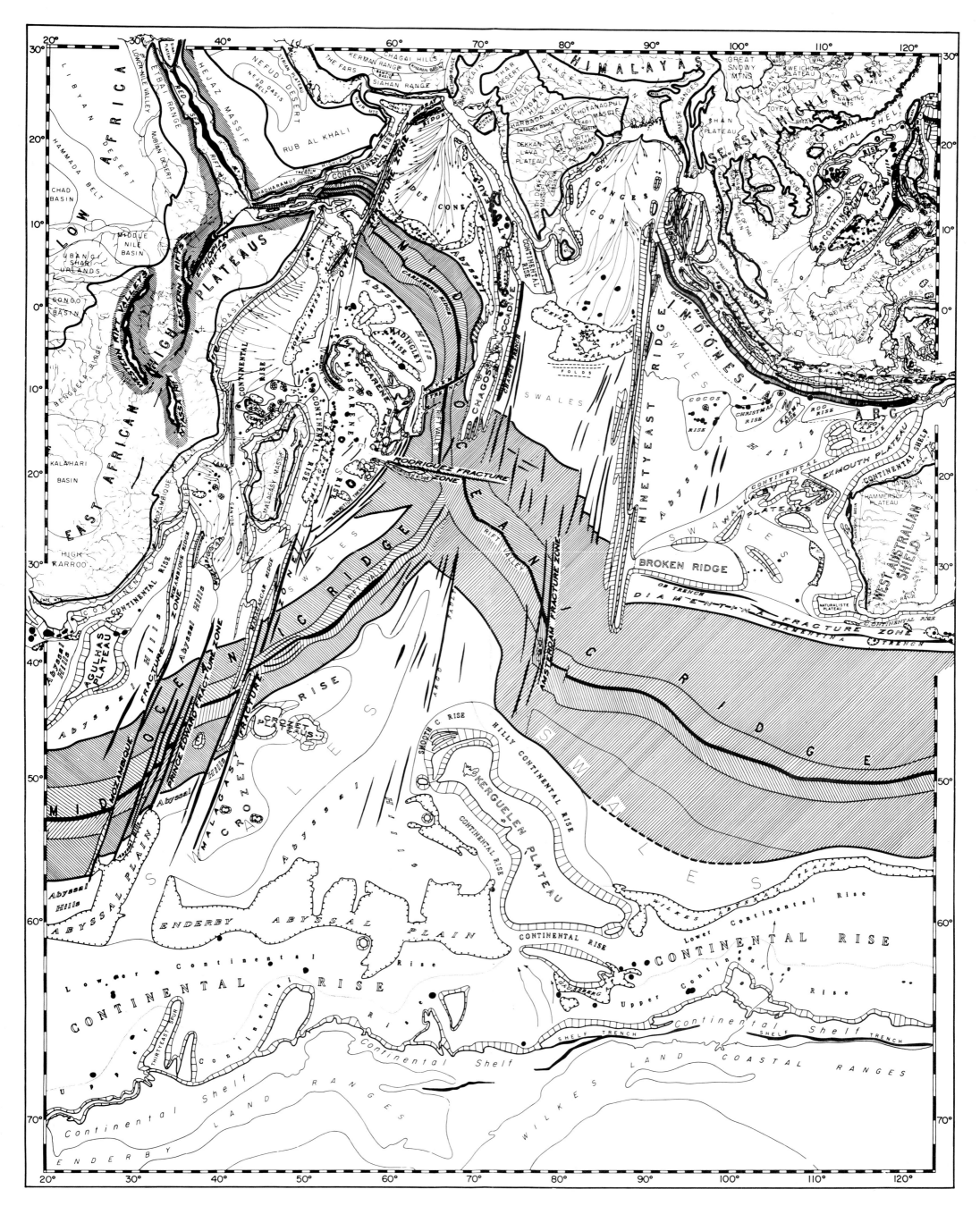

Fig.17.1. Physiography and tectonics of the Indian Ocean. (After Heezen and Tharp, 1967.)

TABLE 17.2

Earthquakes of the Indian Ocean region (Region 33)
(major shocks only)

Date	Epicenter	M	Comments
1823 Feb. 9	off Ceylon		damage
1882 Jan.	Trincomales, Ceylon		tsunami
1928 Mar. 9	Cocos Basin	8.1	
1942 Nov. 10	Prince Edward Ridge	8.3	

Rise near the coast of Antarctica (Balleny Islands). Both main ridges have shorter lateral branches, such as the Kerguelen and Crozet Ridges (Fig. 17.1).

An active seismic zone extends from the Bay of Bengal southward into the deep Cocos Basin of the Indian Ocean. This zone represents a different ridge which may branch off the Andaman active region.

The population density of the Indian Ocean area is slight, and damaging shocks are rare.

EAST–CENTRAL PACIFIC RISE AND HAWAIIAN ISLANDS (Regions 39 and 44)

The East Pacific Rise is of little importance as far as seismic risk is concerned. The most exposed areas are Easter Island and the Galápagos group. Both are volcanic but no disastrous earthquakes have been recorded. Major shocks have occurred at some distance from the main islands.

An interesting volcanic eruption occurred off Juan Fernandez Island on February 20, 1835, at the time of the arrival of the tsunami from the Chile earthquake of the same date. The detailed description appears to correspond to explosive activity of a submarine volcano in Cumberland Bay, Juan Fernández.

The Hawaiian Islands form the crest of an older (presumably Mesozoic) oceanic rise, which continues in the Emperor Seamount Range (non-seismic). Active volcanism exists on the southernmost islands of Hawaii and Maui. Damaging earthquakes are rare; they include the shocks of April 2, 1868 (Island of Hawaii, probable magnitude about 7) and October 6, 1929 (Kona coast, Islands of Hawaii, 6.5). The Hawaiian Islands, by virtue of their central location in the Pacific Ocean, are particularly exposed to tsunami hazard from Circum-Pacific earthquake sources.

APPENDIX 1

EARTHQUAKE REGULATIONS (SECTION 2314) OF THE 1968 LOS ANGELES COUNTY BUILDING CODE

(Reproduced by permission of the County Engineer, County of Los Angeles, California)

SEC. 2314 — EARTHQUAKE REGULATIONS

(a) **General.** Every building or structure and every portion thereof shall be designed and constructed to resist stresses produced by lateral forces as provided in this Section. Stresses shall be calculated as the effect of a force applied horizontally at each floor or roof level above the foundation. The force shall be assumed to come from any horizontal direction.

The provisions of this Section apply to the structure as a unit and also to all parts thereof, including the structural frame or walls, floor and roof systems, and other structural features.

(b) **Definitions.** The following definitions apply only to the provisions of this Section.

SPACE FRAME is a three-dimensional structural system composed of interconnected members, other than ➤ bearing walls, laterally supported so as to function as a complete self-contained unit with or without the aid of horizontal diaphragms or floor bracing systems. ◄

➤ **SPACE FRAME-MOMENT RESISTING** is a vertical load carrying space frame in which the members and joints are capable of resisting design lateral forces by bending moments. ◄

➤ **SPACE FRAME-DUCTILE MOMENT RESISTING** is a space frame-moment resisting complying with the requirements for a ductile moment resisting space frame as given in Section 2314 (j). ◄

➤ **LATERAL FORCE RESISTING SYSTEM** is that part of the structural system to which the lateral forces prescribed in Section 2314 (d) 1 are assigned. ◄

SPACE FRAME — VERTICAL LOAD-CARRYING is a space frame designed to carry all vertical loads.

BOX SYSTEM is a structural system without a complete vertical load-carrying space frame. In this system the required lateral forces are resisted by shear walls as hereinafter defined.

SHEAR WALL is a wall designed to resist lateral forces parallel to the wall. Braced frames subjected primarily to axial stresses shall be considered as shear walls for the purpose of this definition.

(c) **Symbols and Notations.** The following symbols and notations apply only to the provisions of this Section.

C = Numerical coefficient for base shear as specified in Section 2314 (d) 1.

C_p = Numerical coefficient as specified in Section 2314 (d) 2 and as set forth in Table No. 23-I.

D = The dimension of the building in feet in a direction parallel to the applied forces.

D_s = The plan dimension of the vertical lateral force resisting system in feet.

F_i, F_n, F_x = Lateral forces applied to a level "i," "n," or "x," respectively.

F_p = Lateral forces on the part of the structure and in the direction under consideration.

F_t = That portion of "V" considered concentrated at the top of the structure, at the level "n." The remaining portion of the total base shear "V" shall be distributed over the height of the structure including level "n" according to Formula (14-5).

H = The height of the main portion of the building in feet above the base.

$h_i, h_n, h_x =$ Height in feet above the base to level "i," "n," or "x," respectively.

K $\quad=$ Numerical coefficient for base moment as specified in Section 2314 (h).

J_x $\quad=$ Numerical coefficient for overturning moment at level "x."

J $\quad=$ Numerical coefficient as set forth in Table No. 23-H.

Level i $\quad=$ Level of the structure referred to by the subscript "i."

Level n $\quad=$ That level which is uppermost in the main portion of the structure.

Level x $\quad=$ That level which is under design consideration.

M $\quad=$ Overturning moment at the base of the building or structure.

M_x $\quad=$ The overturning moment at level "x."

N $\quad=$ Total number of stories above exterior grade.

T $\quad=$ Fundamental period of vibration of the building or structure in seconds in the direction under consideration.

V $\quad=$ Total lateral load or shear at the base.

$$V = F_t + \sum_{i=1}^{n} F_i$$

where $i = 1$ designates first level above the base.

W $\quad=$ Total dead load including partitions using the actual weight of the partitions or the partition loading specified in Section 2302 (b)

$$W = \sum_{i=1}^{n} w_i$$

EXCEPTION: "W" shall be equal to the total dead load plus 25 per cent of the floor live load in storage and warehouse occupancies.

w_i, w_x $\quad=$ That portion of "W" which is located at or is assigned to level "i" or "x" respectively.

W_p $\quad=$ The weight of a part or portion of a structure.

Z $\quad=$ Numerical coefficient equal to one.

(d) **Minimum Earthquake Forces for Structures:** 1. **Total lateral force and distribution of lateral force.** Every structure shall be designed and constructed to withstand minimum total lateral seismic forces assumed to act nonconcurrently in the direction of each of the main axes of the structures in accordance with the following formula (For forces on parts or portions of buildings and for forces on structures other than buildings, see paragraph 2 of this Subsection):

$$V = ZKCW \qquad (14\text{-}1)$$

The value of "K" shall be not less than that set forth in Table No. 23-H. The value of "C" shall be determined in accordance with the following formula:

$$C = \frac{0.05}{\sqrt[3]{T}} \qquad (14\text{-}2)$$

Except as provided in Table No. 23-I, the maximum value of "C" need not exceed 0.10. For all one- and two-story buildings the value of "C" shall be considered as 0.10.

"T" is the fundamental period of vibration of the structure in seconds in the direction under consideration. Properly substantiated technical data for establishing the period "T" may be submitted. In the absence of such data, the value of "T" for buildings shall be determined by the following formula:

$$T = \frac{0.05h_n}{\sqrt{D}} \qquad (14\text{-}3)$$

EXCEPTION: In all buildings in which the lateral resisting system consists of a moment-resisting space frame which resists 100 per cent of the required lateral forces and which frame is not enclosed by or adjoined by more rigid elements which would tend to prevent the frame from resisting lateral forces:

$$T = 0.10N \qquad (14\text{-}3A)$$

TABLE NO. 23-H — HORIZONTAL FORCE FACTOR "K" FOR BUILDINGS OR OTHER STRUCTURES[1]

TYPE OR ARRANGEMENT OF RESISTING ELEMENTS	VALUE[2] OF K
All building framing systems except as hereinafter classified	1.00
Buildings with a box system as specified in Section 2314 (b)	1.33
Buildings with a dual bracing system consisting of a ductile moment resisting space frame and shear walls using the following design criteria: (1) The frames and shear walls shall resist the total lateral force in accordance with their relative rigidities considering the interaction of the shear walls and frames (2) The shear walls acting independently of the ductile moment resisting portions of the space frame shall resist the total required lateral forces (3) The ductile moment resisting space frame shall have the capacity to resist not less than 25 per cent of the required lateral force	0.80
Buildings with a ductile moment-resisting space frame designed in accordance with the following criteria: (1) The ductile moment-resisting space frame shall have the capacity to resist the total required lateral force (2) If major rigid elements are included in addition to the ductile moment-resisting space frame, the total required lateral force shall be distributed to all resisting elements in accordance with their relative rigidities considering the interaction of the frames and rigid elements	0.67
Elevated tanks plus full contents, on four or more cross-braced legs and not supported by a building[3, 4]	3.00[5]
Structures other than buildings and other than those set forth in Table No. 23-I	2.00

[1]Where wind load as specified in Section 2307 would produce higher stresses, this load shall be used in lieu of the loads resulting from earthquake forces.

[2]Footnote No. 2 is deleted.

[3]The minimum value of "KC" shall be 0.12 and the maximum value of "KC" need not exceed 0.25.

[4]For overturning, the factor "J" as specified in Section 2314 (h) shall be 1.00.

[5]The tower shall be designed for an accidental torsion of five per cent as specified in Section 2314 (g). Elevated tanks which are supported by buildings or do not conform to type or arrangement of supporting elements as described above shall be designed in accordance with Section 2314 (d) 2 using "C_p" = .2.

h_i, h_n, h_x = Height in feet above the base to level "i," "n," or "x," respectively.

K = Numerical coefficient for base moment as specified in Section 2314 (h).

J_x = Numerical coefficient for overturning moment at level "x."

J = Numerical coefficient as set forth in Table No. 23-H.

Level i = Level of the structure referred to by the sub-script "i."

Level n = That level which is uppermost in the main portion of the structure.

Level x = That level which is under design consideration.

M = Overturning moment at the base of the building or structure.

M_x = The overturning moment at level "x."

N = Total number of stories above exterior grade.

T = Fundamental period of vibration of the building or structure in seconds in the direction under consideration.

V = Total lateral load or shear at the base.

$$V = F_t + \sum_{i=1}^{n} F_i$$

where $i = 1$ designates first level above the base.

W = Total dead load including partitions using the actual weight of the partitions or the partition loading specified in Section 2302 (b)

$$W = \sum_{i=1}^{n} w_i$$

EXCEPTION: "W" shall be equal to the total dead load plus 25 per cent of the floor live load in storage and warehouse occupancies.

w_i, w_x = That portion of "W" which is located at or is assigned to level "i" or "x" respectively.

W_p = The weight of a part or portion of a structure.

Z = Numerical coefficient equal to one.

(d) **Minimum Earthquake Forces for Structures:** 1. **Total lateral force and distribution of lateral force.** Every structure shall be designed and constructed to withstand minimum total lateral seismic forces assumed to act nonconcurrently in the direction of each of the main axes of the structures in accordance with the following formula (For forces on parts or portions of buildings and for forces on structures other than buildings, see paragraph 2 of this Subsection):

$$V = ZKCW \qquad (14-1)$$

The value of "K" shall be not less than that set forth in Table No. 23-H. The value of "C" shall be determined in accordance with the following formula:

$$C = \frac{0.05}{\sqrt[3]{T}} \qquad (14-2)$$

Except as provided in Table No. 23-I, the maximum value of "C" need not exceed 0.10. For all one- and two-story buildings the value of "C" shall be considered as 0.10.

"T" is the fundamental period of vibration of the structure in seconds in the direction under consideration. Properly substantiated technical data for establishing the period "T" may be submitted. In the absence of such data, the value of "T" for buildings shall be determined by the following formula:

$$T = \frac{0.05 h_n}{\sqrt{D}} \qquad (14\text{-}3)$$

EXCEPTION: *In all buildings in which the lateral resisting system consists of a moment-resisting space frame which resists 100 per cent of the required lateral forces and which frame is not enclosed by or adjoined by more rigid elements which would tend to prevent the frame from resisting lateral forces:*

$$T = 0.10N \qquad (14\text{-}3A)$$

TABLE NO. 23-H — HORIZONTAL FORCE FACTOR "K" FOR BUILDINGS OR OTHER STRUCTURES[1]

TYPE OR ARRANGEMENT OF RESISTING ELEMENTS	VALUE[2] OF K
All building framing systems except as hereinafter classified	1.00
Buildings with a box system as specified in Section 2314 (b)	1.33
Buildings with a dual bracing system consisting of a ductile moment resisting space frame and shear walls using the following design criteria: (1) The frames and shear walls shall resist the total lateral force in accordance with their relative rigidities considering the interaction of the shear walls and frames (2) The shear walls acting independently of the ductile moment resisting portions of the space frame shall resist the total required lateral forces (3) The ductile moment resisting space frame shall have the capacity to resist not less than 25 per cent of the required lateral force	0.80
Buildings with a ductile moment-resisting space frame designed in accordance with the following criteria: (1) The ductile moment-resisting space frame shall have the capacity to resist the total required lateral force (2) If major rigid elements are included in addition to the ductile moment-resisting space frame, the total required lateral force shall be distributed to all resisting elements in accordance with their relative rigidities considering the interaction of the frames and rigid elements	0.67
Elevated tanks plus full contents, on four or more cross-braced legs and not supported by a building[4, 4]	3.00[5]
Structures other than buildings and other than those set forth in Table No. 23-I	2.00

[1]Where wind load as specified in Section 2307 would produce higher stresses, this load shall be used in lieu of the loads resulting from earthquake forces.

[2]Footnote No. 2 is deleted.

[3]The minimum value of "KC" shall be 0.12 and the maximum value of "KC" need not exceed 0.25.

[4]For overturning, the factor "J" as specified in Section 2314 (h) shall be 1.00.

[5]The tower shall be designed for an accidental torsion of five per cent as specified in Section 2314 (g). Elevated tanks which are supported by buildings or do not conform to type or arrangement of supporting elements as described above shall be designed in accordance with Section 2314 (d) 2 using "C_p" = .2.

The total lateral force "V" shall be distributed in the height of the structure in the following manner:

$$F_t = .004V \left(\frac{h_n}{D_s} \right)^2 \qquad (14\text{-}4)$$

F_t need not exceed 0.15 "V" and may be considered as 0 for values $\left(\dfrac{h_n}{D_s} \right)$ of 3 or less, and

$$F_s = \frac{(V - F_t)\, w_s h_s}{\displaystyle\sum_{i=1}^{n} w_i h_i} \qquad (14\text{-}5)$$

EXCEPTION: One-and two-story buildings shall have uniform distribution.

At each level designated as "x," the force "F_x" shall be applied over the area of the building in accordance with the mass distribution on that level.

2. Lateral force on parts or portions of buildings or other structures. Parts or portions of buildings or structures and their anchorage shall be designed for lateral forces in accordance with the following formula:

$$F_p = ZC_p W_p \qquad (14\text{-}6)$$

The values of "C_p" are set forth in Table No. 23-I. The distribution of these forces shall be according to the gravity loads pertaining thereto.

3. Pile foundations. Individual pile or caisson footings of every building or structure shall be interconnected by ties each of which can carry by tension and compression a horizontal force equal to 10 per cent of the larger pile cap loading unless it can be demonstrated that equivalent restraint can be provided by other approved methods.

EXCEPTION: Ties may be omitted for belled footings having a height not exceeding six feet nor twice the diameter of the bell and for piles supporting one-story buildings of lightweight Type IV-N construction.

(e) **Distribution of Horizontal Shear.** Total shear in any horizontal plane shall be distributed to the various elements of the lateral force resisting system in proportion to their rigidities considering the rigidity of the horizontal bracing system or diaphragm.

Rigid elements that are assumed not to be part of the lateral force resisting system may be incorporated into buildings provided that their effect on the action of the system is considered and provided for in the design.

(f) **Drift.** Lateral deflections or drift of a story relative to its adjacent stories shall be considered in accordance with accepted engineering practice.

(g) **Horizontal Torsional Moments.** Provisions shall be made for the increase in shear resulting from the horizontal torsion due to an eccentricity between the center of mass and the center of rigidity. Negative torsional shears shall be neglected. Where the vertical resisting elements depend on diaphragm action for shear distribution at any level, the shear-resisting elements shall be capable of resisting a torsional moment assumed to be equivalent to the story shear acting with an eccentricity of not less than five per cent of the maximum building dimension at that level.

TABLE NO. 23-I — HORIZONTAL FORCE FACTOR "C_p" FOR PARTS OF PORTIONS OF BUILDINGS OR OTHER STRUCTURES

PART OR PORTION OF BUILDINGS	DIRECTION OF FORCE	VALUE OF C_p
Exterior bearing and nonbearing walls, interior bearing walls and partitions, interior nonbearing walls and partitions over 10 feet in height, masonry or concrete fences over six feet in height[1]	Normal to flat surface	0.20
Cantilever parapet and other cantilever walls, except retaining walls	Normal to flat surface	1.00
Exterior and interior ornamentations and appendages	Any direction	1.00
When connected to or a part of a building: towers, tanks, towers and tanks plus contents, chimneys, smokestacks, and penthouses	Any direction	0.20[2]
When resting on the ground, tank plus effective mass of its contents	Any direction	0.10
Floors and roofs acting as diaphragms[3]	Any direction	0.10
Connections for exterior panels or for elements complying with Section 2314 (k) 5	Any direction	2.00
Connections for prefabricated structural elements other than walls, with force applied at center of gravity of assembly[4]	Any horizontal direction	0.30

[1]See also Section 2312 (b) for minimum load on deflection criteria for interior partitions.

[2]When "h_n/D" of any building is equal to or greater than five to one increase value by 50 per cent.

[3]Floors and roofs acting as diaphragms shall be designed for a minimum value of "C_p" of 10 per cent applied to loads tributary from that story unless a greater value of "C_p" is required by the basic seismic formula $V = ZKCW$

[4]The "W_p" shall be equal to the total load plus 25 per cent of the floor live load in storage and warehouse occupancies.

(h) **Overturning.** Every building or structure shall be designed to resist the overturning effects caused by the wind forces and related requirements specified in Section 2308, or the earthquake forces specified in this Section, whichever governs.

EXCEPTION: The axial loads from earthquake forces on vertical elements and footings in every building or structure may be modified in accordance with the following provisions:

1. The overturning moment, "M," at the base of the building or structure shall be determined in accordance with the following formula:

$$M = J\left(F_t h_n + \sum_{i=1}^{n} F_i h_i\right) \qquad (14\text{-}7)$$

WHERE:

$$J = \frac{0.5}{\sqrt[3]{T^2}} \qquad (14\text{-}8)$$

The value of "J" need not be more than 1.00.

2. The overturning moment, "M_x," at any level designated as "x" shall be determined in accordance with the following:

$$M_x = J_x\left[F_t(h_n - h_x) + \sum_{i=x}^{n} F_i(h_i - h_x)\right] \qquad (14\text{-}9)$$

The total lateral force "V" shall be distributed in the height of the structure in the following manner:

$$F_t = .004V \left(\frac{h_n}{D_t} \right)^2 \qquad (14\text{-}4)$$

F_t need not exceed 0.15 "V" and may be considered as 0 for values $\left(\dfrac{h_n}{D_t} \right)$ of 3 or less, and

$$F_x = \frac{(V - F_t)\ w_x h_x}{\displaystyle\sum_{i=1}^{n} w_i h_i} \qquad (14\text{-}5)$$

EXCEPTION: One-and two-story buildings shall have uniform distribution.

At each level designated as "x," the force "F_x" shall be applied over the area of the building in accordance with the mass distribution on that level.

2. **Lateral force on parts or portions of buildings or other structures.** Parts or portions of buildings or structures and their anchorage shall be designed for lateral forces in accordance with the following formula:

$$F_p = ZC_p W_p \qquad (14\text{-}6)$$

The values of "C_p" are set forth in Table No. 23-I. The distribution of these forces shall be according to the gravity loads pertaining thereto.

3. **Pile foundations.** Individual pile or caisson footings of every building or structure shall be interconnected by ties each of which can carry by tension and compression a horizontal force equal to 10 per cent of the larger pile cap loading unless it can be demonstrated that equivalent restraint can be provided by other approved methods.

EXCEPTION: Ties may be omitted for belled footings having a height not exceeding six feet nor twice the diameter of the bell and for piles supporting one-story buildings of lightweight Type IV-N construction.

(e) **Distribution of Horizontal Shear.** Total shear in any horizontal plane shall be distributed to the various elements of the lateral force resisting system in proportion to their rigidities considering the rigidity of the horizontal bracing system or diaphragm.

Rigid elements that are assumed not to be part of the lateral force resisting system may be incorporated into buildings provided that their effect on the action of the system is considered and provided for in the design.

(f) **Drift.** Lateral deflections or drift of a story relative to its adjacent stories shall be considered in accordance with accepted engineering practice.

(g) **Horizontal Torsional Moments.** Provisions shall be made for the increase in shear resulting from the horizontal torsion due to an eccentricity between the center of mass and the center of rigidity. Negative torsional shears shall be neglected. Where the vertical resisting elements depend on diaphragm action for shear distribution at any level, the shear-resisting elements shall be capable of resisting a torsional moment assumed to be equivalent to the story shear acting with an eccentricity of not less than five per cent of the maximum building dimension at that level.

TABLE NO. 23-I — HORIZONTAL FORCE FACTOR "C_p" FOR PARTS OF PORTIONS OF BUILDINGS OR OTHER STRUCTURES

PART OR PORTION OF BUILDINGS	DIRECTION OF FORCE	VALUE OF C_p
Exterior bearing and nonbearing walls, interior bearing walls and partitions, interior nonbearing walls and partitions over 10 feet in height, masonry or concrete fences over six feet in height[1]	Normal to flat surface	0.20
Cantilever parapet and other cantilever walls, except retaining walls	Normal to flat surface	1.00
Exterior and interior ornamentations and appendages	Any direction	1.00
When connected to or a part of a building: towers, tanks, towers and tanks plus contents, chimneys, smokestacks, and penthouses	Any direction	0.20[2]
When resting on the ground, tank plus effective mass of its contents	Any direction	0.10
Floors and roofs acting as diaphragms[3]	Any direction	0.10
Connections for exterior panels or for elements complying with Section 2314 (k) 5	Any direction	2.00
Connections for prefabricated structural elements other than walls, with force applied at center of gravity of assembly[4]	Any horizontal direction	0.30

[1]See also Section 2312 (b) for minimum load on deflection criteria for interior partitions.

[2]When "h_n/D" of any building is equal to or greater than five to one increase value by 50 per cent.

[3]Floors and roofs acting as diaphragms shall be designed for a minimum value of "C_p" of 10 per cent applied to loads tributary from that story unless a greater value of "C_p" is required by the basic seismic formula $V = ZKCW$.

[4]The "W_p" shall be equal to the total load plus 25 per cent of the floor live load in storage and warehouse occupancies.

(h) **Overturning.** Every building or structure shall be designed to resist the overturning effects caused by the wind forces and related requirements specified in Section 2308, or the earthquake forces specified in this Section, whichever governs.

EXCEPTION: The axial loads from earthquake forces on vertical elements and footings in every building or structure may be modified in accordance with the following provisions:

1. The overturning moment, "M," at the base of the building or structure shall be determined in accordance with the following formula:

$$M = J \left(F_t h_n + \sum_{i=1}^{n} F_i h_i \right) \qquad (14\text{-}7)$$

WHERE:

$$J = \frac{0.5}{\sqrt[3]{T^2}} \qquad (14\text{-}8)$$

The value of "J" need not be more than 1.00.

2. The overturning moment, "M_x", at any level designated as "x" shall be determined in accordance with the following:

$$M_x = J_x \left[F_t (h_n - h_x) + \sum_{i=x}^{n} F_i (h_i - h_x) \right] \quad (14\text{-}9)$$

WHERE:

$$J_x = J + (1 - J) \left(\frac{h_x}{h_n} \right)^3 \qquad (14\text{-}10)$$

At any level the incremental changes of the design overturning moment, in the story under consideration, shall be distributed to the various resisting elements in the same proportion as the distribution of the shears in the resisting system. Where other vertical members are provided which are capable of partially resisting the overturning moments, a redistribution may be made to these members if framing members of sufficient strength and stiffness to transmit the required loads are provided.

Where a vertical resisting element is discontinuous, the overturning moment carried by the lowest story of that element shall be carried down as loads to the foundation.

(i) **Set-backs.** Buildings having set-backs wherein the plan dimension of the tower in each direction is at least 75 per cent of the corresponding plan dimension of the lower part may be considered as a uniform building without set-backs for the purpose of determining seismic forces.

For other conditions of set-backs the tower shall be designed as a separate building using the larger of the seismic coefficients at the base of the tower determined by considering the tower as either a separate building for its own height or as part of the over-all structure. The resulting total shear from the tower shall be applied at the top of the lower part of the building which shall be otherwise considered separately for its own height.

(j) **Structural Systems. 1. Design Requirements.** Buildings designed with a horizontal force factor "K" of 0.67 or 0.80 shall have a ductile moment-resisting space frame. Buildings more than one hundred and sixty feet in height shall have a ductile moment-resisting space frame capable of resisting not less than 25 per cent of the required seismic load for the structure as a whole.

Moment-resisting space frames and ductile moment-resisting space frames may be enclosed by or adjoined by more rigid elements which would tend to prevent the space frame from resisting lateral forces, where it can be shown that the action or failure of the more rigid elements will not impair the vertical and lateral load-resisting ability of the space frame.

2. **Construction.** The necessary ductility for a ductile moment-resisting space frame shall be provided by a frame of structural steel conforming to ASTM A-7, A-36 or A-441 with moment-resisting connections, or by a reinforced concrete frame complying with Section 2632 of this Code.

Shear walls in buildings exceeding one hundred and sixty feet in height shall be composed of axially loaded bracing members of ASTM A-7, A-36 or A-441 structural steel; or reinforced concrete bracing members or walls conforming with the requirements of Section 2632 of this Code.

(k) **Design Requirements. 1. Building separations.** All portions of structures shall be designed and constructed to act as an integral unit in resisting horizontal forces unless separated structurally by a distance sufficient to avoid contact under deflection from seismic action or wind forces. Structural separations of at least one-inch, plus one-half inch for each ten feet of height above twenty feet are considered adequate to meet the requirements of this paragraph.

2. Minor alterations. Minor structural alterations may be made in existing buildings and other structures, but the resistance to lateral forces shall be not less than that before such alterations were made, unless the building as altered meets the requirements of this Section of the Code.

3. Reinforced masonry or concrete. All elements within the structure which are of masonry or concrete and which resist seismic forces or movement shall be reinforced so as to qualify as reinforced masonry or concrete under the provisions of Chapters 24 and 26. Principal reinforcement in masonry shall be spaced two feet maximum on center in buildings using a ductile moment-resisting space frame.

4. Combined vertical and horizontal forces. In computing the effect of seismic force in combination with vertical loads, gravity load stresses induced in members by dead load plus design live load, except roof live load, shall be considered.

5. Exterior elements. Precast, nonbearing, non-shear wall panels or other elements which are attached to, or enclose the exterior, shall accommodate movements of the structure resulting from lateral forces or temperature changes. The concrete panels or other elements shall be supported by means of poured-in-place concrete or by mechanical fasteners in accordance with the following provisions:

A. Connections and panel joints shall allow for a relative movement between stories of not less than two times story drift caused by wind or seismic forces; or one-fourth inch whichever is greater.

B. Connections shall have sufficient ductility and rotation capacity so as to preclude fracture of the concrete or brittle failures at or near welds. Inserts in concrete shall be attached to, or hooked around reinforcing steel, or otherwise terminated so as to effectively transfer forces to the reinforcing steel.

C. Connections to permit movement in the plane of the panel for story drift may be properly designed sliding connections using slotted or oversize holes or may be connections which permit movement by bending of steel.

6. Minor rigid elements. Minor rigid elements within or attached to a structure may be assumed to be expendable and not part of the lateral force resisting system.

References

Aitchison, J. and Brown, J.A.C., 1957. *The Lognormal Distribution*. Cambridge Univ. Press, Cambridge, 176 pp.

Aki K., 1956. Some problems in statistical seismology. *Zisin, Tokyo*, 8: 205–228.

Atwater, T., 1970. Implications of plate tectonics for the Cenozoic tectonic evolution of western North America. *Geol. Soc. Am. Bull.*, 81: 3528–3535.

Barazangi, M. and Isacks, B., 1971. Lateral variations of seismic-wave attenuation in the upper mantle above the inclined earthquake zone of the Tonga Island arc; deep anomaly in the upper mantle. *J. Geophys. Res.*, 76: 8493–8516.

Benioff, H., 1951. Colloquium on plastic flow and deformation within the earth. *Trans. Am. Geophys. Union*, 32: 508–514.

Benioff, H., 1955. Symposium on the crust of th earth. *Geol. Soc. Am., Spec. Pap.*, 62: 61–74.

Bodechtel, J. and Gierloff-Emden, H.G., 1969. *Weltraumbilder der Erde*. Paul List, Berlin, 76 pp.

Bolt, B.A., Lomnitz, C. and McEvilly, T.V., 1968. Seismological evidence on the tectonics of central and northern California and the Mendocino escarpment. *Bull. Seismol. Soc. Am.*, 58: 1725–1767.

Boltzmann, L., 1876. Zur Theorie der elastischen Nachwirkung. *Poggend, Ann. Ergänzgsbd.*, 7: 624.

Boström, R.C. and Vali, V., 1971. Strains and detection in a mosaic earth. *R. Soc. N.Z. Bull.*, 9: 55–60.

Brune, J.N., 1968. Seismic moment, seismicity, and rate of slip along major fault zones. *J. Geophys. Res.*, 73: 777–784.

Bullen, K.E., 1963. *An Introduction to the Theory of Seismology*. Cambridge Univ. Press, Cambridge, 3rd ed., 381 pp.

Burridge, R. and Knopoff, L., 1967. Model and theoretical seismicity. *Bull. Seismol. Soc. Am.*, 57: 341–371.

California, State of, 1908. Report of the State Earthquake Investigating Commission. *Carnegie Inst. Wash. Publ.*, 87(2): 18.

California, State of, 1964. Crustal strain and fault movement investigation. *Dept. Water Resour., Sacramento, Bull.*, 116–2.

Cox, D.R., 1962. *Renewal Theory*. Methuen, London, 142 pp.

Dally, J.W. and Lewis III, D., 1968. A photoelastic analysis of propagation of Rayleigh waves past a step change in elevation. *Bull. Seismol. Soc. Am.*, 539–563.

Davies, G.F. and Brune, J.N., 1971. Regional and global fault slip rates from seismicity. *Nature*, 229: 101–107.

Davies, J.B. and Smith, S.W., 1968. Source parameters of earthquakes and discrimination between earthquakes and nuclear explosions. *Bull. Seismol. Soc. Am.*, 58: 1503–1517.

De la Cruz, S., 1970. Asymmetric convection in the upper mantle. *Geofis. Int.*, 10: 49–56.

De Montessus de Ballore, F., 1907. *La Science Sismologique*. Armand Colin, Paris, 579 pp.

Dietz, R.S. and Holden, J.C. 1970. Reconstruction of Pangaea: Breakup and dispersion of continents, Permian to present. *J. Geophys. Res.*, 75: 4939–4956.

Drakopoulos, J.C., 1971. A statistical model on the occurrence of aftershocks in the area of Greece. *Bull.Int. Inst. Seismol. Earthquake Eng. Tokyo*, 8: 17–39.

Dunbar, C.O., 1960. *Textbook of Historical Geology*. Wiley, New York, N.Y., 2nd ed. 500 pp.

Elsasser, W.M., 1971. Sea-floor spreading as thermal convection. *J. Geophys. Res.*, 76: 1101–1112.

Epstein, B. and Lomnitz, C., 1966. A model for the occurrence of large earthquakes. *Nature*, 211: 954–956.

Ergin, K., 1969. Observed intensity–epicentral distance relations in earthquakes. *Bull. Seismol. Soc. Am.*, 59: 1227–1238.

Esteva, L. and Rosenblueth, E., 1964. Espectros de temblores a distancias moderadas y grandes. *Bol. Soc. Mex. Ing. Sísmica*, 2: 1–18.

Evernden, J.F., 1971. Location capability of various seismic networks. *Bull. Seismol. Soc. Am.*, 61: 241–273.

Gilbert, F., 1967. Gravitationally perturbed elastic waves. *Bull. Seismol. Soc. Am.*, 57: 783–794.

Girdler, R.W., 1967. Red Sea. In: S.K. Runcorn (Editor), *International Dictionary of Geophysics*, 2. p. 1267.

Gross, B., 1953. *Mathematical Structure of the Theory of Viscoelasticity*. Hermann, Paris, 71 pp.

Gumbel, E.J., 1958. *Statistics of Extremes*. Columbia Univ. Press, New York, N.Y., 375 pp.

Gutenberg, B., 1927. Structure of the earth's crust and spreading of the continents. *Bull. Geol. Soc. Am.*, 47: 1587–1610.

Gutenberg, B. and Richter, C.F., 1944. Frequency of earthquakes in California. *Bull. Seismol. Soc. Am.*, 34: 185–188.

Gutenberg, B. and Richter, C.F., 1954. *Seismicity of the Earth and Associated Phenomena*. Princeton Univ. Press, Princeton, N.J., 2nd ed., 310 pp.

Gzovsky, M.V., 1954. Tectonic strain models in earth strain and deformation. *Izv. Akad. Nauk S.S.S.R., Ser. Geofiz.*, 6: 527–545.

Hamada, K. and Hagiwara, T., 1967. High sensitivity tripartite observation of Matsushiro earthquakes, Part 4. *Bull. Earthquake Res. Inst., Tokyo Univ.*, 45: 159–196.

Hamilton, R.M., 1966. The Fiordland earthquake sequence of 1960 and seismic velocities beneath New Zealand. *N.Z. J. Geol. Geophys.*, 9: 224–238.

Hawkes, A.G., 1971a. Spectra of some self-exciting and mutually exciting point processes. *Biometrika*, 58: 83–90.

Hawkes, A.G., 1971b. Point spectra of some mutually exciting point processes. *J. R. Stat. Soc.*, B33: 438–443.

Hayford, J.F. and Baldwin, A.L., 1908. Geodetic measurements of earth movements. *Rep. State Earthquake Investigating Commission – Carnegie Inst. Wash. Publ.*, 87: 114–115.

Healy, J.H., 1967. Crust of Earth. In: S.K. Runcorn (Editor), *International Dictionary of Geophysics*, 1. p.29.

Heezen, B.C. and Tharp, M., 1967. Floor of the Indian Ocean. In: S.K. Runcorn (Editor), *International Dictionary of Geophysics*, p.536.

Heirzler, J.R., Dickson, G.O., Herron, E.M., Pitman, W.C., and Le Pichon, X., 1968. Marine magnetic anomalies, geomagnetic field reversals, and motions of the ocean floor and continents. *J. Geophys. Res.*, 73: 2119–2136.

Herron, E.M., 1972. Sea-floor spreading and the Cenozoic history of the east-central Pacific. *Geol. Soc. Am. Bull.*, 838: 1671–1691.

Isacks, B. and Molnar, P., 1971. Distribution of stresses in the descending lithosphere from a global survey of focal-mechanism solutions of mantle earthquakes. *Rev. Geophys. Space Phys.*, 9: 103–174.

Ishimoto, M. and Iida, K., 1939. Observations sur les séismes enregistrés par le microsismographe construit dernièrement. (1). *Bull. Earthquake Res. Inst., Tokyo Univ.*, 17: 443–478.

Jeffreys, H., 1936. Travel times in seismology. *Union Géod. Géophys. Int., Sér. A., Trav. Sci.*, 14: 3–86.

Jeffreys, H., 1965. Damping of S waves. *Nature*, 208: 675.

Jeffreys, H., 1970. *The Earth*. Cambridge Univ. Press, Cambridge, 5th ed., 438 pp.

Jeffreys, H., 1972. Creep in the earth and planets. *Tectonophysics*, 13: 569–581.

Jeffreys, H. and Bullen, K.E., 1935. Seismological tables. *Bur. Cent. Int. Seismol., Sér. A., Trav. Sci.*, 11: 1–50.

Kantorovich, L.V., Molchan, G.M., Keilis-Borok, V.I. and Vilkovich, E.V., 1970. A statistical model of seismicity and the estimate of basic seismic effects. *Izv. Akad. Nauk, Fiz. Zemli*, 5: 85–102.

Kárnik, V., 1971. *Seismicity of the European Area*, 2. Reidel, Dordrecht, 218 pp.

Kausel, E. and Lomnitz, C., 1969. Tectonics of Chile. *Pan Am. Symp. Upper Mantle, Mexico*, 2: 48–67.

Kawasumi, H., 1951. Measures of earthquake danger and expectancy of maximum intensity throughout Japan as inferred from the seismic activity in historical times. *Bull. Earthquake Res. Inst. Tokyo Univ.*, 29: 469–482.

Khintchine, A.J., 1960. *Mathematical Methods in the Theory of Queuing.* Griffin, London, 120 pp.

King, C.Y. and Knopoff, L., 1968. Stress drop in earthquakes. *Bull. Seismol. Soc. Am.*, 58: 249–257.

Kolmogorov, A.N., 1941. Über das logarithmisch normale Verteilungsgesetz der Dimensionen der Teilchen bei Zerstückelung. *Izv. Akad. Nauk S.S.S.R.*, 31: 1–99.

Le Pichon, X., 1968. Sea-floor spreading and continental drift. *J. Geophys. Res.*, 73: 3661–3697.

Lomnitz, C., 1956. Creep measurements in igneous rocks. *J. Geol.*, 64: 473–479.

Lomnitz, C., 1957. Linear dissipation in solids. *J. Appl. Phys.*, 28: 201–205.

Lomnitz, C., 1960. A study of the Maipo Valley earthquakes of September 4, 1958. *Proc. 2nd Conf. Earthquake Eng., Tokyo*, pp. 501–520.

Lomnitz, C., 1961. On thermodynamics of planets. *Geophys. J. R. Astron. Soc.*, 5: 157–161.

Lomnitz, C., 1962a. On Andean structure. *J. Geophys. Res.*, 67: 351–363.

Lomnitz, C., 1962b. Applications of the logarithmic creep law to stress wave attenuation in the solid earth. *J. Geophys. Res.*, 67: 365–367.

Lomnitz, C., 1964a. Estimation problems in earthquake series. *Tectonophysics*, 2: 193–203.

Lomnitz, C., 1964b. Earthquake risk in Chile. *Bull. Seismol. Soc. Am.*, 54: 1271–1281.

Lomnitz, C., 1966a. Magnitude stability in earthquake sequences. *Bull. Seismol. Soc. Am.*, 56: 247–249.

Lomnitz, C., 1966b. Statistical prediction of earthquakes. *Rev. Geophys.*, 4: 377–393.

Lomnitz, C., 1967a. Time series and earthquake prediction. *I.B.M. Proc. Sci. Comp. Symp.*, pp.129–141.

Lomnitz, C., 1967b. Transition probabilities between seismic regions. *Geophys. J. R. Astron. Soc.*, 13: 387–391.

Lomnitz, C., 1969a. An earthquake risk map of Chile. *Proc. World Congr. Earthquake Eng., 4th, Santiago*, 1, A-1: 161–171.

Lomnitz, C., 1969b. Sea-floor spreading as a factor of tectonic evolution in southern Chile. *Nature*, 222: 336–369.

Lomnitz, C., 1970a. Major earthquakes and tsunamis in Chile during the period 1535–1955. *Geol. Rundschau*, 59: 938–960.

Lomnitz, C., 1970b. Some observations of gravity waves in the 1960 Chile earthquake. *Bull. Seismol. Soc. Am.*, 60: 669–670.

Lomnitz, C., 1970c. Casualties and behavior of populations during earthquakes. *Bull. Seismol. Soc. Am.*, 60: 1309–1313.

Lomnitz, C., 1971. Travel-time errors in the laterally inhomogeneous earth. *Bull. Seismol. Soc. Am.*, 61: 1639–1654.

Lomnitz, C. and Bolt, B.A., 1967. Evidence on crustal structure in California from the CHASE V explosion and the Chico earthquake of May 24, 1966. *Bull. Seismol. Soc. Am.*, 57: 1093–1114.

Lomnitz, C. and Cabré, R., 1968. The Peru earthquake of October 17, 1966. *Bull. Seismol. Soc. Am.*, 58: 645–661.

Lomnitz, C. and Epstein, B., 1966. A model for the occurrence of large earthquakes. *Nature*, 211: 954–956.

Lomnitz, C. and Gajardo, E., 1960. Seismic provinces of Chile. *Proc. 2nd Conf. Earthquake Eng., Tokyo*, pp. 1529–1540.

Lomnitz, C. and Hax, A., 1966. Clustering in aftershock sequences. *Am. Geophys. Union, Geophys. Monogr.*, 10: 502–508.

Lomnitz, C. and Schulz, R., 1966. The San Salvador earthquake of May 3, 1965. *Bull. Seismol. Soc. Am.*, 56: 561–575.

Lomnitz, C., Mooser, F., Allen, C.R., Brune, J.N. and Thatcher, W., 1970. Seismicity and tectonics of the northern Gulf of California region – preliminary results. *Geofís. Int., Mexico*, 10: 37–48.

López-Arroyo, A. and Udías, A. 1972. Aftershock sequences and focal parameters of the February 28, 1969 earthquake of the Azores–Gibraltar fracture zone. *Bull. Seismol. Soc. Am.*, 62: 699–720.

Markhinin, E.K. and Stratula, D.S., 1971. Nekotorye petrologicheskye geokhimicheskye i geofizicheskye aspekt svyaz vulkanizma s glubinamy zemly. *Vulkanizm i Glubin Zemly – Proc. 3rd Volcanol. Conf. U.S.S.R.* Nauka, Moscow, p.15.

Mathéron, G., 1970. *La Théorie des Variables régionalisées, et ses Applications.* Centre de Morphologie Math., Fontainebleau, Fasc. 5, 211 pp.

Medvedev, S.V., 1965. *Engineering Seismology.* Israel Progr. Sci. Transl., Jerusalem, 260 pp.

Menard, H.W., 1964. *Marine Geology of the Pacific.* McGraw-Hill, New York, N.Y., 271 pp.

Mogi, K., 1962. Study of the elastic shocks caused by the fracture of heterogeneous materials and its relation to earthquake phenomena. *Bull. Earthquake Res. Inst.*, 40: 125–173.

Morgan, W.J., 1968. Rises, trenches, great faults, and crustal blocks. *J. Geophys. Res.*, 73: 1959–1982.

Mott, N.F. and Nabarro, F.R.N., 1948. *Report of a Conference on the Strength of Solids, Univ. Bristol.* Phys. Soc. London, pp. 1–20.

Needham, J., 1959. *Science and Civilisation in China.* Cambridge Univ. Press, Cambridge, 567 pp.

Newmark, N. and Rosenblueth, E., 1971. *Earthquake Engineering.* Prentice-Hall, New York, N.Y., 640 pp.

Nowroozi, A.A., 1971. Seismo-tectonics of the Persian Plateau, eastern Turkey, Caucasus, and Hindu-Kush regions. *Bull. Seismol. Soc. Am.*, 61: 317–341.

Ocola, L., 1966. Earthquake activity of Peru. *Am. Geophys. Union, Geophys. Monogr.*, 10: 509–528.

Oliver, J. and Isacks, B., 1967. Deep earthquake zones, anomalous structure in the upper mantle, and the lithosphere. *J. Geophys. Res.*, 72: 4259–4275.

Omori, F., 1894. On the aftershocks of earthquakes. *J. Coll. Sci. Imp. Univ. Tokyo*, 7: 111–200.

Parking, E.J., 1965. *Vicinity of Hayward, California, Study of Earth Movements Determined by Triangulation, 1951–1957–1963.* Report prepared for the U.S. Coast and Geodetic Survey, Washington.

Plafker, G., 1965. Tectonic deformation associated with the 1964 Alaska earthquake. *Science*, 148: 1675–1687.

Plafker. G., Ericksen, G.E. and Fernandez Concha, J., 1971. Geological aspects of the May 31, 1970 Peru earthquake. *Bull. Seismol. Soc. Am.*, 61: 543–578.

Press, F. (Chairman), 1965. *Earthquake Prediction: a proposal for a Ten-year Program of Research. Ad Hoc Panel on Earthquake Prediction.* Office of Science and Technology, Washington, D. C., 39 pp.

Prigogine, I., 1947. *Etude Thermodynamique des Processes Irréversibles.* Dunod, Paris, 259 pp.

Pyke, R., 1961. Markov renewal processes: definitions and preliminary properties. *Ann. Math. Statist.*, 32: 1231–1242.

Reid, H.F., 1911. The elastic-rebound theory of earthquakes. *Univ. California, Dep. Geol., Bull.*, 6 (19): 413–444.

Richter, C.F., 1958. *Elementary seismology.* Freeman, San Francisco, Calif., 768 pp.

Richter, C.F., 1959. Seismic regionalization. *Bull. Seismol. Soc. Am.*, 49: 123–162.

Rikitake, T., 1972. *Earthquake Prediction Studies in Japan.* Geophys. Surv., Tokyo, in press.

Rosenblueth, E., 1964. Probabilistic design to resist earthquakes. *Proc. Am. Soc. Civ. Eng.*, 90, EM5.

Ross, D.A. and Shor Jr., G.G., 1965. Reflection profiles across the Middle America Trench. *J. Geophys. Res.*, 70: 5551–5572.

Sadovski, M.A., 1971. Indicators for use in earthquake forecasting. *Vestn. Akad. Nauk S.S.S.R.*, 11: 11–17.

Santo, T., 1969. Characteristics of seismicity in South America. *Bull. Earthquake Res. Inst.*, 47: 635–672.

Schmidt, P., 1971. Zu Fragen der Erdbebenprognose. *Acta Geodaet. Geophys. Montan. Acad. Sci. Hung.*, 6: 449–457.

Scholz, C.H., 1968. The frequency–magnitude relation of microfracturing and its relation to earth-quakes. *Bull. Seismol. Soc. Am.*, 58: 399–417.

Seed, H.B., Idriss, I.M., and Kiefer, F.W., 1968. *Characteristics of Rock Motions during Earthquakes.* Earthquake Eng. Res. Center, Univ. California, Berkeley, EERC 68-5, 23 pp.

Shreve, R.L., 1966. Statistical law of stream numbers. *J. Geol.*, 74: 17–34.

Steindl, J., 1965. *Random processes and the Growth of Firms – a Study of the Pareto Law.* Hafner, New York, N.Y., 249 pp.

Suess, E., 1885. *Das Anlitz der Erde.* Springer, Leipzig, 4 vols., 2157 pp.

Suyehiro, S., 1966. Difference between aftershocks and foreshocks in the relationship of magnitude to frequency of occurrence for the great Chilean earthquake of 1960. *Bull. Seismol. Soc. Am.*, 56: 185–200.

Tozer, D.C., 1965. Heat transfer and convection currents. *Phil. Trans. R. Soc. Lond.*, A258: 252–271.

Tozer, D.C., 1970. Factors determining the temperature evolution of thermally convecting earth models. *Phys. Earth Planet. Interiors*, 2: 393–398.

UNESCO, 1972. *Report of the Consultative Meeting of Experts on the Statistical Study of Natural Hazards and their Consequences.* Paris.

Vening-Meinesz, F.A., 1964. *The Earth's Crust and Mantle.* Elsevier, Amsterdam, 124 pp.

Vere-Jones, D., 1966. A Markov model for aftershock occurrence. *Pure Appl. Geophys.*, 64: 31–42.

Vere-Jones, D., 1970a. Stochastic models for earthquake occurrence. *J. R. Stat. Soc.*, B32: 1–62.

Vere-Jones, D., 1970b. Discussion on "Stochastic models for earthquake occurrence". *J. R. Stat. Soc.*, B32: 61.

Whitten, C.A. and Claire, C.N., 1960. Analysis of geodetic measurements along the San Andreas Fault. *Bull. Seismol. Soc. Am.*, 50: 404–415.

Wiener, N., 1956. Nonlinear prediction and dynamics. *Proc. 3rd, Berkeley Symp. Stat. Prob.*, 3: 247–252.

Zeil, W., 1964. *Geologie von Chile.* Bornträger, Berlin, 234 pp.

Index